Karen Vanderlaan has two great passions in her life: kids and horses. It is her personal mission to help kids and horses who are in trouble and get them off to a better start in life.

Karen grew up on a dairy farm in Vermont where she attended a one-room schoolhouse for five years. She began riding horses almost as soon as she could walk.

Karen now lives in Utah where she raised her three children. She teaches children and horses.

For my three children.
They changed my life forever.

To my younger sister,
my friend and companion in realizing life's joy
in spite of a painful past.

Karen Vanderlaan

RIPPLES

AUSTIN MACAULEY PUBLISHERS™
LONDON • CAMBRIDGE • NEW YORK • SHARJAH

Ordering Information:
Quantity sales: special discounts are available on quantity purchases by corporations, associations, and others. For details, contact the publisher at the address below.

Publisher's Cataloging-in-Publication data
Vanderlaan, Karen
Ripples

ISBN 9781645362845 (Paperback)
ISBN 9781645362838 (Hardback)
ISBN 9781645368731 (ePub e-book)

Library of Congress Control Number: 2020909124

www.austinmacauley.com/us

First Published (2020)
Austin Macauley Publishers LLC
40 Wall Street, 28th Floor
New York, NY 10005
USA

mail-usa@austinmacauley.com
+1 (646) 5125767

I want to thank my brother and sisters for their acceptance and support. Without them, the remembering would have been much more difficult.

Thank you, Sandy, for insisting that I use my own voice to tell my story. "Editor" is an understatement. Thank you for the endless and unselfish hours you spent and for understanding the tears.

Susan, thank you for the unselfish time and encouragement. Teresa and Sondra, your encouragement and faith kept me plugging along.

Kathy, Lisa, and Kim, your enthusiasm was amazing, you helped me believe.

Bobby, Anna, and Phillip, keep being the best.

Credits

Prologue

Each time a man stands up for an idea, or acts to improve the lot of others, or strikes out against injustice, he sends forth a tiny ripple of hope, and crossing each other from a million different centers of energy and daring, those ripples build a current that can sweep down the mightiest walls of oppression and resistance.

~ Robert F. Kennedy

Ripples. A single pebble dropped in still water triggers an endless series of perfect concentric circles drifting outward toward the end of time. Not so when many pebbles fall. Then the ripples emanating from each fallen stone crisscross, intersect and alter the course of every other ripple. Perfection is lost in the complexity, but in the multitude of patterns, there arises the chance for beauty as well as chaos.

So it is in life. The actions of one infinitely echo in the lives of others. For good or ill. This is the Ripple Effect, and I believe it is true. How else can I explain my life? How else can I explain even this one afternoon?

A twelve-year-old girl in my middle-school class for children with emotional problems wanted to spend her lunch hour in the classroom. I had just been selected as one of two *Teacher Heroes* by our local school foundation for my work rescuing horses. Embarrassed by the accolade, I immediately stored the poster-sized photo essay used to publicize the honor. My young student had seen the poster in my classroom closet and asked to read it.

After lunch, this child became increasingly unruly. Her belligerence escalated as the afternoon wore on, almost to the point that I might be forced to suspend her from school. She—we—survived the afternoon.

After the dismissal bell rang, I straightened the room and picked up the poster to put it away. A mark caught my eye. Someone had smeared a word on the perimeter off the poster and then had attempted to repair the damage, making things worse. It dawned on me that my little student, in holding up the poster, had smudged one word with her thumb. The reason for her misbehavior became clear.

When she arrived the next morning, I asked my staff assistant to teach the class while I escorted the little girl into the hall. I said to her with a smile, "I think I know why you were having a hard time yesterday."

Her little body became rigid and her eyes dropped to her shoes. Then she tossed her head, and with characteristic defiance demanded, "Why?"

"When you were reading my poster yesterday, you accidentally—"

"Suspend me if you want, I don't care." Her words were betrayed by the tears running down her cheeks.

My eyes welled up as I put my hands on her small shoulders.

"It was an accident, sweetie," I whispered. "Don't you know you are worth more to me than that poster?"

She raised her head and stared at me; her mouth opened. I hugged her tightly. She laid her head on my shoulder, and I felt her body relax.

Here was a child whose alcoholic father demanded that she remove her clothes and grant him sexual favors. Here was a physically beautiful child whose mother took her to the area of town where prostitutes gather and used her to attract men. Here was a child surrounded by adults who exploited her at every turn and, worse, made her feel responsible for their exploitations.

Only her feisty spirit protected her from further sexual abuse. Each time she felt backed against a wall, her claws came out. She fought everything. She had spent time in a lock-up facility for drug use. Her only protection from her family came from the supervision provided by the State because she never earned her way off probation.

I hated to think that anything connected with me might add to her misery or to the weight of the responsibilities she already carried for the unconscious adults in her life. She gave me one last embrace and we returned together to our classroom.

Isabelle

Big brother said, "Just wait till you meet her.
She's the good kid, she's perfect."
Isabelle, whose non-father touched her
Whose mother took his side.
No one believed her pain.

Isabelle who is betrayed,
Angry and so afraid—fights back.
Hate-filled words are quickly spewed
Fierce defiance—her protection of choice.

Isabelle—still perfect inside
But the world did not know.

It was the end of the grading period, and I had asked my students to write a paragraph about something they had learned that term. While reviewing their assignments, I came to the paper written by the little girl. My heart sank as I glanced at it; she had written only one sentence. I knew she could do better. Then I read her words, "I learned I am more important than a poster."

I set the papers down and let the tears come. I get so frustrated, knowing that nothing I teach can outweigh the tragic circumstances in which my students live. I question whether my work makes any difference. But, I had made a dent this time.

A young child reached out to touch a story I had shared about horses that I rescued from the meat market. My effort was the conduit through which these animals came to live extended, useful lives. My story, a child's reach—these simple acts had a profound effect on both of us in ways we could not have foreseen. Ripples.

So it is in my life, too. I am going to make it because I am worth more than some people in my life ever knew.

Paradise

Daisies and buttercups,
Sunshine and rain.
Ponies and puppies,
Bambis and garden snakes.

Hayfields by the woods,
Mud between my toes,
All these my world,
All these to love.

I was born in paradise. Our four-hundred-acre dairy farm in the remote Vermont village of West Newbury felt so big and free and alive that I believed we owned the whole world. Given the isolated and free-spirited way we lived, this was a reasonable belief. The world and all of its glory existed just for us.

About two-and-a-half miles from the center of the village, where pavement turned to dirt, a hand-painted sign picturing a life-sized brown and white cow announced, "Milky Way Farm."

I always felt there was something magical about that name. Perhaps my parents selected it when they first beheld their land under the night sky. Far removed from the distortion of city lights, the entire galaxy manifested itself above them, forming an archway of stars, the gateway to infinity. They brought to this corner of the universe all their determination, hopes, and dreams. Together they would make their mark on eternity with the work of their hands and the hoof prints of cows.

Growing up on the farm gave me a more humble perspective. The cows themselves were as big as the universe needed to be, and I agreed with the herd that the meaning of life was simple. Given this disparity, it was inevitable that the farm would live up to all my expectations and impossible that it could fulfill all of theirs.

In the end, Milky Way Farm meant too much to each of us. It became too painful for them to keep and too painful for me to lose. But whatever the future, Milky Way Farm endowed me with the perfect backdrop for my earliest memories.

Our four-hundred acres consisted of rolling hills blanketed with pastures and enormous hayfields wearing various shades of green highlighted in season by buttercups, native daisies, and dandelions.

Our pale yellow farmhouse might have become lost in the swells of this landscape if it were not for an ancient elm tree that anchored it in our yard.

Massive outstretched limbs, many as thick as tree trunks, had defied gravity for nearly a century. From the lowest branch hung a worn wooden swing under which exposed roots bore the scars of generations of children's feet.

An army of gnarled, old apple trees stood at attention behind the house. Long retired, their thick, short branches were no longer pruned to maximize fruit production. Now they served at the will of my brother, two sisters and me—mighty steeds when we charged into battle or comfortable niches to cradle us during the afternoons we wiled away reading, daydreaming or dozing.

Within a short uphill walk from our backyard beat the heart of the farm. A huge, gambrel-roofed barn was painted pale yellow every decade or two to match the house. The lower section of the barn housed the milk room, four horse stalls and two rows of stanchions where forty cows lined up shoulder-to-shoulder, awaiting their turn to be milked, two at a time, morning and evening.

The afternoon shadow of the barn cooled a small stream that wandered leisurely from the high pond, which had been dug generations ago to furnish water for the herd. For us four kids, however, the pond's real value was its endless supply of crayfish, frogs, salamanders, and tadpoles. We caught them, named them, carried them home, housed them in milk cans, and then threw them back so we could catch them again.

Long before the first farmer began cultivating the land for the benefit of cows, Mother Nature crowned its farthest hills with her finest jewels. Sugar maple trees, named to honor the sap harvested in the sugaring process, grew in abundance in the woods behind the pond. A bit south of the sugar maple forest was Blueberry Hill where we gathered wild berries.

Time at Milky Way Farm was measured by seasons that roughly correlated with the calendar. Our seasons, however, changed according to marker events rather than predetermined dates.

Summer began when the cold, biting storms of the early spring softened into warm rains that fell some days in torrents and other days in soft caressing waves. At the first rumble of distant thunder heralding a summer storm, I breathed the scent of rain in the air, grabbed a halter or bridle, and ran to catch my pony. I swung onto his bareback Indian-style and raced through the pastures toward a special hill from which I could command a view of the farm below. We flew upward as the sky darkened from blue to grey. Sometimes the rain drenched us before we reached the crest. Other times we galloped to the top and waited for the downpour. Either way, in the end, I sat triumphantly astride my pony, soaked to the skin, my face turned skyward, licking the rain that wet my lips. In that moment, my hilltop was the apex of the world. I owned it all.

Our return trip shed every pretense of imperial decorum. The challenge was just to stay on. My pony's back was slick, and the rain made him frisky. His body dropped beneath me as he skidded down the steepest slopes then lunged forward to regain his footing. I slipped from side to side, steadying myself by grabbing his mane, clamping my legs around his middle, then sliding again. I laughed aloud. Each time I wiped the raindrops from my eyes, the pony shook his head and his long mane splattered the water back in my face.

Most summers Milky Way Farm offered our family the opportunity to serve as good stewards of the land. Those were the years when Dad would rescue a young fawn that he discovered while mowing the hay fields. Following its instincts to remain motionless in the face of an impending threat, the fawn would forgo ample opportunity to flee as the clanking mower approached. It would drop down and curl up tightly with its legs tucked underneath and its ears flattened against its head. Unfortunately, this camouflage was so effective that Dad might not discover the fawn until after his machinery had injured it. The moment Dad caught sight of a fawn, he shut down the mowers, jumped from the tractor and, cradling the injured baby in his arms, headed for the house.

We kids were too young to appreciate a fawn's vulnerability or consider its poor worried mother. We were thrilled to receive another tiny, spotted pet to bottle-feed and care for until it grew healthy enough to return to the wild. We named every one of these fawns, of course, Bambi.

In the hayloft, my dad built Bambi a miniature wooden stall, which we cushioned with sawdust. We climbed over the sides of the stall and jumped in with a bottle of warm milk or an armful of bandages. Once Bambi healed sufficiently to leave its hospital stall, it followed us everywhere, bounding around or butting against us, begging for its bottle.

The Bambi of my fourth year was our favorite. We somehow managed to convince our black lab to accept this fawn as part of her litter. To nurse along with the puppies, the fawn hunkered low to the ground on its knees, positioning its bottom straight up in the air. Bambi wiggled its head from side-to-side, shoving puppies apart, as it searched for a nipple. Like a good adoptive mother, our lab rolled further over on her back and stretched her legs to accommodate her unusual brood. Once settled in for a meal, Bambi wagged its white, fluffy tail in furious delight. Other than at mealtime, the fawn preferred my siblings and me as its littermates.

A typical New England farm family, we spent many summer days working together in the fields. Beginning when I turned six, I teamed up with my siblings to help bring in the hay. It was our job to roll together three or four of the bales, which lay in parallel rows, each separated by a distance that reflected the success of that season's crop. If it was a sparse cutting, we had to move the bales a considerable distance to create even a small stack.

The three of us that were old enough to walk were still too puny to lift even a single hay bale, but we tackled our mission with a strong sense of purpose and a lot of laughter. Two of us would line up shoulder to shoulder, then charge the long side of a bale, throwing our full weight against its edge so that the bale would roll over a quarter turn, dumping the pair of us on the other side. Progress was slow because each quarter turn required that we muster another charge.

The first years this contribution to the haying effort was minimal, but then having us occupied in the field freed my mom to drive the truck while my baby sister sat beside her. My dad and our neighbors threw the hay bales onto the truck bed and stacked them in a tight and balanced load.

Most summer days, my sisters, brother, and I were left to our own devices. Our favorite pastime was reinventing ourselves as soldiers, pirates, royalty or cowboys. On other days, we were horses. As we romped around the farm with wild abandon, an onlooker might have difficulty discerning whether we were human or equine heroes, except that when we were horses, unraveled hay-rope tails hung from our pants.

Ignoring the itch of hemp on our backsides, we pranced along carrying a long stick in each hand to create the illusion of front legs. We manipulated the sticks in distinct rhythms to mimic the gaits of real horses. My older sister and I tied our hair in ponytails, which swished magnificently when we tossed our heads.

Certainly, no stallion ever galloped more majestically, sauntered more proudly, or looked more authentically equine. I didn't notice the town folk chuckling as they drove past, but years later they reminded me about my imaginative scampering. By then, I could only marvel at the memory of such freedom and joy.

Milky Way Farm celebrated the end of summer with a burst of glory. The trees covering its hills shed their deep green in favor of the yellows, reds, and oranges that give New England its reputation for autumnal magnificence. Fall began for us kids on the sad morning we boarded the secondhand, yellow bus and headed for the only school in our village.

There, in 1963, I began first grade in a one-room schoolhouse built more than a hundred years earlier. West Newbury employed one teacher to teach the thirty students enrolled in grades one through six. During the five years I attended, the same four kids formed my grade.

The school had no running water. In the basement, we had an outhouse-like bathroom featuring a wood plank with a couple of holes for us to sit on. In class, we used a ceramic jug of water for drinks, and everyone brought lunches from home. Each morning, we recited the Pledge of Allegiance, prayed, and checked off a list indicating whether we had brought a handkerchief, remembered our drinking cup, and cleaned our fingernails.

At recess, throughout autumn, open fields surrounding the schoolhouse doubled as the school playground. We made daisy chains, blew dandelion seeds into the wind, and hid in the bushes. We did have a jungle gym, which wouldn't meet any version of today's safety standards, and canvas swings where my sister and I spent endless hours pumping, as high as we could, while singing *Jesus Loves Me* as loudly as possible. The closest we came to a team sport was a hotly contested game of red rover or dodge ball in the barren front yard of the school.

I recall recess in far greater detail than academics. Inside our classroom, I did learn one valuable lesson. *Listen carefully*. Our teacher repeated nothing. She announced each grade's assignment at the beginning of the hour and then expected us to get to work. No talking. We raised a hand for help, one finger up for the bathroom, a cup held high for a drink, and a pencil in the air if we needed to sharpen it. If we were not called on, too bad for us.

I never believed that our teacher particularly liked me, but I don't remember really caring. I had accepted without question that I would never live up to the academic prowess shown by my older sister. By the time I started first grade, her exemplary schoolwork had made her the pride of the school, the teacher, and my parents. She knew so much that she skipped second grade, so although we were only fourteen months apart, she was two years ahead when I entered first grade. My sibling status plummeted as her promotion permeated every aspect of our relationship.

I do remember our substitute teacher because she was the first person who ever read aloud to me. She read *Old Bones*, the saga of a racehorse named Exterminator, and *Vulpese*, the tale of a fox. As she spoke, I felt these stories come alive, and I became a part of each adventure. I could touch the bony frame of the great Thoroughbred; I shared his courage as we thundered down the homestretch. I ached to erase the tragic words when a hunter shot Vulpese. In fact, when our teacher passed the book around so we could see its illustrations, I planned to tear out the final pages. Instead, I burst into tears, furious that I had to accept tragedy as part of life. This gentlewoman responded to my sadness with such understanding that I promised her someday I would write a book that told a story where animals did not suffer so.

Among my fellow students, status was marked by the strangest and simplest things. Some kids' sandwiches were made with tuna fish; others had only jam. Some families had running water; others hauled water from a well. I also discovered, to my surprise, that every kid believed his dad was the toughest and could beat up everyone else's dad. Each of us had to accept the other's declarations, however, because none of us believed our fathers would consider our bragging worth fighting about.

At home, we knew it was fall when the early mornings became so chilly that Dad asked us to bring hot coffee to him while he milked our cows. The question of who had the privilege to carry his mug to the barn was a fighting matter, so many a morning began with heated spats. It never occurred to any of us that we could go together. The coffee run was a solo quest, amply rewarded by a few moments alone with Dad. He always welcomed the beverage and the company.

For about a week when I was in third grade, Dad anointed me with coffee privileges. He knew I was struggling with the concept of telling time, so he carried a wind-up clock to the barn each morning, and when I brought his coffee, he drilled me by changing the hands of the clock between milking each pair of cows. I hated to admit when I finally understood the time because I lost my exclusive right to the coffee run.

The apex of autumn was Halloween. Because the homes of West Newbury were scattered too far apart for trick-or-treating, the village arranged a kids' parade across the Town Hall stage. Each family created costumes and carved pumpkins for judging. The pastor and his wife awarded a vast array of prizes for categories ranging from scariest to cutest and everything in between. With so many categories and such a limited population of children, odds were good that anyone who dressed up and produced a pumpkin would win something.

Snow signaled the advent of winter, and we had plenty of it. Some mornings, intricate crystals frosted our windows. Other times, sheets of ice varnished the entire house. When drifts rose to the middle of the front door, we had to tunnel out to catch the school bus.

As soon as the snow fell, we kids started checking the feedbags. Most of the feed for our cows arrived in burlap sacks that were useless for sledding. We were looking out for the heavy paper bags that held beet pulp, the supplement that helped the cattle hold weight and stay warm in the bitter cold. Beet pulp bags would fly over the crusty Vermont snow. We knew it, and Dad knew it, too.

As soon as we had sufficient snow and enough feedbags, Dad pulled us to the top of a special hill on an aluminum saucer tied behind his tractor. At the highest point, he turned off the tractor and pulled out one of the treasured feedbags. The cold air made the paper crunch when Dad sat down on it. All four of us kids piled on top of him and scrunched together as tightly as our snowsuits would allow. Dad cradled us between his arms and legs.

When we were finally assembled, Dad started pushing and pumping with his whole body, inching the bag forward until he built sufficient momentum for the feedbag to take on a life of its own. It flew over the snow. Each run packed the snow harder until eventually, we thundered toward the barbed wire fence at the bottom of the hill with such speed that we had to bail out to save ourselves. At the last second, Dad tumbled off the bag with four kids clinging to him more tightly than his own skin. Snow enveloped us. We must have made great anchors because we managed to stop our dad just short of the fence.

The annual Christmas pageant highlighted the winter holidays. All thirty kids in the school were featured in the extravaganza, which our school presented on the Town Hall stage. Evidently, I never had a starring role in the nativity because I only recall being one of a cluster of shepherds dressed in burlap feed sacks belted with hay rope. We entered—stage left—carrying cardboard sheep, then paused, pointed upwards at an elongated paper star and chanted, "Behold!" more or less in unison. Then we shuffled past the manger where we took turns pausing and glancing downward, sighing audibly before we filed to the back of the stage and lined up to provide a backdrop for the rest of the action.

Because an enactment of the Christmas story requires only three kings, a couple of taller boys dressed as camels, Mary and Joseph, and a few older girls for the heavenly host, our pageant had a number of shepherds. Being quite shy, I much preferred performing among that crowd. Besides, you just can't be too careful with cardboard sheep.

My older sister, on the other hand, as the pride of the school, relished her turns as Mary, Mother of God. She brushed her long, golden-brown hair into a smooth mantle over her pale blue robe, a blue of that heavenly hue, which easily justified the hours she had spent boiling white sheets in kettles while she concocted the perfect mixture of Ritz dyes.

Once my sister took her place on stage, she knelt beside the feed-bin manger and tilted her head to one side, an idea inspired by her study of Christmas cards which showed Mary's head tipped toward the baby Jesus. My sister's listing head never looked natural to me, but apparently appeared genuine enough for our teacher's standards. She offered my sister the Madonna role several seasons running.

At home, during the holiday, my world felt warm, cozy and right. Dad packed us kids on the flying saucer that attached behind him on the tractor for the quest to find a perfect Christmas tree. On our return trip, we tied the tree to the saucer and rode on top of it.

In the living room, our tree wore the traditional lights, sparkly ornaments, and tinsel, but more importantly, its branches were adorned with homemade cookies. Mom designed and baked rock-hard Moravian cookies that she decorated with frostings of every hue. We kids helped her cut them out and were allowed to paint our share of American flags, horses, wild animals, snowmen, Santa Clauses, and wreaths. In the dawn light on Christmas morning our gifts looked like mountains, and we hungered in anticipation of the coming feast.

Long after the Christmas holiday ended, the snow continued to deepen. It is no wonder that when it finally began melting, our spring would be known as "Mud Season."

One particularly wet April when I was seven, my parents relegated to my younger brother and me the job of bringing in a couple of calves from an outlying pasture. I quickly chose the calf I would escort, knowing that the other was wild as a March hare. My brother was clueless. With a bit of effort, we managed to loop a hay rope around each calf's neck, then start it heading for the barn.

Our return trip was going well until suddenly, and I might add predictably, my brother's calf leaped ahead, pulling and tugging against the kid-sized anchor weighting the other end of its tether. I don't know how or why my brother hung on to that rope after he lost his footing, but he did. He flailed along on his hands and knees until his calf bogged down in a major mud puddle. The calf only stopped pulling after it had cleared the puddle. By then it had stranded my brother face down in the slop. He was just standing when I caught up with them. Black mud dripped off every inch of him.

I fell to laughing so hard I could hardly stay on my feet. My reaction infuriated my brother who burst out crying, especially after I informed him that I knew what I was going to say next day for Show and Tell. He begged me to spare him. I told him that he would be a star. He begged again. No avail.

The next morning, while my brother's angry red face glared at me, I described each detail of the incident to the whole school, laughing until tears ran down my cheeks. Our classmates couldn't possibly grasp the story through my laughter so I had to retell it. All the better for me, all the worse for him. Adopting the airs of our older sister, I even elevated his mishap into a parable about the importance of learning when to let go. So funny then, but a lesson I failed to internalize. How many times in my life would I hang on to something that dragged me through the mud? My brother could have had the last laugh, but he was far too kind.

With the possible exception of the mud-bath renegade, we loved our calves. Calves of every breed have huge brown eyes, sandpaper tongues, swirls of long curly hair on the tops of their broadheads, and perpetually wet noses. Ours, however, were purebred Ayrshires, white-bodied animals with large, dark brown patches. As Ayrshires mature, their horns grow longer than most milk cows and develop a distinctive curve, giving the breed a dignified and regal appearance.

But Ayrshire or not, on a dairy farm, calves are taken from their mothers a few weeks after their birth so that the milk produced by the cows can be sold. We separated our calves from their mothers by leading them to the opposite side of the barn and tying them with hay ropes to rings bolted into the cement wall. Then it was our job to teach each calf to drink Milk Replacer from a bucket.

Young calves will suck on anything so Mother Nature assisted us. When it was my turn, I stuck my fingers into a calf's mouth, and then lowered my hand, with the sucking calf's mouth attached, into a full bucket of replacer. The first few attempts usually failed as the calf jerked its milk-covered face out of the bucket, sputtering and coughing. It didn't take long, however, for each calf to catch on and then empty a whole bucket.

At some point, it occurred to my brother and me that Milk Replacer was no substitute for mothers. We worried and debated about this injustice until we concocted a plan to set the calves' world right. That evening after Dad completed the milking chores and headed in for the night, we sneaked back to the barn and pounded each calf's tether with a rock until the twine shredded and all the calves were loose. The next morning while calves wandered everywhere, my brother and I took turns pointing out evidence that the calves had chewed through their ropes. When Dad looked at us quizzically, we averted our eyes, scuttled out of his line of vision, and tried to appear particularly busy.

Again the next night, we repeated our altruistic effort, this time only daring to release our favorites. The following morning, Dad was on to us. It had not occurred to us that Dad might suspect that week-old calves don't develop escape plans. He lined us up against the barn wall and delivered a farm-reality lecture, pointing his finger right at nose level and declaring once and for all that if we didn't want the burning in our ears to become burning on our rears, the calves must remain tied.

Fortunately, Dad was not a man to hold a grudge. We put the aborted calf-rescue plan behind us as we organized our equipment for spring sugaring, the process that marked the awakening of the earth. On Milky Way Farm it started when warming days triggered the flowing of maple sap. Dad pounded a tap into an unscarred portion of the trunk of each sugar maple tree. Then we kids took turns hanging a bucket on the tap over which we balanced a peaked tin roof to protect the bucket's contents from insects and woodland debris. By the time we finished, hundreds of buckets hung from the trees.

Every morning after the taps were in and the buckets hung, we waited for Dad to finish his milking, then hopped on the tractor beside him and toured the maple woods. He drove close to each tree and emptied its bucket into one of the ten-gallon milk cans strapped to the trailer behind the tractor. We returned to the sugarhouse when the milk cans were full and watched Dad as he poured the sap into a large vat where it boiled continuously until it condensed into a thick, amber liquid—maple syrup.

We transported gallons of this Vermont gold to the West Newbury Town Hall where it was stored until a late spring snowfall provided the final ingredient for the annual square-dance and sugar-on-snow party.

On the appointed evening, the whole town arrived dressed in a rainbow of colorful attire and carrying empty pans. Bandanas around the necks of the men matched their wives' puffy dancing skirts.

Everyone milled around outside, scouting out the cleanest, fluffiest snow with which to fill the pans that were then set out on long tables. When the pans were full, we all fell in line. When my turn came, I scooped up a bowlful of snow then topped it with hot maple syrup that quickly converted to a caramel-like candy. My mouth was already full by the time I left the line for our family table.

When my body could not possibly handle any more gooey, sweet stuff, I downed a couple of the sour dill pickles that were left out beside the syrup to help each kid balance out for another round of sugar-on-snow. Everyone who could survive this dastardly combination took to the floor and formed squares. Professionals called the dance moves, which we kids had all learned from our parents lest we embarrass ourselves.

Years passed as we ticked off each season. The rest of the country urbanized or suburbanized, but time stood still in our storybook New England town. West Newbury could still honestly boast that the village raised its children. Every adult wore the mantle of authority to act as a surrogate parent. On the dark days when trouble befell a kid, the store owner, the mailman, the pastor or a neighbor would chastise or spank, and no child or adult ever disputed this right to discipline.

Under brighter circumstances, all those watchdogs became cheerleaders. Even a small good deed entitled a child to be heralded as a town celebrity, especially when the telephone operator had it all over town that you won at a horse show, your dad saved a man from drowning, or your mom just recorded a song. Everyone knew before you got home. Everybody knew everything. Everyone knew everyone.

The fact is, we could not avoid each other since all community activities took place at the Town Hall. We gathered for fund-raising dinners put on by the Future Farmers of America or the 4-H Clubs. Profits were highly predictable because the whole town could be counted on to show up for the potluck dinner served up by club members.

The Town Hall also accommodated our political gatherings. Rallies were always Republican. There was no reason for the opposing party to meet because our village had only one family of Democrats, and the rest of the town's people considered them just one step away from being Communists.

Most importantly for my family, the Town Hall featured hootenannies. These celebrations were no hillbilly affairs. They were glorious events at which enthusiastic audience clapping, stomping, and singing accompanied even mediocre musicians. Of course, I mostly remember my mother's performances. When she played, we sat together in the audience and glowed, carefully noting how much each neighbor appreciated her songs. We swelled with pride when everyone applauded. She was good; we felt important.

One of the reasons, my mother later gave for leaving Milky Way Farm, was that she wanted a bigger, better life for us. I always wondered if maybe she just wanted a bigger and better audience for herself. I would have loved things to stay just this big, to grow up in West Newbury surrounded by family, immediate and extended. I would have chosen to live in the family house, marry a small-town sweetheart, and pass on the gift of memories to the next generation. In time my mother would choose otherwise, and paradise would be lost.

Family

Big sister, so knowing,
My brother, my pal.
The baby, a soul mate,
Me, the wild child.

Strong arms of my father,
Strong will of my mom,
A unit, a family,
Connected in time.

Milky Way Farm was my father. Dad was a strongly built, clean-cut, muscular man, the quintessential Vermont farmer. His walk was like no one else's. I could always pick him out in a crowd because he carried himself with a purpose, in a ground-covering gait that appeared deceptively relaxed. He had the strongest hands I have ever seen or held. Real man's hands. He never lost his farmer's tan.

Despite possessing all the attributes of the most masculine man, Dad had the heart of the gentlest person. He saw the world through clear blue eyes that unfailingly managed to discover the wondrous in the ordinary. He wanted us to share his insights, most particularly his love of wildlife.

Dad declared that time spent with family, friends or a neighbor was never wasted time. No wonder, I can't think of a single person who did not value his friendship. At the slightest hint of need, Dad dropped everything to assist a friend. He was the first in line to milk cows for an injured dairyman or take food to a sick neighbor.

Once he rescued an entire barn full of cows. All lined up for milking, the cows had stretched their necks through stanchions to access their feed while they awaited their turn. The barn's rotten floorboards gave way beneath them like the trap door of a gallows, leaving the row of cattle dangling by their necks. Not a single hoof touched the ground.

Dad and the farmer positioned a tractor to support the remainder of the barn floor, then rigged up an ingenious series of pulley ropes to hoist each cow from her noose and carefully lower her to the sub-floor. Every cow survived. The next day, Dad joined several other neighbors to help repair the barn.

On top of his farm work, Dad served as fire chief, game warden, town policeman, and coach of the local baseball and basketball teams. He rescued baby deer in the spring, calves born in winter, and drunken teenaged boys whenever the need arose. He once jumped into a partially frozen river to save a drowning man.

That winter day, Dad was on duty as the police officer. The occurrence of some minor crime sent him chasing the suspect. In an attempt to escape, the fugitive jumped into our river. The water was so shockingly cold that he could not move, much less swim away. Instinctively, my father dropped his gun belt, jumped into the water, and dragged the man to shore. Apparently, frigid water makes a bad man weaker and a good man stronger. At the end of the affair, my dad discovered that his gun belt had been stolen. Man saved; gun lost. Maddening, but a fair exchange from my dad's point of view.

As busy as he was with this myriad of vocations, Dad never ran out of time to care for us. During the years we lived on the farm, he was the one who tucked us in at night, comforted us when we were sick, removed our slivers, dabbed iodine into every scrape, dried our tears, and spanked our backsides when we deserved it.

The highlight of each day was dinner together around our heavy oak farm table. We were a raucous crowd when we first assembled in our seats. Then at the sound of Dad's chair pushing back from the table, conversation ceased and all heads turned to watch him rise. As he stood solemnly at the head of the table, Dad paused to absorb the energy of our silence. Then he began. Each word was spoken with such precision that at first, we had a hard time telling if he was reciting the opening lines of narrative poetry or sharing his most profound thoughts. Eventually, his voice fell into the rhythm of a poem like *The Midnight Ride of Paul Revere* or *The Village Blacksmith*, or he pulled from his pocket special pictures from *Life* and *Time* magazines. The graphic depictions of starving children tended to appear on liver-and-onion nights.

I don't know whether every American household considered liver and onions a food group but mine did. The only way I could gag any of it down was to smother the liver in mashed potatoes and swallow it whole. More than one liver-and-onion night, we kids were ordered to remain seated at the dinner table to clean our plates long after our parents had finished. More than once we were told to remember the starving children in China. We wished with all our hearts that those poor kids could have the liver, not only the liver on our plates but all the liver that would ever be.

After dinner, we gathered near my father and waited for him to pick up the lucky kid whose turn had come to sit on his lap as he watched TV until our appointed bedtime. Then Dad escorted us upstairs and made rounds to each bedroom. Ceremoniously he pulled the covers right up to each of our chins. If we had colds, Dad rubbed Vicks Vaporub on our chests, placing a final dab under our noses before tucking us in. As the smell permeated the room, we felt safe, warm and loved.

There were four of us kids, and not one of us would have described our status as separate but equal—we all knew who stood at the top of the pecking order. Linda, the oldest, preceded me by fourteen months, an interval apparently sufficient to anoint her with supremacy in almost all things, almost all the time.

Although she was just a toddler when I arrived, Linda had already been declared precocious and was widely admired for her outgoing personality and self-assurance. A typical oldest child, she was born mature. Even as a young kid she rarely missed an opportunity to extract from an insignificant incident some pearl of wisdom, which she imparted to her siblings, or rather her underlings, with great ceremony and intermittent contempt. As one of the ill-informed underlings, it was impossible for me to comprehend the price of her maturity or appreciate when her bossiness served to protect us.

The fall of my eighth year during deer hunting season, my paternal grandfather arrived from Connecticut with a good friend. The hunt was such an important event that they came together every year, and we knew my grandfather's buddy so well, he insisted we call him, "Uncle Pete."

One afternoon toward the end of one season, Linda and I ambled over to their trailer to see how their day had gone. Because Grandfather was still manning his spot on a far hill, it was Uncle Pete who responded to our knock and called for us to come in. Uncle Pete patted his thighs and motioned to me to sit in his lap. He teased and bounced me a bit, then chuckled, "You love your Uncle Pete, don't you?"

"Yeah," I giggled as he started to tickle me.

Linda had settled on the floor to watch TV. Abruptly she jumped up and demanded, "We have to go. We're late. Mom will be really mad if we don't hurry and get the horses fed."

I resisted briefly, but she was emphatic, and I never wanted to be in trouble with Mom. I shrugged, jumped down, and we headed home. As we hurried through the field, I could hear that my sister's breathing was much faster than mine. Then she stopped. She was breathless as she spoke.

"Yesterday after Uncle Pete killed his deer, I was in the barn with him when we heard Dad's gunshot. Uncle Pete grabbed my hands and put them down the front of his pants and told me to pray that Dad had bagged a deer." She said no more, but the look in her eyes spoke volumes—about horror, embarrassment, and shame.

"You should tell," I whispered.

"I can't and neither can you, Uncle Pete said Dad would go to jail. It would be our fault. We have to stay away. Do you hear me?"

Words failed me, but the pact was made. We ran home to feed the horses.

I found it easy to trust in my sister because we were the best of friends. We imagined together. I willingly deferred to whatever world she dreamed up so long as it included our ponies. We rode all over our farm and into town, each adventure more glorious than the last. Then suddenly, she outgrew me.

I was never so aware of the outgrowing as the day Linda blew the whistle on the group of us playing doctor. After she told, my dad gathered us all, including the neighbor's kids, around our big oak table. It was a dark, dark moment. He lectured. We squirmed in our chairs while our heads hung lower and lower. The end of innocence was also the end of all the fun with my big sister.

After that lecture, my remaining childhood memory of my older sister was her reading to us at night. Besides the substitute teacher, Linda was the only person who ever read to us. I loved books and couldn't wait to snuggle under the covers and reflect on the previous night's chapter as I waited for her to locate the correct page and resume the story. It came naturally to Linda to read dramatically. After all, she relished discovering any drama hidden in real life. I still have *Keep a Silver Dollar,* the horse story I most remember her reading.

Having lost my first, best companion to puberty, I looked down the family pecking order and shifted allegiance to my brother, Ted.

Ted was born seventeen months after me. For the most part, he shared my suspicion that we had been dealt a lesser hand, growing up sandwiched between two sisters. Once Ted and I bonded, however, we unearthed all kinds of hidden advantages in our birth order. We dubbed ourselves "The Middle Ones," a less-than-original title, but to us, it signified an allegiance of power and ensured our exclusivity.

Prior to the necessity of finding a new best friend, I had thought little of my brother. He was totally eclipsed behind the long shadow cast by my older sister.

He was just a skinny, hipless kid, always running to keep up, always hanging on to his pants as he ran. By today's standards, his baggy jeans might appear stylish in a cargo-pant sort of way, but back then, his jeans hung low because they were either hand-me-downs or purchased large enough to last for years.

Each new day evolved into a scavenger hunt for Ted. He filled his pockets with so many rusty nails, worms, bits of string, and rocks that he would have to jettison most of the bounty before he could mount a horse or climb a tree. We knew he was itching to join us, but always he hesitated. He had to weigh the value of his newly acquired treasures against the fun we were having, and the decision never came easily. The longer he debated with himself, the further behind he fell. We never waited.

Instead, during the years when Linda and I were joined at the hip, Ted was our favorite target for dirty tricks, inspired in part by Mom's insisting that we include him despite our whining that he never played any game the right way. Like the times when we harvested blueberries for Imperial Feasts. He popped every berry he picked straight into his mouth, contributing nothing to the communal bucket. He would become so focused on stuffing his cheeks that he would wander smack dab over a fire-ant hill.

My sister and I could see what was coming, and we smugly maintained our silence as poetic justice ran its course. We were all focused, his two eyes on the berries, our four eyes on the anthill, each ant's hundreds of eyes on Ted's feet. We smiled and nodded at each other as we waited, knowing that our brother would be stomping, dancing and punching at the ants once they summitted his shoes and bit down on his shins. Of course, all his tromping around on top of the anthill called up an army of reinforcements, guaranteeing that the situation would get worse before it got better. Perhaps my brother should have learned to be more careful, but he didn't. Certainly, my older sister could have imparted a pearl about fire ants, but she didn't. We just hoped that he would lose his taste for blueberries or at least for berry picking with us.

Other evenings, we would entice Ted into tagging along to investigate the forest. We kept up a front of false camaraderie until the shadows darkened. Then we began chanting in our lowest, spookiest voices, "The wolves are coming, the wolves are coming."

Once we had created enough tension to scare ourselves, we took off for home, leaving Ted behind screaming, "Wait, wait for me." Fortunately for him, if any wolves did reside in the woods of Milky Way Farm, they ran very slowly or had no taste for a little boy who was so skinny that he couldn't keep up his pants as he raced for home.

Then, my sister became serious and left me without a playmate. I suffered from her abandonment until I realized my brother, who was still tagging along behind me, was dying to assume my former role as the underdog. After all, the bottom rung still elevated him from bearing the brunt of our jokes.

Left to our own devices, I realized that I enjoyed running side by side with Ted, and he wasn't actually slow. If it hadn't been for the head start that trickery gave us, he probably could have outrun my sister and at least kept up with me.

Fortunately for me, Ted also had an imagination vivid enough to match my own. He and I invented one game after another. His hero was Abraham Lincoln; mine was Marquis De Lafayette. No matter that they had existed generations apart in history. At Milky Way Farm, Lincoln and Lafayette roamed the hills of our farm together, conquering the British, the Indians, the Confederates, and various dragons we encountered. Lincoln, of course, deferred to Lafayette in strategic decisions, and Lincoln always agreed to go second.

About the time I turned ten and my brother nine, we formed the Daredevil Club with the neighboring farm boys who were close to our age. I was the only girl. I assumed the position of the leader, bestowing on myself whatever illustrious title fit my current mood. I maintained this status because I would touch any disgusting creature, climb any tree, and most importantly, take any dare. Our dares ranged from disgusting-but-benign to life-threatening. Once a dare was on the table, the challenged member had to either accept it or endure unending scorn.

On a boring afternoon, one member might challenge another to taste an unpronounceable spice from the pantry. A taste was no measly sprinkling on the tip of the tongue. It meant downing whatever size spoonful the darer handed to the daree, and I can attest that gagging down a tablespoon of red pepper flakes feels more life-threatening than benign.

In addition to executing household dares, a good part of each club meeting was devoted to reconnoitering and secret missions in the open fields or nearby woods. Discovering a puffball in a cow pasture triggered an automatic dare. In New England, puffballs are natural phenomena, mushroom-like masses that can grow as big as basketballs. The dare required the challenged member to kneel down and ceremoniously plunge his hand inside the puffball. If he was lucky, his gesture released a puff of brown powder harmlessly into the air. If it was not his day, his hand slid into a mass of rotten brown slime with a remarkably distinct and disgusting odor that might not wash off for days. Still, no member ever hesitated.

Our barn inspired a second automatic dare. Every Dare Devil had to jump from one of the two trap-door openings in the hayloft situated ten feet above the barn's ground level. In preparation for the jump, we pried each door off the loft floor, set it aside, and then threw down as much hay as we considered necessary to ensure our survival. One Dare Devil stationed himself by each opening, and on count the designated jumpers stepped into the abyss, dropping feet first into the hay. The dare was not complete until each member had jumped and then helped clean up every trace of our safety net by feeding the hay to a hungry cow.

One afternoon when a jump was scheduled, I started tossing down the hay. I failed to notice my father standing underneath the trap-door until I had covered him in a shower of hay. Even before the last wisp had settled on the barn floor, he shouted, "Get down here this minute."

When he realized what we were intending, he tanned my hide—not because the hay had fallen on him, but out of disbelief that we took such risks. From that day forward, Dad forbade jumping.

But he hadn't said anything about running the rafters. My status as president, chairman or queen of the Dare Devil Club remained unchallenged because I could run the rafters of our barn faster than anyone. The rafters, providing the horizontal support for the gambrel roof, ran down each long side of the milking barn about thirty feet above the floor. They were constructed of two-by-six boards set on end and spaced about three feet apart. The rafter runner had to measure each footfall to span the three-foot void and land on the two-inch surface of each board.

Right foot, left foot, right, left. The runner picked up momentum while focusing on the other end of the milk barn a hundred feet away. Looking down would be fatal to the effort, and for that matter could be fatal to the runner. The temptation to look down varied with the conditions underfoot. At times the barn was full of hay. At other times, it was empty.

Because only one club member tackled the rafters at a time, a comparison of speed required the waiting Daredevils to count aloud, "One-thousand-one, one-thousand-two, one thousand..." The accuracy of the count was not critical; it was a foregone conclusion that the race was mine. I was the only one who actually ran over the rafters, and I only ran because I was relentless in my efforts to prove myself. I never fell. Of course, when my father eventually heard rumors about rafter running, he sternly and emphatically disallowed that dare, too, and removed the ladder with which we had accessed the rafters.

The Dare Devil Club regularly assaulted the wooded hill across from our farm then marched single-file to our favorite meeting spot. As the highest point in the near vicinity, it offered a panorama of the surrounding fields, an array of creatures, a variety of climbing rocks, and quick access to escape into the trees. No one else ever ventured up the hill, so the escape value of our location went untested.

One afternoon after we had regrouped on our summit, I found myself at a loss for any plausible need to maintain order and silence. Then I came up with the idea of a swearing contest. I sat the club in a tight circle and instructed each member to take a turn reciting the curses he had overheard his parents mutter as they milked cows, sheared sheep or worked on fences. Each member took lots of turns because we had heard all kinds of swearing. The epithets we recited, however, were not the vulgar words overused today but rather pure swear words like, "Shit," "Son-of-a-bitch," and "Damn it all to Hell." These words had power and saying them, gave us power. Well, they gave us a little power, but not enough to protect us if we were overheard. Before we took our turns, we often paused to look behind ourselves, knowing that we would be eating soap if we got caught. After we exhausted our repertoires, we rested a while, relishing the momentary sensation of adulthood.

Daredevil training came in handy the summer when I visited my father's family in Connecticut. I accompanied my cousin to her day camp so that she could show off the array of camp animals, including deer, pigmy goats, and a black bear that belonged to one of the counselors. The bear lived in a chain-link cage about eight-feet square. The top of the cage was covered with a piece of plywood that had a hole just large enough for the bear's head to stick out when he stood on his hind legs.

After lunch when all the campers assembled in the picnic area, my cousin stole me away from the group to demonstrate how cool it was to feed the bear. Although the bear was technically off-limits to campers, the counselors had left a tempting supply of his special pellets in a bucket by the cage.

When the bear saw my cousin pick up a handful of pellets, he immediately reared up and stuck his head out of the hole in the plywood, anxiously awaiting his treat. My cousin stepped up on the stool next to the cage and extended her hand toward him. Instead of licking the pellets out of her hand, the bear grabbed her outstretched arm and began pulling her toward him. The stool toppled over, her legs kicked furiously, and she screamed with a pitch and volume that only one in the jaws of a bear could justify.

Spurred by her peril, the Daredevil spirit roared inside me. I grabbed the handle of the pellet bucket and jumped on the stool from where I wielded the bucket with the authority of a hammer thrower, swinging it over my head with my full ten-year-old might smack across the bear's face. Pellets sprayed everywhere, but the bear ignored my first effort. My cousin's screams intensified. Without flinching, I bashed the bear's face again, then again and again, until I think I knocked that bear silly. He released my cousin and shook his head, looking for all the world like the bewildered victim of the whole affair.

Hearing all the screams and commotion, the counselors came running. The first to arrive stared at the blood covering my cousin and passed out cold. Second on the scene was the owner of the bear who stopped short and wet his pants. A crowd gathered before anyone mustered the where-with-all to examine my poor cousin's arm. The bear had chewed from her wrist up past her elbow. An ambulance was summoned and she was whisked away.

Confronting the bear was nothing compared to the discomfort I experienced dealing with the attention the bear rescue brought me. My cousin's parents, my grandparents, and even a newspaper reporter made me tell and retell the tale of my heroism. Although attention embarrassed me, cards, gifts, a plastic horse, and newspaper articles eased my self-consciousness. I ceremoniously accepted a savings bond and a much-desired plastic horse as tokens of appreciation for the great save. In truth, all the hoopla, money, and praise paled when compared to the plastic horse. I would take on a bear any day for such a prize.

Fortunately for my ever-daring body and soul, my commitment to dare deviling, shifted into a safer balance as my relationship with my baby sister began to blossom. Only through the grace of God did she come into my life.

After Ted, my mother had not wanted another child. Mother had lost a great deal during the first couple of years after his birth. One fateful morning, a neighbor had come to visit and share a cup of coffee with Dad. When she stood

up to leave, she flicked ashes from her cigarette into the burner on our gas stove. Midmorning that day, Mom took us girls out with her to ride the horse while little Ted rode with Dad on the tractor. When we returned to the house, Linda and I settled down in front of the TV to watch *Rocky and Bullwinkle*. Then Mom's screams filled the room, "Go, find your dad!"

Terrified by her terror, we ran out to the driveway, sat down and cried. We had no idea that our house was going up in flames. Within minutes, Dad arrived with Ted. He threw Ted to Mom who caught him, then Mom grabbed us and ran to the end of the driveway. We watched in horror as our beautiful, four-story home burned to the ground. After weathering over one hundred years of history, it was reduced to ashes in a matter of hours by a cigarette butt. The only things salvaged were a melted spoon and a horse-head ashtray. Every memory, every treasure my parents owned was lost. It was too much for Mom.

When my mother realized she was pregnant a few months later, she stole away to the barn, found the veterinary instruments used for the cows, and attempted to perform an abortion. She had not realized that Dad was already in the barn throwing hay to the cows. When he rounded the corner and discovered my mother, he knew immediately what she intended. In an effort to assuage her misery, he promised her two Arabian horses if she would let the baby live. They each made good on their promises. In a few months, I had a sister, and my mother received a magnificent Arabian stallion and the mare of her choice.

Considering the miraculous intervention which ensured her life, it was no wonder my baby sister grew up to look exactly like an angel, or rather a cherub, though perhaps a skinnier variety than is usually depicted among the clouds of Heaven. Her soft smile transformed her otherwise impish face into the picture of gentleness. Her wide-eyed gaze exposed a soul that came into this world possessed of both wisdom and sadness.

As soon as she learned to stand up, it became apparent she would be tall for her age, graceful and beautiful. The rest of us kids would grow strong and muscular. Teresa would remain refined and willowy.

I began to take notice of Teresa when she was about two. Prior to then, Mom had kept her in the backroom of our house. There, Mom fed and changed her fourth child three times a day. The rest of the day, a wooden baby gate separated Teresa from the family. I had watched the way she pulled her small body up and stared through the gate, and I thought she looked exactly like a pet store puppy. Surely, my mother must have changed my sister's clothing when it was soiled, yet I remember only a pair of little red stretch pants, day after day.

Once Teresa was old enough to toddle around outside, my shadow took on the shape of my baby sister. She followed me everywhere, probably because I let her. Then I discovered how much I loved her.

As the years passed, I came to believe that our friendship began a very long time before, perhaps in some epoch that I could no longer remember. Teresa brought joy to my existence; I provided protection for hers.

We rode horses together, double and bareback. She sat behind me as we explored trails, jumped jumps, sang songs, and relished the simple joy of life.

I insulated her from Mom's temper. Like when Teresa got so involved in capturing and smashing the potato beetles in the garden that she wet her pants. My mother reprimanded her with disgust, but not wanting to interrupt her own activity, ordered me to take my sister into the house, change her, and spank her.

Inside, I removed Teresa's wet pants and put on dry ones, but I only pretended to spank her, clapping my hands to imitate the sound of smacks. We covered our mouths with our hands to suppress the sound of our giggles.

Other days, it was Teresa's fine hair that triggered Mom's anger. It was always so tangled and matted that once, despite Teresa's tears and protests, Mom cut it off. To ease Teresa's sorrow, I asked Mom to cut my hair as well. We both looked awful, but we looked alike.

Truth was, the tempo of all our lives perpetually rose and fell according to the whims of our eccentric, high-strung and self-centered mother. Mom came from a privileged background, growing up in a Washington, D.C. suburb that prided itself on education and civility. My grandfather was a physicist who had worked to develop the atomic bomb; my grandmother was renowned as a gracious hostess. Mom described herself as a rebel and prided herself in escaping her private-school, debutante world.

There seemed to be something deliberate in the way my mom's housekeeping was the polar opposite of her mother's. My grandmother's residence could have graced the cover of *Good Housekeeping*. She served breakfast with silver, and her sheets and pillowcases were ironed before going into the closets. Mom was not interested in any tasks traditionally assigned to women.

Mundane things never mattered to her. She particularly considered housecleaning beneath her. Because she allowed her cats the run of the place, we, kids, routinely scrubbed cat feces from the tub before we bathed.

Mom seemed to care that the house appeared presentable only when her parents were coming to visit. By that time the cleaning job had escalated far beyond conventional cleaning methods. Frantically, Mom conscripted us for the effort. She had my father park his dump truck beneath the upstairs window. We watched in horror as she tossed our treasures out the window, and we sobbed as Dad drove them away.

In much the same way that my mother scorned gentility, she seemed uncomfortable with her femininity. She stood five-foot-six inches tall, but her slim, athletic body rarely stood in one spot for long. I can only picture her in motion. She never wore makeup and never needed it. Her hazel eyes burned with passion that radiated unobstructed because she nearly always confined her thick, dark hair in a barrette or braid.

I remember the day when I first became aware that Mom was beautiful. Momentarily, the world stopped. That afternoon, we were all hurrying to bring in the hay during a thunderstorm. My mother wore a sleeveless shirt. I stared at her wet, bare arms and shining face. She moved with that exquisite quality of grace in motion that converted even an act as simple as hay hauling into something of a dance.

It was Mom's personality, however, that most impacted our lives. Something in her core forever burned, fueling her life with perpetual intensity. If she took an interest in something, she had to conquer it. Even creativity became a competitive sport. When she helped us carve pumpkins, she produced wizened cowpokes, cigar-smoking comedians, apes or witches. No wonder our jack-o-lanterns won the community Halloween contests every year. No wonder our townsfolk congratulated Mom on the ribbons that had been awarded to us.

For dress-up classes at the horse shows, Mom handcrafted costumes that transformed her children into knights, cowboys, Indians, Arabian sheiks, traveling minstrels, and princesses. The year I was a tournament jouster, Mom created armor from heavy poster board covered in aluminum foil and emblazoned my shield with the pale yellow and black colors of Milky Way Farm. She draped my pony in an old bedspread plated with glittering armor. I rode off convinced that my wooden sword could slay any dragon—or at least my little brother.

Everything fell by the wayside as Mom poured herself into her projects, but once she had mastered a challenge, she moved on, and she never looked back.

Apparently, small children—including her own—didn't make the grade as worthy of her interest. She rarely displayed affection toward any of us—through word or touch. On the other hand, I noted early in life her love for cats. Mom often wandered around the house carrying one, or if she were sitting, a cat would most likely curl up on her lap and purr in response to her caressing and gentle words.

I do remember once when I was about eight that my mother held my hand. She had taken me to the doctor because I had stepped on a nail. As the doctor cleaned the hole in my foot, Mom offered her hand for me to grip so I could withstand the pain of the procedure. I held her tightly, thinking to myself that the doctor could take all the time he needed. Pain was immaterial. But when the doctor finished dressing the wound, she withdrew her hand, telling me she admired my bravery. I clung to her praise more tightly than I had grasped her hand.

Praise from Mom was hard to come by. Far more often she would lose her temper, and when she did, she destroyed things. When I was four or five, she dismembered my beloved stuffed rabbit, the only plush toy I ever owned. While my sister was napping on the sofa, I had used a pair of scissors to cut her long, wavy hair. I had just mastered the art of snipping and had no idea that I was committing an unforgivable and unforgettable criminal act until my mother's fury made it apparent.

Mom lifted my rabbit off the couch where it lay beside me in a floppy heap. She stood directly in front of me, grasping the rabbit below its shoulders so that its ears, arms, and legs hung limply. She picked up the scissors in her other hand. I watched in silent horror as she slowly and deliberately chopped off each arm and leg, then stabbed deeply into its belly exposing the fluffy stuffing. Finally, she hacked its face into bits as she repeated, "This is your own fault, and this is what happens when you use scissors the wrong way."

My toy and my heart were scattered in pieces around her feet. I turned away sobbing as she stepped over the shreds and left the room.

If anything got out of hand while Mom worked in the kitchen, utensils would fly. One afternoon as she was shaving kernels off corncobs to freeze for winter meals, my brother and I ran in to tattle about our most recent spat. Mom looked up from the corncob and glared at us. Then she raised the knife to shoulder level and hurled it against the kitchen wall where it stuck momentarily before it fell to the floor and bounced toward us. Our words still hung in the air as we flew out the door.

Mom's penchant for punishment was, however, tempered by her desire to teach us. Late one summer day, after we had spent hours in a muddy stream building dams, digging trenches, and throwing mud balls, we charged into the house, hoping that dinner was ready. Instead, we ran into Mom emerging from the laundry room with an armload of freshly washed clothes. Justifiably livid about our muddy tracks and handprints, she herded us out, hosed us off, and then sent us to bed without supper.

Within an hour she summoned us downstairs. The moon was about to eclipse the sun. She had fashioned a special lens, which would allow us to safely observe the disappearing sun. As the world darkened before its time, we took turns observing. Between turns, we looked at each other with eyebrows raised in expressions of marvel that reflected not so much our appreciation of nature's phenomena as the miracle of Mom's reprieve. We were far more impressed with the fact that Mom set aside her punishment than with the eclipse, but when the magic ended, she sent us back to bed, still hungry.

As part of her search for deeper meaning in life, I remember Mom taking a mail-order Bible study course. She spent hours filling out the assignments and even more time reviewing her work when it was returned with comments. When the postman began delivering religion to our door, Mom began delivering us to the local Congregational Church. We had to attend regularly because we sang in the choir and were enrolled in Bible classes. Later, Mom began attending a Baptist Church in nearby New Hampshire. When she became convinced that it provided the enlightenment she sought, we were allowed to attend with her.

Our Sunday drives together to the little church in New Hampshire were the highlight of my weeks. Mom played word games with us in the car, pretended that the car was an airplane and sang songs with us. Once at the church, she sat beside us. I vied for the seat next to her as often as possible.

Horses

"Riding a horse is not a gentle hobby
to be picked up and laid down like a game of solitaire.
It is a grand passion
It seizes a person whole, and once it has done so, he will have to accept that his life
will be radically changed."

Ralph Waldo Emerson

It is impossible for me to describe me without horses—except for the few incidental things that I acquired from my birth order or inherited from my parents. I was born in between a precocious sister and a daredevil brother, who was followed by the angel. I looked most like my dad. Not pretty, for sure, but athletic. I had his Dutch nose and muscular body. It was from my mom that I acquired my determination, stubbornness, and intensity.

I could swim halfway across Hall's Pond and sprint fast enough for my mother to nickname me, "Runs Like A Deer." It was not just to be head of the Daredevil Club that I touched all those weird creatures. I actually loved them. Frogs, snakes, June bugs—nothing gave me the creeps. But outside the club, I was painfully shy, easily embarrassed, and worked too hard to please everyone.

My hair was a mess. I had the most unfortunate habit of rolling my head back and forth on my pillow to rock myself to sleep. By morning, the hair on the back of my head resembled a rat's nest. To make me presentable for school, Mom had to tear through the tangled mass with her brush. She hated it, I hated it, my hair hated it. Compared to my older sister, with her neat and tidy tresses, I looked pretty sorry even after the cleanup.

Fortunately for me, horses never cared how I styled my hair. They seemed to know instinctively that my heart was theirs. They understood how I loved their feel and their smell, how I saw beauty in their movement, how I found peace in their presence.

They also provided my closest connection to my mother. She had been raised by people who knew nothing of horses but who could afford to indulge her passion for them. When she reached adolescence her parents bought her two horses and her father built a barn for them.

Even as she grew up in the East, her heart had soared westward. As a child, she read all the novels by Will James, subscribed to *Western Horseman* magazine, and memorized the training techniques of legendary western bronc busters. She described herself as a self-made cowgirl and took pride in the degree of horsemanship she achieved.

Luckily for us, our mother wanted to share her passion for riding with her offspring. There were always horses in our lives. The first one I remember was Flicka, a retired camp horse from upstate. Flicka was a big-boned, bigheaded old mare, the likes of which never appear in anyone's daydreams of equine beauty. She was, however, a solid citizen who understood her job as our caretaker perfectly.

If Mom tacked her up, I could ride Flicka alone by the time I was five. To mount I had to climb high enough on a fence so that the saddle was below eye level. Then I launched myself onto Flicka's swayed back, landing atop the saddle like a sack of potatoes. After a bit of a scramble to adjust myself into an upright position, I flailed my legs furiously to get us started. We then plodded to the far reaches of the farm and beyond.

One afternoon, I plopped off Flicka onto the dirt road leading to our house. I doubt that she had done anything to precipitate my fall. Most likely, I was nodding off or fiddling around and lost my balance. Then I dropped off like an apple falling from a tree. Flicka stood quietly over me, blocking traffic while I dusted myself off and reconnoitered. I had no clue how to get back on without a fence. After several aborted attempts of the running and leaping variety, I managed to scramble aboard by climbing hand over hand up Flicka's mane, then getting a toe into the dangling saddle straps. Finally, one knee reached the stirrup and I shimmied on up from there. These efforts to resolve my mounting dilemma must have stupefied the drivers of the vehicles that stopped on the road because none of them got out of their cars to rescue me.

Within a couple of years of this inauspicious beginning, my older sister and I could really ride. We had a small herd of ponies that we galloped around bareback or tacked up in Civil War saddles that Mom had collected. These McClellan saddles were barebone affairs consisting of a leather-covered wooden tree, wide wooden stirrups, and a couple of straps for attaching the cinch. This Spartan, but sturdy design, indicated to me that General McClellan lacked any concern for his cavalry's comfort and even less for mine. In his defense, I doubt that the general anticipated his saddles remaining in circulation a hundred years after the war ended, but, on our longer treks, I would have appreciated a bit more thought about padding.

McClellan's tack never confined our imaginations to The War Between the States. Once aboard our saddled ponies, we became Arabian princesses, Knights of the Round Table, pioneers, Indians, outlaws, bandits or other recently conceived heroic figures.

Through our expeditions, we came to know our fields and trails as intimately as the backs of our hands. On each wooded path and game trail, we built jumps out of branches, logs or brush. We often ended our escapades in the yard of the neighbors who saved cookies for us, and sugar lumps for our ponies. No matter how far we rode, we could still hear the clanging of the heavy old farm bell that Mom rang to summon us home for dinner.

Horses even accompanied me to the West Newbury School, in my imagination at least. I insisted that every book I read featured horses. Because our library's collection was quite limited, I had to read Marguerite Henry's and Walter Farley's novels over and over. In the end, I knew The Black Stallion and The Godolphin Arabian so intimately that I could draw these fabulous creatures with every detail Marguerite or Walter had described.

As I sat at my desk, a horse galloped through my mind every time I was bored. Since I was bored often, I doodled my notebooks full, recording the essence of each steed that stole my attention from the blackboard. I saved enough drawings to wallpaper my entire room with my equine sketches.

In the spring of the year that each of us would turn nine, Mom gave the birthday child a foal to raise. Each foal was the offspring of my mother's Arab stallion crossed with Smoky, our mixed-breed, blue roan pony. The foal born in 1965 would be mine.

I was still eight during the first week in May when our pony mare was ready to deliver. Her bag had filled and was leaking the first drops of milk, signaling an imminent birth. We four kids had been granted permission to sleep in the barn so that we could experience the foal's arrival. Early that evening, we headed up the hill carrying piles of blankets. Even three-year-old Teresa tagged along, dragging her pillow with her. We mounded up thick beds of hay and piled all the bedding on top, then wiggled down between the blankets and snuggled together, talking, giggling, and arguing. Linda, though only ten, was well on the road to becoming the serious one. She kept us in line, and at her insistence, we finally settled down.

When we quieted, we could hear the night symphony of the barn: gentle cows chewing their cuds, horses stomping in their bedding and softly blowing through their nostrils, automatic waterers occasionally refilling, and hay rustling as cows and horses munched. I breathed in the pungent odor of the animals along with the sweet smell of hay and oats as I blissfully drifted off to sleep.

I awoke to find my colt already up, nursing, and dry. Any disappointment I harbored about missing his birth dissipated immediately with the sight of him. He was the most glorious creature I had ever seen.

The family made fun of him, calling him, "Pink" because of his coloring. His coat was strawberry roan, light, reddish-brown flecked with white. He had a wide blaze running down his face, tall white stockings on three of his legs, and a patch of white around the other knee. Perfect. I named him Milky Way Moon Dust in honor of our farm. Dusty for short.

I was completely responsible for my foal. I brushed every inch of his body over and over, intending to make his coat outshine that of the Black Stallion. His baby fuzz would take months to develop any luster, but I did manage to make it stick down in a rather unnatural but tidy manner. I also taught Dusty to lead and to let me pick up his miniature feet. I didn't know it then, but all of that effort constituted imprinting, teaching Dusty to accept all the things humans would expect of him.

I learned from Dusty as well. When I asked too much, he spread out his spindly legs, lowered his head, dropped his ears out to the side, and flatly refused. Shut down. Through this passive resistance, Dusty was imprinting me with the patience, kindness, and forgiveness that horses had a right to expect of me.

The arrival of Dusty marked a new chapter in my family relationships. My little sister, already my shadow, adored Dusty, too. In no time, Teresa, Dusty, and I became inseparable. As a result, I lost interest in the Daredevil Club and demoted my brother, who had no desire to keep pace with Dusty worship. Ted didn't want to spend his free time attending to a colt or singing songs about him. My little sister did. Of course, since she was not yet four, the songs had to be simple. Really, really simple:

"Dusty boy, Dusty boy, Dusty boy, Dusty boy,
Dusty boy, Dusty boy, Dusty boy, Dusty boy!"

This favorite tune went on through several verses, the lyrics always the same. We sang as a duet.

Dusty had barely turned five months old when my patience ran out—I could no longer wait to teach him about a rider. I lifted Teresa onto his back. He didn't seem to mind, so I led him around his stall. This arrangement made perfect sense to me. Although he was still quite young, Teresa weighed almost nothing. And neither Teresa nor Dusty ever complained. My parents, however, saw my training quite differently. They reprimanded me severely for endangering my sister. Dusty had to wait more than a year before he would again enjoy the privilege of carrying a rider. Poor Dusty, poor me.

One winter day before Dusty turned two, Teresa and I were out in the corral to observe him. Dusty was milling around the barnyard with the other horses, who were anxiously waiting to be brought in for dinner. Something spooked the herd into running. My little sister tripped right in Dusty's path. Instead of crushing her, Dusty jumped, clearing her little body as she instinctively covered her head. Because her face was pressed on the frozen ground, I couldn't determine her status. Frantically, I ran to her, expecting the worst. It was apparent, however, as I helped her up, that Teresa had escaped unscathed. Our eyes met, my fear melted away, and simultaneously we burst into smiles. We declared Dusty a hero. The next day, during show-and-tell, I described Dusty's miraculous leap. I proclaimed that he had saved her life, and I confess I may even have sung his song. Heaven forbid. But love knows no bounds.

Many were the accolades I received as Dusty and I grew up together. People, whose names I didn't even know, approached me at Dusty's first County Fair to congratulate me on the skill that it took to stay on that naughty boy as he reared and pranced around.

After our first eighth-place ribbon in the bareback class, we went on to become consistent winners at fairs and shows. The little stinker never gave me a free ride, but he did make me believe I was someone special. I would come to feel that sitting on his back was the most natural place to be. Imagine how I felt when I overheard my mother tell Dad, with pride in her voice, "Karen can stay on anything with hair." I hung on her words—if only she had ever told me she was proud of me.

The next summer I turned eleven, a woman named Ann arrived at Milky Way Farm and brought a mare to be bred to Mom's stallion. She had selected him after watching him at a show. I am not sure if Ann had been impressed by his performance in one particular class, or if she was just overwhelmed by his versatility and his endurance. Mom cared so much about all-around championships that she routinely entered her stallion in every division from western barrel racing to English pleasure, from costume to carriage classes. But, if Mom was the consummate competitor, her stallion was the classic show horse. Together they relished every challenge and usually accumulated enough points to end up either champion or reserve champion of the show.

The arrival of Ann opened new worlds for me. She had been to places and had done things about which I knew nothing—hardly amazing considering that my horizons were limited to our farm. What she knew about horses, however, was exceptional.

Ann stayed in the house with us for the summer while she looked after her own two horses. She cared for her animals so differently, with expertise and thoroughness I had never before witnessed. She used four or five different kinds of brushes, each with its own name and purpose. Grooming was a top to bottom effort, one brush at a time. In the end, her efforts unveiled a sleek and shiny equine figure that would have met even Walter Farley's standards.

Ann blanketed her horses for cold nights. She wrapped their legs and tails to protect them when they traveled in the horse trailer. She rode in English saddles, and her fancy Thoroughbred mare had come to America from England on an airplane. I watched her exercise those big, beautiful horses and wanted more. I never tired of hearing about her jumping competitions or riding with her.

During her free time, Ann gave me riding lessons. She also taught me about taking responsibility. She suggested that I pick up glass, wire, and metal scraps around the farm because such litter could hurt the horses. I felt myself growing up a bit as I looked for ways to make things better, for my parents, as well as for the horses. I began to help out without being asked. I amazed myself.

But, I was jealous of Ann's relationship with my mother. They were close friends and spent hours together. I hung out on the fringes of their time, accepting leftovers. I was heartbroken when Ann left to get married. Still, I had made a connection with her that would last through many years of my life and survive some very big bumps in the road.

The following fall my parents began fighting. The farm was making no money, and my family fell into debt. That winter came early and was especially hard on Mom. Feeling trapped by mounting snow, mounting debt, demanding bill collectors, and demanding children, she voiced her unhappiness with escalating force.

As always, Dad responded with confidence that things would work themselves out in time. For my mother, however, time had run out. She left at Thanksgiving Holiday to stay with Ann, who by then was living in Aspen, Colorado with her husband and baby daughter. Gone for three weeks, my mother wrote only once. She never called.

Music

Music makes pictures
And often tells stories
All of it magic
And all of it true

~ John Denver

By the time my mother returned from Aspen, she had refocused her life. Formerly, her focus had centered around herself, cats, horses, the farm, Dad, and us. In that order. All these were swept aside when she became a local celebrity, playing guitar and singing at hootenannies, town meetings, and political conventions.

Mother's original music reflected her conservative political philosophy. She was a staunch member of the Daughters of the American Revolution and the Young Americans for Freedom. During the sixties, she joined the campaign to encourage then-Governor Ronald Reagan to seek the Republican nomination for president. She and Dad collaborated on a song, they titled *Modern Paul Revere* which would become Reagan's campaign theme song. When Reagan died in 2004, their song was played at the finale of a tribute to Reagan on the Larry King Live show.

Far more importantly for us kids at Milky Way Farm, Mom occasionally sang about us. In one verse of a simple ballad she wrote,

My little farm and family,
Gifts from heaven just for me
My heart is singin' 'cause I'm free
I love life and life loves me.

So it could have happened that the horses, the farm, us kids, and even the cats could adjust our status behind Mom's new passion and her talent. Certainly, we were all thrilled to be memorialized in song as her "Gifts from Heaven."

Then in the spring of my eleventh year, I heard Mom announce that her pre-music existence had been miserable. Her words terrified me. How could her heavenly gifts have devolved into the source of her misery? My fear grew as I sensed Mom withdrawing from us and pouring herself into music.

Probably, it was inevitable that at one of her political conventions my mother would discover Bunny. This twenty-three-year-old musician had already lived beyond Mom's wildest dreams. Bunny collected Harley Davidson motorcycles and vintage cars, including a black Cadillac hearse. She dressed in silver-studded black leather, boots with steel toes, and a black helmet. She carried knives strapped to her boots.

Off and on that first year, Bunny thundered up to the farm on a motorcycle or drove up in her hearse. Either way, a cloud of dust billowed behind her. She stayed in the vacant trailer south of our main horse pasture.

We kids had never seen anything like Bunny, and after we overcame our surprise, we were drawn to her like metal to magnet. We clamored for her attention, but Bunny chose to keep to herself, at first. Eventually, Bunny appeared to warm to our adoration. On rainy days she played board games with us—Monopoly and Sorry. When the weather permitted, she put our imaginations to the test in inventive versions of hide-and-seek or cops-and-robbers. She recited versions of Cinderella that were so clever and exciting that Disney's version paled. And she talked in Pig Latin. No doubt about it, Bunny was fun. She even allowed my little sister to climb onto her lap, never complaining if Teresa had wet her pants.

Underneath her *Hell's Angel* veneer, Bunny was stunning. When her helmet came off, chestnut-brown hair dropped to her waist. Its highlighted waves created the effect that the sun itself moved with Bunny, an image made more convincing by the power of her intense blue eyes. Her body exuded strength without compromising the soft curves of femininity. She had long accepted the deference accorded her beauty as a birthright.

But there was something even more mysterious and captivating about Bunny, something different from anyone I knew, before or since. She projected an addictive presence, utterly self-serving, but alluring none the less.

Only my father remained immune to Bunny's charm. In fact, he didn't appear to like Bunny much, and his distraction felt strange because he generally liked everyone.

Bunny and my mother spent more and more of their time writing lyrics, practicing songs and performing. Fellow musicians declared their harmony extraordinary; audiences loved them. As a duet, they recorded my mother's first album, *Torch of Freedom*. Although they recorded it in the late sixties, this album was no hippie affair. It spoke of patriotism, not peace. It praised the government, not the dissidents.

Prior to Bunny's arrival, my musical exposure had consisted of a few well-worn country albums by Hank Williams and Marty Robbins, some marching band records, a bit of classical music, and my mother's original songs. Around the time I turned eight, Mom had begun teaching me simple chords for the guitar. As soon as I could strum a tune, Teresa sang along. We had spent hours belting out our favorite songs, like the hit tune about Dusty—"Dusty Boy, Dusty Boy."

Once I heard Bunny play, I concentrated on learning the guitar with a vengeance. Her playing mesmerized me; her fingers danced on the strings. I sat at her feet as she introduced me to Peter, Paul, and Mary. I met Joan Baez, Buffy Saint-Marie, Joni Mitchell, Pete Seeger, Arlo Guthrie, and the entire cast of Woodstock. These songs moved me more deeply than the words of the people from my past. Perhaps Bunny's guitar gave their thoughts more meaning and the musicians' greater sincerity.

For the remainder of my eleventh year, Bunny continued to reside at our farm, and the longer she stayed, the worse my parents' fighting became. Milky Way Farm refused to make money. Dad still envisioned a light at the end of the tunnel and remained steadfast in his belief that his hard work would pay off. Mom saw only debt. They had borrowed against the cows, the tractors, and the land. My mother captured the depth of her misery in a dismal song describing a woman alone, trapped and dying in a car that was stuck in a snowstorm. Winter and debt made her even tougher than usual to be around.

We sought refuge in Bunny's music when the shouting intensified. She listened to our fears and her patience calmed us. I remember all four of us kids racing to the barn to escape the sounds of our parents' fury. Bunny gathered us together, and we sat cross-legged in a semicircle in front of her. Our terrors melted away as we gazed into her eyes while as she sang sweet, comforting children's songs. She winked at us and smiled knowing smiles, knowing we were torn apart by our parents' fighting. She offered her music as our port in the storm.

Bunny cultivated our trust to get what she wanted. She wanted our mother. How could we know that once she got her, Bunny would become a storm in which there was no port.

That fall, Mom and Bunny left. Making matters worse, the local school board decided that our one-room school should house only first through fifth grades. We four sixth-graders would be bussed to the *big* school in nearby Newbury.

All of us transfers felt intimidated by the larger school and terrified by the masses of unfamiliar kids, but I was the most miserable. I could not shake my despair over Mom's absence and Dad's sadness. It left me without the energy to play, so I avoided my classmates and hated recess. My new teacher wrote notes of concern to my father and insisted that I at least walk the fence around the perimeter of the schoolyard just to get fresh air. I suppose I looked like a prisoner with a reprieve from solitary confinement under order to exercise in the compound. I doubt that a prisoner could have been more miserable and forlorn.

But I was not the only child in our family who was suffering. Ted was far more demonstrative about his pain. His school papers were often covered with angry scribbles. At home, he would throw himself in the dirt and pound the earth, screaming.

Then one day, as Linda and I stood together outside the *big* school, fire trucks roared by with sirens screaming. We overheard rumors that the one-room school was ablaze. We stared at each other and whispered simultaneously, "I bet it's our brother."

Ted had gone to school with matches in his pocket. Around lunchtime, he raised one finger to indicate a need to use the bathroom. When permission was granted, he descended to the basement and lit the insulation on fire. Then he returned to his seat and resumed his spelling. When smoke from below filled the classroom, the teacher ran downstairs. She had extinguished the flames before the trucks arrived.

The incident was never discussed at home, but the school district called in a child psychologist who worked out a program between the school, my father, and my brother. Ted told us that during his therapy sessions, the psychologist continuously struck matches, trying to keep his pipe lit. The irony of this ritual was not lost on my brother, even if he was only ten years old. After two such meetings, my father rose and declared that they would not be returning.

A new counselor was called in. This wise man used the time with my brother to create a cool dinosaur project that was displayed at the little schoolhouse. I didn't get it. It seemed to me that his diorama should at least have featured Smoky Bear holding a sign to remind the kids about the danger of matches. Heaven knows what would have happened to Ted if Mom had been around, but I'm certain it wouldn't have involved a diorama.

Mom refused to return for Christmas. Our kitchen never filled with the smell of Christmas cookies, so the tree decorations were scant and dull. There was no big turkey dinner. Gifts did appear under the tree, but no one had wrapped them. Dad tried to make Christmas morning special, but we could see how much he was hurting.

With Mom gone and Dad suffering, I sought solace anywhere I could find it. One place was the Baptist Church in New Hampshire we had recently joined with Mom. It was not the religion that gave me comfort, but rather one special member of the congregation, an older woman who nicknamed me, "Little Buddy" and called herself Aunt Ruth. Especially during this time when I so craved parental affection, I would have done anything to please Aunt Ruth or to repay her gentle friendship. She never asked for anything.

Knowing our mother was absent, Baptist Church members offered to pick up any of us kids who wanted to attend services. Of course, I wanted to go. I would get to spend time with Aunt Ruth.

One Sunday when there were no clean clothes anywhere in the house, I dug out my previous Sunday's dress from the laundry piled in the hall. I soaked it in the bathroom sink and scrubbed it with hand soap, rubbing one spot of cloth at a time against the knuckles of my other hand. It took a long time and almost a bar of soap to cover the entire dress. Grimly determined in my cleaning effort, I didn't notice the blisters forming on my knuckles until they burst and bled on the skirt. My heart ached as I started scrubbing again, but I switched hands and rubbed the bloodstains against the knuckles of my other hand until the spots rinsed down the drain.

Once I walked into the church, I no longer cared about the blisters, and it was obvious that Aunt Ruth did not care about the dress. Truth be told, no matter what I wore, I looked like a scrawny little tomboy, which was exactly the reason Aunt Ruth originally sought my friendship. She motioned me over to her pew where she had saved a place for me. Our legs touched because I pressed myself close to her, oblivious to the empty space on either side of us. We didn't need to, but we shared one hymnal, and my emptiness disappeared, at least for the moment.

To dispel the agony of my mother's absence during the rest of each week, I kept busy galloping Dusty around our pastures. The passage of time transformed the farm from snowfields into acres of newly mown hay. We galloped on. Sometimes Teresa came along, and we rode double and bareback.

Her small, fragile body hugged my sturdy one. After the spring daisies bloomed, we adorned Dusty's head with a bridle of braided hay rope in which we had woven freshly picked flowers. To complete the illusion of wild princesses, we tucked daisies in our own braids before we took off across the field. As usual, we sang at the top of our voices.

Lonesome though I was, I remained a free spirit, grounded in Paradise at Milky Way Farm.

Paradise Lost

This used to be my playground
This used to be my childhood dream
This used to be the place I ran to
Whenever I was in need of a friend

~ Madonna

When school ended, my world forever changed. My mother returned with Bunny from wherever they had been. Mom had mailed us a few postcards, but because we didn't know anything about a place called Nashville, the pictures meant nothing to us. The cards, however, reassured us that Mom thought of us. Bunny even wrote. She sent the sweetest notes to Teresa. Instead of words, which my little sister could not yet read, Bunny drew tiny pictures to tell her stories.

The day after Mom came home, she announced that we kids would soon be joining her on an adventure. We all wanted adventure, we wanted to be included, and we wanted to please our mother. Mostly we wanted everything to be okay, so we promised to be ready when it came time to depart.

Upon their return, Bunny seemed to have chosen me as her little pal. I felt honored. I did everything to foster her affectionate feelings for me. If she suggested something needed to be done or she wanted something, I could not act fast enough. She had given us so much comfort while my parents had fought that I convinced myself she must love us.

In June, the day of my twelfth birthday, my parents gave me a Breyer horse, the one I most coveted from this extensive collection of life-like plastic horses. This white Arabian stallion could have been modeled after the horse of my dreams, the one I envisioned when we pretended to be horses.

That same afternoon, Mom packed our belongings and loaded her horses in our makeshift trailer. Despite his despair in knowing that Mom was leaving him, Dad had spent every spare moment of the past several months converting an old blue International truck from a bakery transport into a six-horse van.

Oblivious to all this effort on his behalf, when it was Dusty's turn, he flatly refused to walk up the ramp into the trailer. Mom tried to load him several times, eventually losing her temper and whipping him. Then Dad jumped in to salvage the situation. He thought he could climb on Dusty's back and ride him in, but Dusty planted his feet in front of the ramp and would not budge. It was a comical sight, this big, sturdy man kicking wildly at my small, unresponsive pony.

I had been watching the whole sad scene from the shadows of the barn because I was ordered to stay out of the way. But I stepped forward when Dad gave up and dismounted. He handed me the lead rope, shook his head, and asked me to hold Dusty for a bit.

The other horses, having already stood in the van for quite a while, were becoming impatient. I could sense a disaster brewing as their stomping escalated. I spoke seriously to Dusty about his poor manners, and then I walked him up to the edge of the ramp. I stepped up; he followed. Then I led him to his spot, tied him, and kissed his nose. I whispered in his ear, "Thank you, thank you."

Everything loaded, my mother, her most beloved cat, Bunny, her German shepherd dog, our six horses, and we four kids headed out for the adventure Mom had promised. It did not occur to me that I would never come back to Milky Way Farm or that, as I waved to my father standing alone in the driveway, I would not see him for a very long time. His nurturing presence would be forever stolen from me.

Dad should never have stepped back from our lives. He should have understood that we needed him to keep holding our hands, and tucking us in. Along with our father, we were leaving behind the innocence and naivety, joy, and freedom I had cherished. Mom never looked back.

Bunny and Mom had set their sights on Nashville to become country music stars. It took, however, much longer to arrive in Tennessee than they had anticipated. Our first stop was at Mom's parents' home in Maryland. We kids stayed with our grandparents while Mom and Bunny drove on to Tennessee with the horses. Four days later they returned for us and for the crates our grandfather had constructed for our belongings.

That next afternoon, the big blue International truck broke down in Atkins, Virginia, one of those back-water towns where dogs roam freely in the streets and people live in trailer houses with junk cars as front-yard ornaments. None of us could possibly have imagined that we would be marooned there for three long weeks while the repair shop struggled to locate the parts needed to repair our old truck. While we waited, we ate peanut butter sandwiches, morning, noon, and night. Following our supper sandwiches, we set up cots and slept inside the horse compartment of the van. We had christened the truck "The Big Blue Monster."

We kids wiled away the days climbing around the broken cars and boxcars, abandoned behind the auto repair shop. The backlot where we played had long ago succumbed to the ravages of poison ivy. As farm kids, we were well versed in the danger lurking in each shiny, colorful leaf. However, because our entire temporary playground was enveloped in the vines, none of us could avoid getting a rash.

Ted's exposure was different. He deliberately rubbed poison ivy leaves all over himself, hoping that if he got badly infected, Mom would take us home. Unfortunately, Mom remained indifferent to his ten-year-old strategizing. She rubbed salt into the open blisters that covered his face and body, then she simply ignored him when he curled up in agony in the back of the van. Perhaps Mom and Bunny played their guitars a little louder to drown out his crying. For whatever reason, they practiced constantly.

As time in Atkins dragged on, real trouble began. The summer heat became unbearable and truck parts were delayed again. As temperatures rose it became harder to sleep in the back of the van. We roasted. My mother had no patience with us kids and yelled at the slightest provocation—and sometimes without one. For a woman whose passions had ruled everyone's life, such totally uncontrolled chaos was her worst nightmare.

Then one scorching afternoon, we lost Teresa. It dawned on all of us at about the same time that she was missing. We spread out as Mom instructed and began calling for her. Moment by moment, our search became more frantic until we were shouting with all the volume that panic engenders. Bunny found her.

It was years before Teresa told us that earlier that same day Bunny had smacked her over and over for wetting her pants. Teresa was still six years old. She had outgrown the red leggings, but her body remained diminutive and childlike. Teresa had worked hard to grow up, and she kept up in many ways, but she could not conquer bedwetting. The secret beating turned her childhood upside-down. When Teresa curled up between the crates that held our belongings, she had fully intended to disappear forever.

No wonder Bunny had searched so rabidly. She had to steal a few moments alone with Teresa to buy her silence. Bunny promised two model horses for my sister's birthday and two more for Christmas. Bunny kept that promise, along with every other promise she made, good or bad. But for the present, Teresa's inexplicable sadness overwhelmed us all. Mom's adventure lost any final remnant of its charm.

I will never forget one small act of kindness that resurrected in us kids a fragile ripple of hope. An evening or two after the search for Teresa we were playing inside the truck waiting for the bread and peanut butter to be brought out for supper when we heard knocking on the side door. As we scrambled to the open windows, we peered into the faces of a middle-aged couple holding an aluminum pan full of steaming macaroni and cheese. They were presenting to us the first and only hot food we ate during our three-week stay in Atkins. We were overwhelmed with gratitude and appetite.

Even a bad dream eventually comes to a close. The parts arrived and the repairmen installed them post-haste. Our hosts had probably had their fill of Vermont squatters. Still, they lined up in front of the garage to wave us off.

When we arrived in Nashville, we drove around in seemingly endless circles until we had asked for directions often enough to zero in on a treeless street, lined on both sides with indistinguishable plank shacks situated on narrow, barren lots. The scene looked as alien to me as a foreign country—one I had no desire to visit.

Mom and Bunny managed to single out one of these pitiful structures and parked the Big Blue Monster in front of it. Mom came around to the back of the van and opened the door to the horse compartment where the four of us kids had been traveling. Not one of us moved when the door opened. We just stood there and stared at the little house.

In the twilight, it was obvious that the paint had peeled away so long ago that it was impossible to determine the color it had once worn. We would only be able to identify our house by the pair of broken windows next to the front door.

After a minute or two, Mom ordered us out, and we marched single-file behind her to the front door. One after the other we filed in, each carrying a cot to sleep on. We kids set up cots in the first room, the one with the broken windows. Mom and Bunny assembled their cots in a separate back room. We did not unload the truck because Mom assured us we would move again very soon.

All night as we lay on our cots, our ears filled with the sounds of city streets or, more accurately, the clamor of city slums. Car tires screeched, sirens wailed, and stray dogs howled while the neighbors screamed and swore. None of us had ever seen, heard or smelled anything like this. In spite of the stifling heat, we pulled our covers tightly around us, trying not to leave any part of our bodies exposed to the terrifying visions that engulfed us.

In the morning, the enormity of our loss descended upon us. No more family mealtime rituals, no more homegrown food, and no more Dad declaring each meal the best one ever. We ate in silence, seated on our cots. Our food came from dented cans and damaged cardboard boxes purchased at a discount outlet. Once Mom and Bunny found a part-time job singing at an Italian restaurant they sometimes brought home pizza that they salvaged off of the trays left by customers. The mealtime tension was worse than the food. My sensitive little sister began throwing up.

One evening, when Mom prepared another round of grilled-cheese sandwiches, she overlooked me. She had just taken a sandwich out of the pan and started eating. I could hear everyone chewing, but I did not dare say a word. One after the other, Linda, Ted, and Teresa stared at me, then averted their eyes, attempting to hide behind their sandwiches. But chewing stopped. You could have heard a pin drop anywhere in that barren shack. The silence caught Mom's attention. She surveyed the room. When she realized I had nothing to eat, her curses tore through the silence as her sandwich flew across the room. I burst into tears, assuring her it was okay. The sandwich lay in pieces on the floor. No one moved to touch it. No one moved at all.

It wasn't just mealtime that had changed. My mom's self-absorbed, self-focus narrowed even further as Bunny fought her for control of their music career and our household. Their relationship reduced itself into a raw power struggle.

Although Mom was older than Bunny by ten years, Bunny abandoned any pretense of respect for Mom's seniority. Bunny's words twisted our whole reality as she convinced Mom that she was clearly inferior and greatly flawed. We could sense our mother capitulating. First, we noticed her weeping in frustration after a practice session when she couldn't get a complex bar of music right, at least "right" according to Bunny.

Later, we watched in horror as Mom groveled, cried, and pathetically crawled on her knees, while tears and snot ran down her face.

What had become of the pride of our Town Hall? Where was the self-assuredness that had served as such a constant in our lives? Our strong, proud, powerful mother was begging for help while Bunny pounded her with insults, demanding that Mom play the music one particular way. Then seconds later, Bunny changed everything she had just ordered. My insides churned. I tasted bile in my mouth as I witnessed one horrific, degrading scene after another. Even I could see how Bunny orchestrated each no-win situation. Even I could see that Bunny reveled in prolonging every agony she initiated.

Needless to say, we four children were no match for this master of mind games in the throes of destroying our mother. Bunny casually accepted our misery as collateral damage, unavoidable injury to the poor unfortunates trapped within their war zone.

Soon, it was Bunny who told us what was expected. If we made the slightest mistakes, she ridiculed us. If things weren't picked up, we were slobs; if we didn't think ahead, we were stupid. Bunny's tone, even more than her words, cut deeply into our tender souls. Mother never intervened on our behalf, but then she, too, was trying to survive Bunny's wrath. We followed our mother's footsteps and submitted.

The addictive charm Bunny had used to win us over either evaporated or morphed into venom. I came to think there were two Bunnies; one good and one evil. None of us knew, from moment to moment, which Bunny we would get.

Being the sensitive, insecure child that I was, I internalized the whole affair as my fault. Perhaps each of my sisters and my brother felt the same, but no one compares emotions when survival is at stake. All I could focus on was my own shortcomings. All I heard in Bunny's tirades was one declaration after another that our problems arose because I was bad. I figured that I was not loved because I was not loveable. My child's mind twisted her condemnations around until my child's heart came to believe that if I could become good, I could make everything okay. Given such an impossible goal, a sense of failure soon overwhelmed me.

Worse yet, I began believing Bunny's pronouncements that I deserved punishment. So, since I could never be good enough, I contemplated ways to punish myself, intending that self-mutilation would alleviate everyone else's suffering.

At night, fleas were biting us all. Constantly. Because the itching drove me nuts, I scratched the bites until I scraped all the skin off my ankles. Then, I poured salt on the rawest places, creating sores so deep that they eventually formed lumpy, white scars all over my lower legs.

If I felt responsible for some, especially, bad things, I cut myself with a pocketknife and left a trail of blood in my wake. I was never brave enough to do any real damage with that knife so I determined that salt served as a superior punishment. The pain lasted much longer.

Days rolled into weeks. Mom and Bunny left us alone at night in this house of broken windows with only Bunny's dog for protection. They cruised Nashville in the "Big Blue Monster," seeking their musical fortune or at least looking for a spot to play for wages. They returned in the wee hours of the morning and slept late. When they awoke, they started at it again, practicing hard and fighting continuously.

I cannot be sure how long we stayed in this dismal space, maybe only a month, maybe an eternity. Maybe both. The toll on us was enormous. We had lost touch with the earth. On the farm, it was not our mother we ran to for solace but rather Mother Earth—her hills, forests, and fields. These were the spaces where our horses consoled us. Now our horses were boarded at a beautiful nearby horse farm, but neither Bunny nor Mom ever took us to see them. Cutting off contact with my soul-mate Dusty severed my connection to my soul. I hardly noticed as the summer crept onward.

Then Mom and Bunny announced we were moving to Fairview, a small town about twenty minutes outside of Nashville, my mother, with help from her parents, had purchased a farm. Perhaps, this farm had once operated with dignity, but years of neglect had erased any trace of it. Weeds and thorn bushes covered the fields, and the fences lay in ruin. Because the seller's tenants still resided in the farmhouse, we would have to live in the barn, assemble our cots in its lower section, wash ourselves from a spigot, and eat our meals in the feed room. An unbelievable upgrade.

But the dark cloud under which we existed followed us to the farm. Every request to perform a task was shouted as an order and followed by, "*NOW*!" No one dared delay even for a second. One evening after Mom yelled, "Come eat, *NOW*," Teresa came flying up from our sleeping quarters without a stitch of clothing. The whole family stared at her in shocked silence. For once everyone smiled. Innocence had crossed paths with obedience. A vulnerable little body trying so hard to be good. She tore my heart out.

The inconveniences of residing in the barn became insignificant when we picked up our beloved horses and ponies. Once I could touch them, I could get back in touch with life. As soon as the horses were unloaded, Mom sold The Big Blue Monster, replacing it with a station wagon and a small, two-horse trailer. Good riddance.

The return to the country reinvigorated us sufficiently to foster a collective commitment to resurrect our land. We started by shoveling years of petrified manure out of the barn. The challenge turned me into a tenacious and stubborn worker. At twelve years old, I would tackle any man's job—like digging postholes for the new fence, pounding nails into boards, and chopping weeds. I, however, had to accomplish each task without a man's tools.

Before we could put up the new fence, I had to scratch out two-foot deep postholes with a hand shovel. The ground was a bed of rocks and baked hard. Each time my trowel hit a fieldstone, I would kneel down, grab the shovel blade in both hands then bash and pry at the rock, gouging the earth around it in an effort to create that first whisper of movement indicating some hope, I could dislodge it. Tears ran down my cheeks and blisters erupted on my hands. I never gave up. I never asked for help. I would heft the rock out. Afterward, I measured each hole to be sure it reached the proper depth. The only standard I accepted was perfection.

Despite the overwhelming energy we all expended, the land gave back to us tenfold. We had space again, with trees, a stream, and fifty-six acres for riding. I discovered a long path that we named "The Snake" because it wound through dense woods but had soft enough footing to permit galloping. Dusty memorized every curve in that path and the hill ahead. Each time he ran the gauntlet, he burst into the clearing and charged upward. On a rainy summer day, the hill was a nearly perfect vantage point from which to relish the taste of rain. But it was not Milky Way Farm.

Once the Fairview farm began to take shape, my routine relaxed into occasions when I could escape all day with Dusty. I awoke before anyone else, eager to savor the quiet of the early morning hours. No one was yelling insults, no one was crying. I slipped out from under my blankets and dressed quietly then tip-toed out of the barn, afraid to disturb the silence. I located my pony in the herd, slipped on his bridle, and swung onto his back. Then we headed for the edge of our property where I kept an old blanket hidden. I slid off, threw the blanket over the barbed wire fence, hopped back on Dusty, and we cleared the pasture fence. Our objective was the next field where I had discovered a stand of wild blackberries flourishing on our perimeter fence. There, Dusty and I breakfasted together. I downed the berries, Dusty attacked the grass. No words were possible, but none were necessary. Dusty knew without question that he remained my dearest friend.

Summer ended and school started just before we were able to move into the farmhouse. The days of our one-room school where we knew everyone and everyone knew us had ended, even for the little kids. In the Tennessee school, we had as many students in one classroom as had attended the whole West Newbury School. Everyone talked funny. They labeled me a "Yankee," and I got in trouble for not saying "ma'am" and "sir." I didn't know where "yonder" was or what kind of word "y'all" was.

As if school wasn't torture enough, Bunny's tirades escalated into a constant diet of disparagement. Perhaps her real coup was destroying our sense of family, our connectedness with each other. It became my greatest fear that the shortcomings of my siblings might spill over to me, thereby reducing me to even less than I already was. Bunny pitted each kid against the others until any one of us would tattle on another, hoping against hope that Bunny's censure of the targeted child might provide at least a moment's respite. Within a few weeks, Bunny's conditioning completely isolated each of the people crowded in our tiny farmhouse.

My insatiable need to feel loved made me Bunny's unwitting accomplice. My brother and sisters sneered at me, accusing me of being Bunny's favorite. I coveted the title, but it came at a great price. Any time Bunny thought my siblings had messed up some chore, part of berating them included bragging that I would not have performed so poorly. Bunny then relieved them of the privilege of performing that job and assigned it to me. The list of my chores grew longer; the depth of their resentment grew deeper. Bunny ordered them to stand by and watch me work while she ticked of her litany of foul labels and nicknames.

Bunny called Linda a "teen pregnancy waiting to happen"; I was the "pathetic crybaby"; Ted was a "slob"; and Teresa was a "sneaky bed wetter." How ironic that within a few years so many of Bunny's dire predictions for my siblings would come true in my life, not theirs. I would become all the "bad" that Bunny saw in each of them.

Our first Christmas in Tennessee was a far cry from our celebrations at Milky Way Farm. Even though Bunny had made it clear that she was against the whole holiday idea, Mom let us pick a half-price tree from the closest tree lot on Christmas Eve. We could not know that our sorry dried-up selection would be our last tree. Years later, Teresa made one feeble attempt at a holiday ornament when she decorated a large pinecone with shiny marbles. Mom never again baked cookies.

That Christmas morning, we each received a riding crop from Bunny. We were surprised but thrilled by her gift. A riding crop can be an effective aid in training a horse when used judiciously to reinforce a command. All of us felt proud, thinking that Bunny considered us sufficiently accomplished to be entrusted with such a tool. After the other gifts were opened, Bunny had us hammer a nail in the paneling by each bedroom doorway. Each of us hung our own whip next to our bedroom door.

Evidently, Bunny didn't understand about horse training, or child training either for that matter. One day, in the midst of one of her tirades, Bunny motioned me toward my room and with a tone of utter disgust, demanded, "Get your crop."

Surprised but silent I walked to my room, lifted the whip off its nail and brought it to her. She took the whip from my outstretched hand without a word. Then she placed her hands on my shoulders and turned me around. Slowly and deliberately, she raised the whip and smacked it down on my backside and legs. Instinctively, I covered my back end with my hands. The whip then landed across my palms, again and again. I cried out with each blow. When Bunny finished, she thrust my crop at me and instructed me, "Hang it back up."

I was as horrified and humiliated as I was hurt. I walked past my siblings in a march of shame down the hall to my bedroom. I placed the whip on its nail, walked into the room, and closed the door.

The incident, with the riding crop, was not the first time Bunny had hit me. She first laid her hand on me when I left the front gate open. Mom drove up the driveway with Bunny on the hood of the car. I laughed, thinking how funny they both looked. Bunny jumped down, ripped off her belt, grabbed my shoulders, twisted me, and beat me. Mom did nothing.

After the crop incident, however, I lost track of all the insignificant or imagined transgressions that triggered whippings. Perhaps a light had been left on, or someone forgot to flush the toilet. Maybe we forgot and flushed the toilet when Mom and Bunny were sleeping. We may have left a piece of clothing on the floor or a halter out. Every beating left marks; angry red welts across our legs, buttocks, and hands. Often, these welts turned into bruises that remained sore, unsightly, and embarrassing long after each beating ended. The memory makes them ache still.

Linda once left her horse tied to a post as she hurried to the restroom. He spooked, reared back, and broke his halter. Bunny whipped Linda so severely that she could not dress for gym. Red and purple welts covered her back, buttocks, and legs. The next time Bunny went in to beat her, however, Linda challenged her, demanding that Bunny never, ever hit her again. Bunny didn't. Instead, she shunned her. It was as if Linda ceased to exist.

If only the rest of us had possessed such a sense of self-preservation. But we feared the shunning more than we feared the pain. Even young children have an innate sense that the true antithesis of love is not hate; it is indifference. We three younger kids still clung to a wisp of hope, or an inextinguishable need to be loved.

Mornings became everyone's worst nightmare. Teresa still wet the bed. Initially Bunny had simply humiliated her by insisting that she sleep in cloth diapers and plastic pants. Later Bunny refused to let her take off the wet diapers and made her wear them to school. As if the smell of urine-soaked diapers did not create enough of a stigma, I watched Bunny select clothes for Teresa that accentuated the diapers.

Teresa began getting up early to hide in her dresser any bedding that got wet when her diapers overflowed. The distinctive odor of stale urine, however, ensured that once or twice a week Bunny would discover the soiled sheets. She grabbed Teresa and demanded she get her riding crop. Meanwhile, Bunny dragged one of the kitchen chairs to the center of the living room. When Teresa returned, Bunny stripped her, then shoved her onto the chair.

Bunny ceremoniously shrouded Teresa's skinny, little, naked body by draping the soiled sheets and wet diapers all over her. The stench of stale urine permeated the room, but even more potent was the smell of our fear. Bunny stalked in circles around Teresa, holding the riding crop aloft. When the real horror began, the rest of the family slipped away, but I watched dumbstruck.

My feet were nailed to the floor. My eyes bore my sister's witness because my heart told me that Teresa needed whatever strength my presence had to offer. I swallowed a cry as the first smack of the whip opened the floodgates of my gentle baby sister's wailing. The pitch of Teresa's cries, like the severity of her welts, rose and fell according to the degree of force Bunny selected. Foam built up in the corners of Bunny's mouth. Venom spewed from her lips along with spatters of saliva. I can't quote Bunny's words but I remember how I felt when I heard them. I felt more pained than when I rubbed salt on my ankles or when blisters burst on my hands as I dug postholes with a hand shovel. Hot tears welled up behind my eyes, but if I made a sound, Bunny would stare directly through me and smack Teresa again.

Finally, Bunny threw the whip at Teresa. Bunny ordered her to hang it up, take care of the sheets, and get ready for school. Bunny then turned and walked away as if nothing happened. Bunny forbade our helping our little sister so Teresa would be left in that chair in the middle of the room with the soiled linens draped all over her body. She was racked with unstoppable sobs. She was only seven years old.

Teresa's welts, wet diapers, and humiliation had to be obvious to her teacher and classmates. Still, no one from the school ever questioned her about what was going on in our family. In fact, no one asked any of us, and we never thought to tell. A sense of isolation grew along with our misery.

Bunny did not always beat us with our riding crops. The whip ceremony required premeditation. Bunny needed time for our anguish to build—the interval while her target retrieved a whip from its nail. If Bunny's rage arose spontaneously, her lashing out was instant. She once grabbed Ted around the throat, choking him and kicking him with her steel-tipped boots because his room wasn't clean. Another time, Mom and Bunny caught him playing with matches. It was crazy, but Ted ran. Once they caught him, they threw him down, and while he shielded his face, both Mom and Bunny beat him repeatedly with two-by-fours. They could have killed him, and when they were finished, he looked as if they had tried.

The most degrading incident for me occurred one Sunday afternoon as I walked down the hall from the bathroom. Perhaps, I had flushed the toilet at the wrong time. Whatever I had done did not please Bunny, and she intended that I know it. Her first harsh rebuke brought tears to my eyes, and as her rage intensified, I wept. I had always been overly sensitive and cried easily. Bunny repeatedly condemned my crying as the hallmark of a weakling.

Bunny fell silent as she glared at me. Then she drew up her hand and smashed her fist into my face. I felt my lip break open and blood spurted as I flew backward and slammed onto the floor. The wind was knocked out of me, so it took a moment before I could stand. Then I cowered before Bunny with downcast eyes, astonished by the stream of bright red blood running off my chin and on to the floor. Slowly, quietly, and deliberately, Bunny spoke, "Tell anyone who asks that you fell from your horse." Then she pushed past me and walked off. Shame overwhelmed me. The sharp pain on my mouth was engulfed by the intense heat which emanated from the remainder of my face. I never fell off my horse. Riding was the one thing at which I was best. Please, please don't make me humiliate myself before the world. But I never said a word, and it was a long time before I could even raise my eyes from the blood pooling at my feet.

That it never occurred to me to disobey Bunny—to speak the truth about my lip or my life—speaks volumes about our topsy-turvy world. Bunny's every whim dominated us. After our mother had acquiesced, she never once stood up for us. We were so thoroughly indoctrinated by Bunny's repeated condemnation that "we got what we deserved," that we all came to believe we deserved what we got. No one ever asked why.

Self-destructive obsessions resurfaced in my damaged psyche. I internalized everything Bunny said about me as my own personal truth: I not only made endless and stupid mistakes, I was bad. So I focused on changing the very core of me, hoping that becoming good would afford me the power to end everyone's suffering, especially my little sister's. Really we were all miserable, but Teresa's pain was so palpable, and her humiliation was so total.

Each day, I would do my chores and extra on top of that. I would spend hours after school, working around the house and farm until after dark. I mowed the lawn, swept the house, cooked meals, did the laundry, cleaned the barn, and organized our horse trailer. To make time for all the chores, I did my homework on the bus. I imagine my schoolmates were playing around me as we rode home, but I don't remember. I had no friends. I had only the fear for my family.

Whatever rules Bunny instituted, I abided by them. I never complained about the out-of-style clothes she required us to wear, even though the other students ridiculed me constantly. Day after day I wore floor-length skirts, men's dress shirts, and tennis shoes, all acquired from the Goodwill Thrift Store. Never once did I get a new dress. Never once did I even roll up my skirt the way my older sister did as soon as she got to school. I accepted the burden of looking like a dumpy misfit in a school filled with girls sporting tight polyester pantsuits.

The only person who would hang out with me was another outcast who regularly declared herself retarded.

Fortunately, I had lucked into an incredible teacher. My first year attending this school was her first year of teaching. She seemed committed to doing what she could to alleviate my school woes. Each day during recess, she permitted me to remain in the classroom with her. Intuition told her how I agonized about free time with my peers. Unfortunately, this was a decade when teachers did not ask personal questions so, while she understood that long skirts alienated me from the other kids, she had no way of knowing that they hid so many whip marks and bruises. Still, her simple kindness meant a great deal. She praised my good grades and even wrote to me a couple of times that next summer. She encouraged me to look beyond the present and to aspire higher. When I confided in her about my dream to become a veterinarian, she provided me information about the profession. She told me about several of the better universities in the South. I even wrote to Auburn for catalogs and information about their vet program.

During the week, I stayed up past bedtime and prepared treats for Mom and Bunny to enjoy when they returned home from work in the wee hours of the morning. Bunny and Mom performed six nights a week at The Bayou, an upscale nightclub whose patrons dined on gourmet Cajun food and danced. I had memorized Bunny's harmonies so that when she visited her mother, or if she felt sick, I could sing backup for Mom. Because we had no sheet music, I sat by my mother as we performed. By watching her fingers as they formed each series of chords on her guitar, I could follow her lead without making mistakes.

During the year that I filled in at The Bayou, no one ever said a word about one of the musicians being only thirteen years old. The nightclub had contracted for two musicians; our pay was for two musicians. If I played well enough for the contract, the owner looked the other way.

For my own part, I loved being needed, even on the occasions when one of the heavier drinkers fell into our microphones as he floundered around trying to keep the beat of songs like, *The Night They Drove Old Dixie Down*. It was my job to straighten up, then resume playing while Mom carried the tune for the other dancers.

Not infrequently, Country Western celebrities came to the Bayou for dinner. I met Loretta Lynn, Marty Robbins, and Lynn Anderson. Although they tolerated the introduction, they were there to dine and dance, so they never sang with us.

Even on weeknights, we would often play till one in the morning. In exchange for staying up long past bedtime, I enjoyed hours of my mother's attention. No matter that chores and school came early the next day.

I longed for some equivalent to the Bayou that would afford me the chance to earn Bunny's favor. In her mind, my fatal flaw, my Achilles' heel, was sensitivity. My eyes filled when she insulted me, and I wept when she beat me. How could I prove that I had overcome such a flaw? The only way I could figure was to let her beat me and learn not to cry.

When I eventually proved to be a stoic, Bunny declared that she was proud of me. She would whip me in front of my siblings just to show them how tough I had become. They hated me. Bunny used me. I idolized her. It was all wrong, but it was what it was. Bunny had mastered the art of manipulation; I had not even mastered being a teenager.

Toward the end of the first year of the contract with The Bayou, Bunny got religion and was "saved." Almost immediately thereafter, she dragged us all to a local Southern Baptist Church to hear her new minister. Brother Tidwell fit every conceivable stereotype of the old Southern preacher. He opened each door by first wrapping a handkerchief around the knob. I asked him once why he did this and his reply was, "Just in case some nigger had touched it."

Brother Tidwell shouted out sermons of "hellfire and damnation" while sweat poured off his bald head and dripped past his temple. Only the big white handkerchief that repeatedly mopped his brow spared us from being splattered by sweat when he paraded down the aisle, throwing his head side to side to emphasize each point. Even more than his message, his breath and body odor permeated the church. All ten families in the congregation noticed.

To me, Brother Tidwell seemed a pathetic, little, fat man with a pathetic little following. But Bunny heard his message differently. After visiting with him privately a couple of Sundays, she came back saved. She may have looked the same to us, but change was in the wind.

The music Bunny and my mother composed switched to hymns that praised God, Jesus, and salvation. I had to adapt my game plan for gaining Bunny's approval. I mimicked Bunny's fasting, praying, and studying the *Bible*. I would go without eating a couple of days a week, stay up all night examining the *Bible* with her, and privately pray that God would accept some responsibility for making me "good." Of course, none of these actions stood any chance of lessening the impossible burden I had assumed of saving my entire family, so I continued to feel like a failure. I couldn't save myself and I couldn't save my little sister. I only hoped that if I could get God on my side, maybe He could save us all.

Studying the *Bible* with Bunny required concentration that far surpassed any effort required by school. After Mom and Bunny gave up their jobs playing at The Bayou, Bunny and I were able to begin studying around midnight while the rest of the household slept. Bunny declared this time sacred and excluded my siblings. No wonder I relished every moment.

Bunny and I sat opposite each other at our kitchen table. We opened our matching *Bibles* and pulled out an array of colorful markers and pens for color-coding our discoveries. An eerie silence fell over the room as Bunny and I read silently. Suddenly Bunny would blurt out an explicative of awe and wonder about how a specific scripture touched her, or related to a previous verse, or provided her with newfound holiness.

I struggled to keep up, having to affirm her incredible finds and decipher her selected passage upside down so that I could color code my own *Bible* correctly. I never understood the source of her awe, nor did I feel holy. I just felt very, very tired, especially when the sun came up, Bunny went to bed, and I left for school.

The religion to which Bunny introduced me focused on the dark side of Christianity. She whispered constantly about evil spirits and casting out demons. Religious martyrs particularly intrigued her.

She had borrowed a very old manuscript titled, *Fox's Book of Martyrs,* which documented people from the fifteenth to the early eighteenth centuries who had suffered torture and death for their beliefs. Week after week, Bunny searched Nashville's antique bookstores, hoping to procure her own copy of this treasure. Seeing her disappointment, I decided to copy the borrowed volume, word for word, as a gift for her. I worked in the evening prior to our *Bible* study, printing each page by hand.

I had completed almost two hundred pages when Bunny located and purchased a copy of the book for herself. I was devastated; months of effort suddenly rendered worthless. I threw my pitiful, handwritten pages in the trash where they filled the can. Bunny questioned me about all the papers. Because I couldn't handle her ridicule, I told her I had made a mistake. She cautioned me about waste, and that was that.

During this same period, Bunny insisted that I read the *Satanic Bible* and another book about Satan worshipers. The latter book described a cult that grabbed innocent girls off the streets and raped them. As part of their ceremonies, the worshipers chopped off their own little fingers. The image scared me to death. I found myself checking constantly to make sure that any strangers I encountered all had their little fingers intact. My fears combined with all this studying, fasting, and sleep deprivation left me so hungry and tired that I don't know why my school performance didn't suffer. I certainly did.

Once religion became the focus of our lives, the whole family became a Gospel band. My mother picked guitar and five-string banjo. Bunny used the guitar and keyboard while Linda strummed the autoharp. I played twelve-string guitar and spoons. Ted learned the bass guitar, and little Teresa kept rhythm on the drums. We all contributed to singing harmony behind my mother's strong lead voice. The "Glory Land Band" had emerged. We traveled to various churches, sang and played our "Jesus" music, and chanted, "Praise God and Glory Hallelujah!" We even recorded an album.

For the cover of the album, we needed an appropriate family portrait. We drove to the horse park where we often rode. I had written a song that, not surprisingly, featured a horse, a white horse like the animal I owned at that time. To draw attention to my song, my horse Chenaniah was to be included in the jacket photograph.

Typical of Bunny's efforts to discredit us, she awarded Ted the privilege of sitting on my horse for the photograph. So, it was poetic justice that during our first attempt at the picture, Chenaniah ran away with him. For the rest of the sitting, Bunny permitted me to hold my horse's bridle. As the day wore on and the temperature rose, we grew more and more miserable. It took all afternoon to get even one acceptable shot. Mom and Bunny titled the album, *Travelin' On*. I don't know how well it sold.

I do know that life at home remained anything but Godlike. Practices were hell. Bunny ridiculed whomever she decided had messed up, blaming that person for wasting everyone else's time. Resentment rose in those who were not the immediate target of her ill will as the session limped on for hours on end.

Occasionally, a rehearsal went well. I remember one good session on the morning of my little sister's tenth birthday. Afterward, Teresa and I were giggling, playing around, and just enjoying the crisp, sunny, autumn day. Then Bunny whooshed in, and for no apparent reason, demanded that Teresa get her whip. We stared at Bunny in astonishment. Teresa obediently brought her the whip, hoping against hope that Bunny intended a birthday spanking. Bunny grabbed the whip and cracked it down ten times on Teresa's rear end and hands. These were no affectionate pats. Bunny hit hard. Then she walked out. She left my sister with ten red welts, once again, making a point of hitting my sister in front of me to demonstrate that I was too insignificant to stop her.

We were supposedly dedicated to God. We sang about His mercy and forgiveness, but we did not live with mercy and forgiveness. Sadly, I still believed, God condoned everything that was happening to us. After all, Bunny was the one who claimed the direct relationship with God. All we knew of Him, came from her.

Escape

If I were really your child,
I guess I would do things right.
If you loved me, really loved me,
You would not inflict or permit the pain.

So, maybe I was left on the doorstep,
Or maybe, you just needed another farmhand.
'Cause if I were really your child,
I wouldn't so badly need to escape.

But, in the dead of night,
There is one who knows my sorrow.
Into my dreams—we're off in flight.
He comes for me, my chance to getaway.

My Pegasus—imaginary salvation.
Take me to where it is all okay.
But—when we finally reach Heaven
I fall from grace, and back to my hell.

During the four years I lived in Tennessee, our horses remained my bedrock. They afforded me intervals of joy in my waking hours and escape during my dreams.

The first couple of years at the new farm, I spent hours each day on Dusty, dreaming of our Olympic future. I could ride him with or without saddle or bridle, over jumps, into rivers, anywhere.

Mom had enrolled us in the United States Pony Club. Membership provided us the opportunity to associate with other horse lovers, become more accomplished riders, and compete. We were living in poverty compared to the other Pony Club kids, but having the opportunity to participate in, Dusty made me feel like royalty. Everything is indeed relative.

I first became aware of the difference in social status between these more privileged children and ourselves when we traveled out of town for team rallies. My brother, sisters, and I remained in our motel room and ate meals out of cans while the other team members dined at restaurants. I suspect this difference bothered my older sister more than me. I was happy just to be a part of all of this—on the road with Dusty, four or five brushes, leg wraps, tail wraps, and my knowledge.

We proudly wore our local club's blue and white colors on our T shirts and saddlecloths as we competed in events that resembled, in a scaled-down version, the Olympic horse sport called, Eventing. The magnitude of scaling down corresponded to the age and riding ability of each Pony Clubber.

As in the Olympics, our first phase was Dressage. Any similarity to the international competition ended with that title. An Olympic dressage test resembles power-ballet on horseback—performed in a sand arena instead of on stage. The Olympian, formally attired in top hat, shadbelly, and tails, rides a precisely executed series of movements that elegantly demonstrate the horse's training, strength, and flexibility.

But, Olympic riders were not born with top hats. They, too, came up through the ranks, and for many, the ranks included the Pony Club. Hard work, attention to detail, commitment, and a dream. It was a dream I shared. A dream of a partnership with a special horse that would carry me to the top—to Mount

Olympus—to the games. So even at this lowest level Pony Club Rally, I performed with my sights set on glory. The series of lopsided circles and uneven diagonals that I trotted and cantered comprised a relatively short performance that would challenge the attention span of even the most devoted parent.

Cross Country, the second phase, involved galloping through open fields over natural obstacles, including brush, logs, ditches, and water. In the Olympics, cross country obstacles can be death-defying, like ditches spanning an eight-foot chasm and flanked by solid timbers over which a horse can barely see.

From the viewpoint of a novice Pony Clubber, the shallow divots he or she jumps appear just as ominous. Dusty and I, however, with years of ditch hopping under our belts, had no problem. We were the pair the team could depend upon to ride clean.

The rally ended with the third phase, stadium jumping followed by the victory gallop during which my heart swelled with pride. On my pony, I was anyone's equal and no one in Pony Club ever treated me as anything less.

Unfortunately, because Dusty was the best horse we owned, Mom and Bunny asked me to sell him when finances got tight. After all, they pointed out, I was outgrowing him. I could see right through their rationalizations and was devastated. My fourteen-year-old perspective told me it was impossible to outgrow your best friend. Besides, Dusty and I were performing at the top of our game.

But as hard as I worked at riding and as much as I cared about Dusty, I was working even harder to become good. Emotional survival dictated that I care more about Mom and Bunny's approval than my pony. So I agreed to sell Dusty to another girl in our Pony Club.

In exchange, Mom and Bunny found an outlaw horse that had bucked off and killed a man. This mare was a light, dapple-grey Connemara with one ear partially torn off and a scar that ran across her entire face as a result of the fatal accident. Her owner, a Hunt Master wearing his red coat, had beaten her many times. One day out of retaliation, or fear or fright, she bucked him off and he died.

Mom and Bunny explained to me that if we didn't take the mare, she would be destroyed. Bunny accepted her and named her Outlaw. In an effort to be the "good" girl again, I agreed to ride her in Pony Club.

I don't actually know if horses see color, but I would have sworn that red-colored objects terrified her. For that matter, she reacted badly to a myriad of other objects and many other hues. As a result, I was the only one who ever rode Outlaw. Everyone else refused, expressing a very realistic fear of being hurt. The fact was, Outlaw was always on the verge of an outburst. As a result, it was hard for me to bond with her. She lacked the gentle dedication and sheer joy in performing that was the essence of Dusty. At best, she would do her job, but she never lost her underlying distrust of humans.

As far as I could tell, Outlaw had only one friend. She loved one of our barn cats, which she allowed to sleep on her rump as she grazed in the pasture. I did grow to appreciate Outlaw, and I ended up keeping her until she died an old mare. She only bucked me off once.

I kept track of Dusty and visited him after he reached thirty years of age. He lived a beautiful life and retired at a quality horse farm in the lush rolling hills of middle Tennessee. Thank heaven for happy endings, at least for some. For my own day-to-day existence, I could not foresee any good way to survive each day, much less imagine happily-ever-after. But in my dreams, I did fly.

For several months, a winged, white horse would soar into my room at night to pick me up and carry me off in search of Heaven. As he landed by my bed, he awakened me by blowing low and soft through his nostrils. He would stand motionless as I deftly grabbed a hold of his mane and leaped onto his back. We took off without making a sound, and as we flew I was safely cradled between his powerful wings. Each nightly journey was arduous, mysterious and exhausting. When, at last, we found Heaven, we fell from the sky, and my dreams ended.

Shortly after the dreams ceased, I encountered the real-life, flesh and blood version of my Pegasus. We were visiting friends of my mother who raised Arabian horses and who had expressed an interest in purchasing a mare Mom owned. They were taking us on a tour around their farm when I saw him turned out in a lush grassy pasture. He was dancing solo, tossing his head, prancing around, and showing off. He had attitude. Like Outlaw, he appeared almost white, but, while her dapples were grey, his shone like polished silver. Our eyes met for a second. He took off; I was swept away. I could think of nothing else as I willed fate to bring us together.

Several months later, my mother traded her Arabian mare for this horse. She wrote up a payment plan and promised that the horse would be mine as soon as I finished paying the bill. Until then he would be my responsibility, and no one else would ride him.

When we picked him up, the previous owners informed me that my dream horse had a dangerous habit of rearing and had fallen over backward several times when a rider had tried to mount him. I suppose that I should be thankful for this otherwise terrible vice, without which we certainly could not have afforded such an animal. I listened attentively, accepting the challenge of a partner whose respect I would have to earn one step at a time.

My dream horse arrived with the registered name Ahab. Because my years of *Bible* study taught me that Ahab was an evil king, I became obsessed with finding a more auspicious name for my exotic new horse. While sitting in church one Sunday thumbing through my *Bible*, I came across a verse about an Old Testament musician, named Chenaniah. With religion and music such integral parts of my existence, I considered Chenaniah the perfect name for my treasure.

Even with his new name, Chenaniah remained extremely spirited and tended to be obstinate, but life had made me determined, and Dusty had taught me patience. Chenaniah's propensity for indifference was no match for my desire for a teammate. I worked with him on the ground until he first tolerated me, then accepted me, and eventually loved me. By the time I felt ready to mount him, he stood quietly. Chenaniah never reared with me.

In time, Chenaniah helped me recapture much of the magic I had experienced riding around Milky Way Farm. Teresa and I rode him double all over our Tennessee property. We even jumped him double. I sat in front; she wrapped her arms tightly around my waist. I gloried in the feeling that I was taking care of her.

2 LITTLE GIRLS

Our lives, heavy and weighted,
Yet the four hooves beneath us gave us wings
So our spirits could soar—
Free to dream, imagine, dance, and sing.

Her small arms around me,
Hold tight as she clings
I want to make it right,
Make the horror go away

The galloping horse,
My sister—my friend,
Our lives would change, of course,
But now, this moment of time,
Was ours—to be, to laugh, to be free

No Escape

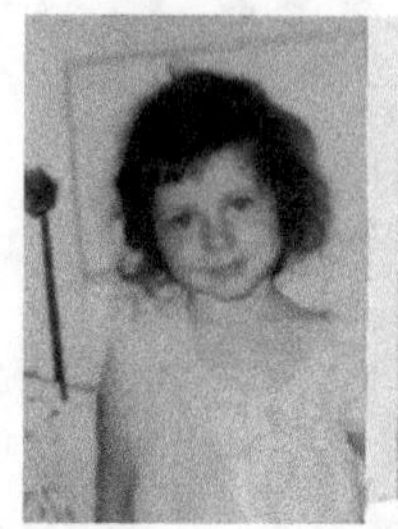

How does a little girl
Decide not to grow up?
If she can run, climb and play
Can she will away inevitable maturity?

How does a little girl,
Believe it is evil to come of age?
Are we all bad,
Some just sooner than others?

I could not be with the horses all the time, so I invented several alternative means of escape when I was home. As I went through the motions of coping with my day, I fantasized that I had been dropped off with these people as an orphan. They worked me as a slave and beat me when I didn't perform as expected.

I escaped into this fantasy often because my heart told me that if I had truly belonged, my life would look different. Real parents would not stand by while their babies were hurt. Real parents would put their children first. In a real family, people would laugh, hug each other, and enjoy being together. Fantasies, however, cannot cure real life. Time kept passing, and I was growing up with a very tough reality.

Well before I turned fifteen, I had been indoctrinated with the attitude that men were not okay people. Bunny and my mother had nothing but derogatory comments to make about dating, marriage, having children, and men in general. I compounded their negative assertions about men with my own religious confusion about purity. I decided to opt-out of growing up.

Although I lived in a house full of women, no one had even spoken to me about physical maturation. Linda, who continued to prize her role as my conscience, had attempted to educate me. Horrified, I hurried away, hushing her. The little she had told me made me particularly anxious to avoid the menstrual cycle thing. But alas, I could not escape.

At fifteen, I got my first period. I opened the bathroom cabinet to look for a tampon. With so many women sharing one bathroom, feminine hygiene products were readily available; knowledge, however, was not. I withdrew the tampon from its box, briefly considered reading the directions, but became too embarrassed by the diagrams. I inserted the tampon, cardboard packaging and all. I could hardly walk, but I had to be alone. I left the house, limped to the barn, and climbed up to the hayloft where I spent the day laying in the hay, crying miserably.

Amidst all our man-hating, it seemed rather strange that Bunny began to date a fellow she met at a singing engagement. He was a quiet, well-mannered, handsome man. More importantly for our future, he was Pentecostal, a denomination best known for holy rollers and noise. His church had a full band in the choir loft. His services were emotionally charged affairs where some members spoke in tongues while others clapped, cried out, and chanted Amens. Outsiders who could not relate to their *Bible*-toting, long skirts, long hair, and sandals, referred to the believers as "Jesus Freaks." Under Bunny's direction, we graduated from Brother Tidwell's Southern Baptist congregation into the boyfriend's big-city Pentecostal church.

There was a chance that Bunny's boyfriend could have brought a breath of fresh air into our home, but such was not the case. He ignored us kids and made my mother crazy with jealousy. I mean "crazy with jealousy" quite literally.

One afternoon while Bunny and the boyfriend were visiting in the backyard, Mom flew out the screen door with gun in hand, screaming that she was going to blow off Bunny's boyfriend's head and then her own. This wasn't the first time we kids had seen Mom in a rage, but it terrified Bunny's boyfriend. His face turned brilliant red then lost its color completely. We slipped off into the house as Bunny jumped on Mom. After Bunny wrestled the gun away, Mom fell apart. She crumpled to the ground sobbing and babbling incoherently.

After the boyfriend regained his senses, he absolutely insisted that my mother get professional help. Bunny agreed. Mom would do anything Bunny said, and—being crazy relieved her of the burden of coping with her responsibilities—her children—us. So, she allowed Bunny and the boyfriend to pack her off in his car. Linda, Ted, Teresa, and I watched from the kitchen window as they drove her away. Bunny shouted back to us that they would soon return. They had Mom admitted to the Seventh-day Adventist hospital outside of Nashville.

Shortly afterward, I don't know why or how Dad showed up and moved in with us. Bunny moved out, but not without some gun brandishing of her own. Years of tension between them erupted in a shouting match during which Bunny grabbed a pistol and threatened to shoot my father. When he refused to back down, she fired off a round which imbedded itself in the hallway floor. Dad ordered her out, and out she went.

I visited Mom at the hospital a couple of times. I hated what they did to her. Her stories about being strapped to a table when she received shock treatments broke my heart. She told me that her doctor described her singing gospel songs each time she awoke from a treatment.

The visions in my mind may have been worse than her reality, but maybe not. I felt so protective, but so utterly helpless. My longing for assurance that my mother loved me escalated out of control. The child in me could not grasp that my needs, born of neglect during Mom's most rational years, could not possibly be satisfied during the time of her own personal crisis.

The void in me became terrifying. Numbed by years of chaos, I sank into a deep, dark hole. During the day, I went to school, relieved to have the distraction. In the evenings, however, I pulled the blinds in my mother's room, turned on gospel records, sat in her rocking chair and spent hours rocking in the dark.

Seeing my despair, my father tried to comfort me, tried to convince me that all this "Jesus" stuff was wrong. He sat across from me in the darkroom and spoke of his great love for me, describing how he had cared for me when I was a colicky baby, how he would rescue me from my mother when she couldn't take my crying. He told about rocking me all night long, then going out at dawn to milk the cows. I could remember his kindness back on Milky Way Farm, but now his love felt too remote. Four long and painful years had passed without a word from him. Four years ago, he had given us to Bunny, even though, he knew she was not a good person. Too much water had run under the bridge that separated us.

Dad should have focused on our present lives instead of reminiscing about our past. And he should have asked questions. Lots of questions. But he didn't ask, so he knew nothing about our lives. We didn't tell, yet we couldn't forgive him for not knowing. His ignorance meant that the only misery to which he could relate was my mother's. How had we made her so unhappy? Unspoken answers ached in my heart.

On the other hand, Bunny no longer lived in our house. She had discarded her boyfriend, as he no longer served any purpose. No longer did I have to witness her torturing my little sister; no longer did she order us to retrieve riding crops with which to beat us. Instead, she called to ask how I was feeling, and I yearned to believe her concern was genuine. She told me how God was working in her life, and I came to feel that she could be the connection through which God would start working in mine.

Summer was coming to a close when Mom returned home. She had converted to the Seventh-day Adventist religion, which required her to attend church on Saturday, accept a new spiritual leader, and become a vegetarian. Her doctor was Adventist and she had made some new friends who also professed that faith. Dad stayed in Fairview, started a concrete business with a friend and built a little cabin in town.

While Mom was still in the hospital, my parents had decided to send me to a Seventh-day Adventist boarding school in Mississippi for my junior year. Mom had never been swept away by the Pentecostal ideas and now she desperately wanted me away from that church, from Bunny, and from the whole "Jesus Freak" movement. I cried, fumed, and growled, but I was well entrenched in the role of the martyr. I had no choice. I would go.

The school required each prospective student to have a physical. Mom brought me to her Adventist psychiatrist for the exam. He took one look at me and declared me, "Healthy as a horse." He then asked my mother to leave the examining room. As soon as she closed the door, he leaned forward and looked straight into my eyes.

Instead of checking my vision, he whispered, "What right do you have to be hurting your mother?" I blinked in astonishment, but I couldn't respond. He was the one who strapped Mom to a table for shock therapy. How could he think I was the one hurting her? We stared at each other in silence.

Eventually, he opened the door and motioned for my mother to reenter. When she walked into the exam room, he shrugged, turned both palms upward, then slowly shook his head side to side. His gestures implied that talking to me was hopeless. Mom responded by pointing toward the busy street and muttering to me through gritted teeth, "It would be easier on me if you would go out and get hit by a car."

The doctor's question had left me speechless, but my mom's declaration left me breathless. I gasped, reeling from her verbal blow. The room was full of pain. She felt only hers; I felt only mine.

Within days, I departed for Pine Forest Academy in Chunky, Mississippi. If I had not been so determined to be miserable, I could have enjoyed being there. It was situated on a huge farm where pinewoods that sheltered the entire campus. Charming wood frame buildings, scattered along a dirt road, served as a chapel, dormitories, a cafeteria, a hospital, and a dairy. A couple of matching private homes housed the school's administrative staff.

Despite these bucolic surroundings, my spirit boiled. I was determined to remain faithful to my Pentecostal beliefs, which were my connection to Bunny. The Adventists would not allow my music until I altered the words to my favorite gospel songs to match their religious beliefs. But even as the new verses adapted to their doctrine, my mind rebelled.

Worse yet, the school permitted no running or playing in the creek and no boys for friends. Being a girl, I was not even allowed near the dairy. So all the beauty of a farm surrounded me, but I experienced none of its essence, none of its freedom. I was not permitted to be me.

I had gone off to school with my old guitar, Jesus music, my *Bible* highlighted like Bunny's, and my commitment to fasting. I also brought a contraband slip of paper containing Bunny's phone number. I called her collect a couple of times a month. She always accepted the charges and told me how God grew in her life and worked miracles through her.

When we spoke, Bunny pointed out particular scriptures that spoke to my "persecution" by the Adventist non-believers. We sent tapes back and forth and wrote letters that we called "Epistles" to make them sound more Biblical. More and more I felt as if I was her chosen one. I had a role in her rebellion for God, and she described me as a modern version of her beloved martyrs from *Fox's Book of Martyrs*. I knew the others well. After all, I had hand-copied a good portion of their book.

I knew the *Bible* more thoroughly than those teaching my religion classes. They could not understand why anyone who knew the *Bible* so well would resist converting to their Adventist religion. Instead, when I fasted, it made everyone nervous, so fasting made me important. People noticed me. I was making a real statement until the dean and the dorm mother made a special trip to my room to forbid all-day fasting. I could skip breakfast and lunch, but, they insisted, dinner was mandatory.

I called home about once a week. Teresa always filled me in on our horses. Then I had a few moments to speak with my mother. She did her best to steer our conversation toward routine small talk, but I would not miss a chance to tell her how much I loved her. As soon as she heard these words, she said goodbye and handed the phone to someone else. She never repeated the magic words; she never, ever said, "I love you, too." Linda once got on the phone and ordered me not to tell my mother I loved her because it upset her. Heaven forbid; how could I stop?

As with many Adventist schools, Pine Forest Academy was affiliated with a hospital. To help pay for tuition almost all of the students worked in the hospital, the school cafeteria, or the dairy. I was assigned to the hospital where almost all the patients were geriatric.

I had one particularly wonderful patient named Mrs. Bernard, who was partially bedridden. I came to dearly love her, perhaps because she reminded me of my own grandmother. Both women were quiet, gentle, and loving. Both spoke to me of God, His mercy and their love for Him.

Mrs. Bernard's husband visited every week and cared for her basic needs. I walked into the room one afternoon and interrupted the most intimate act I had ever witnessed between a man and a woman. Mr. Bernard's gentle hands were shaving her withered legs. She smiled at me as she welcomed me in.

A few weeks later during my evening shift, Mrs. Bernard fell in the hall and could not get up. When I found her, I helped her to her feet and half-carried her to her room, but I could not lift her onto her bed by myself. The best I could do was to continue holding her up while I yelled for help. Hearing my calls for assistance, another student aide finally arrived. I supported Mrs. Bernard under her arms while the other girl lifted her legs. We laid Mrs. Bernard gently on her bed and adjusted her body to make her as comfortable as possible. Then I started searching for the doctor.

The head nurse thought he might be working at his farm. She gave me vague directions and off I sprinted. I must have run a mile or so before I saw him plowing his cornfield with an old, red tractor. When I reached the doctor, I was so out of breath that I bent over, panting for almost a minute before I could describe Mrs. Bernard's plight. To my horror, this pillar of the Adventist community listened disinterestedly to my report without speaking or reacting. He would not even get down from his tractor. When I finished, he shifted his tractor back into gear, shrugged matter-of-factly and said, "She's old. She's going to die anyway."

I stared into a face so devoid of compassion that there was nothing more to say. I turned and hurried back toward the hospital. I could hear by the sound of the tractor's engine behind me that the doctor had resumed plowing. Mrs. Bernard remained in such agony that she never spoke or got out of bed again.

My work in the Adventist hospital introduced me to both extremes of life. Not long after, I shared the pain of one ending her journey, I witnessed the miracle of another just beginning hers.

Given that all the hospital's patients I had seen were geriatric, I was shocked when a fifteen-year-old girl was admitted to the hospital to give birth. Word was that the young mother intended to give up her baby girl. I spent most of my shift staring at the newborn through the otherwise empty nursery window. The baby looked so vulnerable with her hands curled up in front of her face and her tiny pink lips pursed together. Someone had pasted a pink bow in her black hair. How I would love to take that tiny baby, to love her, and to have her love me back.

A day later, I heard that the mother decided to keep her baby. She named her Tiffany Michelle. I never forgot Tiffany. She had triggered in me a reverence for motherhood that I have never lost. From Tiffany on, I wanted my own baby. I had not, however, figured out how that might happen because I was still committed to hating men. Never mind, I knew it was in the cards; someday I would be a mom.

The brightest event of that dismal school year occurred as a result of one of my few conversations with the boys attending the school. At Pine Forest Academy, girls and boys were usually segregated. Our interactions were so limited and so naïve that most of the students actually believed the rumor that pregnancy resulted from taking vitamin E and holding hands. Having been raised on a farm, I tried to assure my classmates that this combination of events put them in no danger, but most remained convinced that handholding constituted a considerable risk.

That afternoon, several boys had teased me about a paper I wrote describing my Pony Club competitions. Somehow, the next day they conned a neighboring farmer into loaning them his old mare. She wasn't really much of a horse; her back was long, her legs short, and her hair was shaggy and matted. At that moment, however, she ranked as the most beautiful equine in my world. Dress and all, I swung up on her back. Overwhelmed by the chance to prove my skill and feel the movement of a horse's muscles beneath me, I kicked and the mare responded. Off we galloped to loop the school grounds. Heading back, I caught a glimpse of the dean frantically motioning for me to ride over. He was not pleased. His greatest concern was for my loss of decorum. Riding around with my dress flying in the breeze was hardly ladylike, and ladylike behavior was highly prized at Pine Forest Academy.

I had to control my elation throughout his lecture. I had ridden again, and I had impressed my peers. One of the boys, who most relished teasing me the day before, even wanted to be my boyfriend. No thanks.

Perhaps, I departed Pine Forest Academy knowing a bit more academics. Certainly, I left knowing a lot more about myself and about life. I went home inspired by the knowledge of love that could outlast death or spring forth with birth. And I left harboring my first twinge of cynicism toward any religion whose leader could drive off on a tractor in the face of real need.

Away from Bunny

Life ain't no easy freeway Just
some gravel on the ground You
pay for every mile you go
And you spread some dust around

John Denver

The summer after Chenaniah came into my life I turned sixteen, got my driver's license, and needed a job. An older southern gentleman who served as Hunt Master for the local organization, with which my Pony Club fox hunted, hired me to exercise his hunting horses, clean stalls, and condition his leather tack.

He lived with his wife on an enormous plantation that had had the good fortune to retain all the charm of the most gracious period in Southern history. Stately white columns adorned the front of the three-story brick mansion. Ancient magnolias and huge weeping willows shaded its expansive lawn.

An aura of gentility radiated from the house to the two-hundred-year-old barn. Time had given the entire structure a certain patina. I loved to stroke the hand-polished stall doors, polished smoothly by so many hands. As I walked down the brick floor of the center aisle, I slid my boot over a shallow rut slowly formed by two centuries of horse hooves meandering down the center aisle to and from their stalls.

My employer was at all times a proper gentleman. His daily attire was as impeccable as his manners. His wife was a lady in every respect, quiet, welcoming, and poised. She wore only dresses and rode only sidesaddle. She once devoted an entire afternoon to teaching me how to ride in her antique tack, and then she tailored a sidesaddle skirt for me.

The hunting horses were Irish bred with names like Kilarney and Kilkenny. Although they were big-boned, energetic, and fit animals, they remained tractable enough for me to safely include Teresa in their exercise sessions. I loved to take her to work to ride with me. On the hottest days, we even took the horses swimming in the pond.

Working at this magnificent farm, afforded me a whole new sense of freedom and my paychecks were providing me a semblance of independence. But the price of my growing up took an odd turn during my second week of commuting the forty minutes to work. Our old Ford Fairlane stalled at a traffic light. When I couldn't coax the engine into turning over, the truck driver behind me began honking. The tension was building and someone else leaned on a horn. Then in my rearview mirror, I saw the trucker get out of his cab and swagger toward me.

Assuming he was intending to lend a hand, I rolled down my window and sighed with relief when I heard him say, "Looks like you need a push out of the way and a jump. Want some help?"

"Yes, thanks so much."

His hand reached into my window and grabbed my breast. As he squeezed, a huge smile crossed his face, and he gloated, "I'd love to help you."

Snapping out of a momentary stupor of both shock and terror, I cranked up my window with greater speed than either Ford motor company or my assailant could ever have anticipated. I trapped his arm, and then grabbed the pocketknife I kept for scraping bot-fly eggs off the horse's legs. It lay on the seat beside me. The truck driver jerked his arm out the window and shook his hand as he turned toward his truck. He glanced back once over his shoulder, still smiling. I rolled the window the rest of the way closed and opened the knife. I had a death grip on the knife handle with one hand and the steering wheel in the other.

When the light turned red, the trucker rammed my back bumper, shoving my car into the intersection. I turned and stared at the faces of the drivers into whose path I lurched. I could see by their gestures that they were honking and cursing but they moved in slow motion. My world had become silent. Any noise that was not muted by my closed windows was eclipsed by my fear.

My senses returned in time for me to realize that the impact of the truck combined with the slope of the road were sufficient to carry me through the intersection if I would just let off the brake—if I could just lift my thousand-pound foot—"Move foot, move."

The car glided forward and I eased it to the curb and stopped. The trembling in my hands spread through my whole body before it finally quieted. I leaned forward, rested my forehead on the wheel.

This was it. The first time a man had touched me—all Bunny's haranguing against the male gender suddenly justified—all my Mom's condemnations of men now vindicated by a truck driver who got his kicks by mauling a vulnerable teenaged girl— a classic case of manhood at its worst, sexuality at its lowest common denominator.

When I regained my composure, I walked to the nearest store to call my boss. I explained my tardiness as engine trouble. Then I called my mother and asked for help with my car. Though she sounded annoyed to be interrupted in her current project, she soon arrived with jumper cables. We got the Fairlane started and I headed on to work.

Mom never understood why I was so upset about a dead battery, and I never told her about the guy in the truck. In this of all instances, she would probably have risen to my defense, but for me, the incident was too horrifying to revisit and too embarrassing to describe. I buried it in my subconscious where it festered along with my other insecurities.

I was not about to let one misadventure ruin such a lovely summer, but the naivety and trust in mankind that the village of West Newbury had fostered in me had been shaken to the core. I made my final payment to my mother to pay off Chenaniah and swore to myself that no one would ever take him away from me.

Bunny had moved to Nashville, about twenty minutes from where I worked at the Hunt Master's plantation. At least one night a week I sneaked away to see her after work. No one noticed that I left work a little early and arrived home a little late. During our conversations, Bunny described the nightclub where she had to work to pay her bills and explained that God would forgive her for singing worldly music because He had a bigger plan for her. She told me stories about strange people she contacted, people who healed by laying their hands on a sick person, people who could see the spirits of dead people and people who spoke in foreign tongues. Each of these things sounded to me just as the *Bible* had described. Some evenings we sat with our *Bibles* and resumed our studying and underlining. Now I became frantic to absorb each inspired insight God gave to Bunny.

Bunny encouraged my visits, and we chatted like old friends. Perhaps, I filled a bit of the empty space created in her life when my dad reclaimed my mom. It is equally possible that Bunny was just plain vindictive. Because my father had taken my mother from her, she would take me from my parents. Who knows, but she paid me every kindness and her influence on me grew to be enormous.

When my parents forbade my seeing Bunny, they both became my enemies. I was unwilling to give up Bunny or her beliefs. Hook, line, and sinker, I had swallowed her version of the Pentecostal religion, emphasizing the deeper, darker meanings in scripture. She had fixated on demonic possession, casting out demons, and laying on of hands. Finally, she wanted to share it all with me. For years I had been desperate for this connection, now it was all I had.

My parents knew I still contacted Bunny. So for my senior year of high school, they shipped me even farther away. This time to California, to the home of Ann, the woman who had shown me the larger world of horsemanship back in Vermont.

My father drove me to Nashville's Greyhound bus station and sat with me in a vast, dirty, overcrowded depot that reeked of an eternity of broken dreams. Newspaper pages and empty food containers lay scattered around the passengers awaiting their transit and the homeless waiting for another day to pass. I made myself as small and inconspicuous as possible, hoping that none of those frightening individuals would notice me. Hours later, I boarded the bus as my father's figure disappeared from sight.

For two long nights and three endless days, I lived in the window seat of that westward bound, Greyhound bus, scarcely daring to get off to go to the bathroom. I was terrified that I would take too long and be abandoned on a curb somewhere in the middle of nowhere.

In Nevada, I disembarked briefly. As I washed my hands, I glanced into the broken mirror in front of me. I did not even recognize the reflection, which looked exactly like the people who had frightened me so back in the Nashville terminal. At some subconscious level, the thought registered that no one could be more alone than the figure staring back at me, the one who had just flushed a dirty toilet in a decrepit bus depot halfway across the Nevada desert.

I trudged back to the bus and stepped inside, pulling myself by the handrail and noting again how pressure-filled my ears when the doors sealed me inside. During the short time I had been in the restroom, the sun had baked my seat. As the bus started moving, I had to cover it with someone's discarded newspaper before I could sit down. All the snacks, my dad had packed, had disintegrated into stale crumbs. My clothes smelled. I could no longer cross my legs because of the prickly stubble they had sprouted, and my feet had swelled until my shoes no longer fit. California was too far from home.

Much of the weariness and despair that had been growing inside me dropped away when Ann met me at the bus stop. I even felt a glimmer of hope as we drove up the gravel driveway leading to her rambling hilltop home. As soon as we carried my bags in the house, Ann walked me down to a lovely wooden barn that housed her three horses and her daughter's pony. Ann was now raising

Thoroughbreds. Her stallion and two mares were grazing in spacious pastures shaded by eucalyptus trees.

In the barn, I met Ann's seven-year-old daughter, a perfect child, a fairy girl. She smiled at me, and I held her hand as we ambled back to the house.

I was content to live at Ann's, but I wasn't the same kid I had been when I had so idolized her back at Milky Way Farm. I was determined to stay in touch with Bunny and did—without Ann's knowledge. Bunny still accepted my collect calls and told me she was moving to Georgia where she planned to form a new gospel-singing group. Her promise to keep a spot open for me kept me going. She related new stories about speaking in tongues, casting out demons, and miracles God continued to perform through her. I promised to do all the right things, pray all the right prayers, and keep all the right commandments. I fasted, prayed, and begged, but still, God did no work through me.

At school, I joined the Agape Club, a nondenominational organization whose members gathered to pray, read the *Bible*, and sing gospel music before classes and during lunch. I felt certain Bunny would approve of this club and would be proud that I attended the local Pentecostal church when I could find someone to pick me up.

On the other hand, Ann and her family had become Mormons. At their urging, I sat through missionary lessons, fasted and prayed, studied *The Book of Mormon*, and accompanied them toward services. Privately, I prayed for a sign, a lightning bolt or thundering in the sky that would show me God's truth. How come praying, fasting, and studying revealed so much to so many, but so little to me? Others described visions, healings, and closeness to a God who illuminated the right path for them. Experiencing none of those miracles, I suspected something was wrong with me. God didn't like me.

I felt torn, not between different religious doctrines but between different religious people, each of whom told me that all I needed was to take a leap of faith. I wanted more than anything to take that leap, but I knew not where to aim myself. Though my heart was willing, my mind told me that whatever direction I chose would reflect merely faith in people, not faith in God. But pleasing these people was important, almost as important as finding God.

I particularly wanted to please an English lady whom I had met through Ann and whose three small children I tended. In her, I discovered a new and different brand of woman. In her, there was no guile and no hypocrisy. I do not believe, I ever heard her raise her voice toward anyone, not her husband or her children. She understood my hunger for love and she reached out to me. She also understood my need for time alone and let me spend evenings behind their home in the small backyard shed which they had fixed up to serve as a spare bedroom. Ann's friend lived fully in accordance with her Mormon faith, and I had faith in her.

So, for lack of answers to my prayers, I agreed to be baptized into the Mormon Church. Ann would be relieved; my English friend would be happy; the missionaries who had spent so many evenings teaching me would be rewarded. I would adopt their sensible religion and thereafter conform to the highest values of people, I highly valued. The "Jesus" music, miracles, casting out of demons, and speaking in tongues would have to wait. Bunny need never know; she was three thousand miles and several months away.

My friends in the Agape Club were certain the devil had influenced my decision. Still, even after I joined the Mormon Church, they didn't turn their backs on me. They just offered to pray for me. Like them, I spent a fair amount of time wondering about my decision.

I was sitting in my room reading the *Bible* one evening when I heard Ann hang up the phone. A moment later, she tapped softly on my door, then entered. I could tell by the look on her face that she had something important to tell me. She sat down on the bed beside me, pausing long enough for us both to feel uncomfortable.

"I just got off the phone with your dad. He asked me to tell you that their divorce is final. It's not really a surprise is it? After all, they have been separated for five years."

The silence that followed her declaration was so awkward that Ann stood up. It seemed to me that she had decided it was better to avoid my answer. Instead, she rested her hand on my shoulder for a moment before she left. I stared out the window, watching the landscape blur as my eyes filled. Tears ran down my cheeks and streaked on my shirt where they fell. The last glimmer of hope that Mom and Dad might reconcile had just died. The ache in my heart turned to anger. Anger—the emotion that protects. Say what you will about not shooting the messenger, all I could feel was fury at hearing such news from Ann. Anger overshadowed the pain of my broken dreams.

I waited until Ann's house was empty to phone home. It seemed to take eons, especially because the three-hour time change made me desperate to get a call through to my little sister before it was too late. As usual, Teresa answered the phone picking up on the second ring.

Over top of her greeting, I spit it out, "So Ann tells me Mom and Dad are divorced."

Teresa answered quietly, "Yeah, it's over, and Dad has a girlfriend so he hardly ever comes around."

The volume of the conversation went back up. I growled, "I can't believe, they made Ann tell me. They just don't have the guts to be honest with me."

There followed a long pause, honoring the pain we each felt. Again the soft voice, "You're right. I have something else to tell you. First off, Chenaniah is fine."

Her disclaimer set off an alarm. "What happened?" I whispered. My anger had evaporated, no longer of use, no longer appropriate.

"Last weekend, I was jumping him in the arena and he slipped and fell in the corner where it's always muddy. At first, he couldn't get up, but now he's fine."

With mounting concern, I begged, "What about you? You don't sound fine."

"When Chenaniah fell, he landed on top of me, and when he got up, I couldn't move my leg. It broke right above my knee."

"Oh no!" The volume was up again, but I spoke out of desperation, not anger.

She continued quietly, "Luckily, the neighbor's kids were overriding my pony because no one else was home at our house. They got me up and helped lay me over her back. It was just like when we pretended that you were the kidnapped maiden."

"You probably looked a lot more like a dead rustler freshly cut down from the hanging tree." I chuckled, trying my best to picture her peril rather than her pain, "How did you get to the hospital if Mom wasn't home?"

"Mom didn't think it looked serious so I didn't go. She propped me up in the kitchen on two of those blue metal chairs and gave me some pillows from the sofa. My knee kept swelling up bigger and bigger, and then it turned red as a ripe tomato. The worst problem was that I couldn't get to the bathroom."

"How did you?" The question of the bathroom quest became the crux of our conversation. How does one get down a hall to the toilet on a swollen, broken, un-cast leg? I was choking as I asked, and I couldn't figure out if I was about to laugh or cry.

"Well, I waited 'til I was really desperate to go, otherwise I couldn't make myself move my leg off the chair. The first time I held on to the edge of the table to pull myself up, then tried to hop on my good leg. But, no way. It hurt too much. Eventually, I figured out how to get out of the chair butt first. I'd lower my fanny to the ground, and lift my leg down. Then I scooted backward down the hall pushing off with my good leg and my hands. I'd get on and off the john the same way. I'd back up to it, put my hands on the seat and push up. Really, though, the harder part was getting organized on the kitchen chairs when I got back because the pillows kept falling off the chair seat when I tried to lift my leg up on them."

I couldn't believe her words. Still choking, I was now also crying. It was so like Teresa to describe the situation without mentioning her pain.

I learned as we continued talking, that Mom had left Teresa in those two chairs for four days and nights. Thank heavens my mother's parents arrived for a visit over spring break. The joyful greetings they were exchanging when they walked into the house, stopped cold when they caught sight of Teresa, the blue chairs, and her knee. By then it had swelled to four times its normal size and taken on the tomato color she had described. Without even unpacking, my grandfather carried Teresa to their car and sped off for the hospital. The hospital staff openly condemned my mother's neglect of the injury, but Mom remained steadfast in her indifference.

I had called home so that Teresa could alleviate my pain. Now I ached that I was again powerless to ease hers. Thousands of miles separated me from my family, but nothing, not even Ann, could insulate me from their ill will toward each other.

It took quite a while for me to shake off the weight of so much heartache. Lucky for me that Ann gave me the space to grieve and at the same time included me in her family's highlights. She took me along to a John Denver concert in San Francisco. Because John was a friend of Ann's, he had mailed us all front row seats and backstage passes. I was beside myself.

Back in Tennessee, back when secular music was forbidden, I would sometimes sneak out to the barn to listen to his music. I had purchased his albums secretly. I loved to listen to his gentle voice sing about the good stuff of life, all I imagined life should be.

At the concert, we were so close to the stage that I could see each chord his fingers formed on his guitar. Later, backstage, Ann introduced me to John and his wife. As he shook my hand, I whispered, "I play your songs."

Still holding my hand, he paused, looked into my eyes, and nodded. Making it clear he was according me the respect of one musician to another, he answered, "I bet you play them well." Then he smiled. I had met the first person in my life who lived up to all my dreams, and the memory of that moment sustained me for a good while.

Toward the end of the school year, I gave my old guitar to a friend in the Agape Club who couldn't afford one. Then I spent the last of my savings on a new twelve-string guitar. I would be heading for Georgia and Bunny. Everything needed to be in order when I became a member of her gospel band. Besides, I badly needed a friend and a guitar can feel like a friend. Having played since I was eight, the shape and weight of the instrument in my lap were familiar. My fingers found comfort touching the strings and forming chords. No one needed to know that the twelve-string doubled as my security blanket.

At the end of the academic year, my father attended my high school graduation with his new wife and two of her daughters. Dad's wife looked a bit like John Denver's but other than that, she did not impress me. Following graduation, we drove to their new home in Arizona. My brother met us there, and we stayed for a couple of days before we returned to Tennessee.

The night before we left, Dad called me into his room and began a conversation with the kind of awkward trivial inquiries that warned me something of significance would follow. "Do you have everything packed?"

I answered, still waiting for his agenda to surface—Dad didn't seek me out for small talk. After a pause punctuated by an audible sigh, he started, "Listen, I want you to understand that if you go to live with Bunny, I'll disown you."

Bunny's name had not once been mentioned during our past few days together. In fact, my dad had not brought her up for more than a year. There would have been no point in discussing Bunny because we both knew how we felt about her and our feelings were not the same. Dad still had no idea that Bunny had beaten us. His instincts about Bunny's religion made him fear for my safety but he never explained why. We were both aware of one thing—if Dad were correct, even if I should avoid Bunny at all cost, my dad was not offering me an alternative. No home with him.

As I listened to my dad, my eyes narrowed and my emotions intensified. Who was this stranger attempting to manipulate my life and conditionalize his love? There followed another silence. I was speechless, and Dad had nothing more to say.

In my heart, I knew he wouldn't disown me. It just wasn't in him. So we parted, both knowing I would be going back to Bunny.

Back to Bunny

Like a death grip
She holds my being.
Her power is far too strong,
I am too weak and needy to resist
Such magnetism.

Only with her is there a place for me
I convince myself I am wanted So,
like a dog returning to its vomit I
go

The next day, Ted and I left on an Amtrak train. In contrast to my westward trek, this cross-country trip was one of the most peaceful and spiritual times I had known. We had no sleeping arrangements so when the heat of the late afternoon sun diminished and twilight took its place, we made our way back to the club car. I retrieved my guitar from its case and Ted and I took turns playing and singing throughout the night. I don't remember if we sang, *Me and Bobby Magee,* but our evening inspired its words.

We shared fond memories of childhood on the farm and caught each other up on the past school year. More than talking though, Ted and I made music. We played and harmonized on every song we knew, as our captive audience of one grey-haired man in an old grey shirt nodded in rhythm to the tunes he recognized. Some made us cry, some made us laugh until we cried.

From the Nashville train station, I headed back to our Tennessee farm, my little sister, and Chenaniah. Ted returned to the home of Carl Greenhill.

By all appearances, Mr. Greenhill was a good Christian man being an elder of the Seventh-Day Adventist Church. Unfortunately, he was the extreme opposite. Mr. Greenhill was a child predator. For the three-year period that Ted attended the Adventist high school, he lived with the Greenhill's. Because Mom didn't contribute to her son's board, perhaps Mr. Greenhill assumed he had the right to take his fee out in trade.

Ted spent those three years staying away whenever possible, locking doors, and warding off the advances of this pious man, sometimes to the point of physical altercations.

Linda was living in Chattanooga where she attended Southern Missionary College, earning a teaching degree.

While I had studied in California, Mom had been traveling back and forth between the farm in Tennessee and Austin, Texas, where she sang lead with her new singing group. She had become a more and more accomplished musician and was widely acclaimed as the finest female banjo player in the nation. The more successful her music career became, the more she complained about having to drag her youngest child around with her. In fact, because of the inconvenience, Mom had discontinued the physical therapy for Teresa's leg and insisted that the orthodontist remove her braces prematurely.

Knowing that Mom considered even one child quite an albatross, I harbored no illusions that she would relish resuming any maternal responsibility for me. All her concerns focused on the homeless fiddle player she had hooked up with at a nightclub in Texas. He sat around our farmhouse, smoking like a chimney, bragging about his former stardom, and telling dirty jokes.

It was obvious that I needed to stay out of the way and cost no money. I felt as if I was well on the way to accomplishing both objectives when I obtained a telemarketing job selling a tire sealant to auto repair shops. The product was easy to sell, and I did well.

One day, on a whim, a fellow worker and I decided to call a few of our customers to see how they liked the product. We figured the follow up would be good for public relations.

One after another of our customers reported their dissatisfaction. Either they had not received the product, or if some small portion of their order had been delivered, it was worthless, green goop. My friend and I were shocked. Once we concluded that our employer was running a big scam, we approached our supervisors together. They assured us that the singular people with whom we had spoken were hardly representative of their thousands of customers around the world. They promised to look into the complaints.

A month later, we recontacted the customers we had called, and several dozen more. Their stories were identical. No attempt had been made to rectify the problems. My co-worker and I quit, but not before we had agreed that each of us would call the local authorities.

About midsummer, Mom, her fiddle player, and thirteen-year-old Teresa moved to Reno. Nightclub jobs were readily available there and Mom had purchased a trailer house on the outskirts so that she and her boyfriend could shack up together.

Mom's trailer was tiny, just one bedroom. My little sister, always the afterthought, was allotted a minuscule space in the hallway between the kitchen and Mom's room. Teresa's few clothes hung at the end of her cot and privacy was nonexistent.

As much as I missed Teresa, it was a relief to have Mom's fiddle player out of my life. I had the farmhouse to myself for the rest of the summer, and I loved it. I had lived among so many people and had been so lonesome. Now I lived alone and felt so peaceful. The whole farm was mine.

I acquired a new job, pressing records in a factory in Nashville. When I drove home from work, no one told me what to do. I selected my own groceries and lived on grilled cheese sandwiches. Each night I placed the paper towel holding my sandwich over the chipped part of the veneer on the kitchen table then sat down with a sigh of satisfaction. I felt like the lady of the manor, reigning from the head of my banquet table.

My routine with the horses was equally self-indulgent. Bunny had forfeited Outlaw when she left our farm, so I inherited the mare by default. Of course, I also had Chenaniah. I loved to ride late at night when the dark made the quiet more profound and mysterious. I was aware of each footfall of my mount and could tell whether he stepped on rocks, leaves or clay. When we approached the swamp, the sounds of peeper frogs and crickets harmonized with my horse's rhythmic breathing to create a marvelous harmony. I chuckled to myself once, crediting the insects with far greater range, talent, and rhythm than Mom's fiddle player had ever demonstrated.

If there was a full moon, I could make out the paths just well enough to gallop along. I navigated each hill and turn as much by memory as by sight. My nightgown billowed out behind me while my bare legs pressed against my horse's sides. Having the freedom to do anything I wanted, this was everything I wanted to do.

I spent so much time at home that it was inevitable I would run into the squatters who were living in the hollow below our farm. Heaven knows how long this poor woman and her two children had resided there, in a condemned, wooden shack. During the four years, we had owned the farm, I had heard rumors about how this family bathed in the creek and ate whatever food the woman could obtain by begging house to house. Perhaps, the town fathers had left her alone because she added a bit of local color to the community and inspired countless odd tales. I saw her for the first time when she knocked on my door.

I knew immediately that my visitor was our squatter because she looked exactly the way I had heard her described. Her greasy, disheveled hair absolutely refused to be held down by the hairclips scattered around her head. Her once-pink, shift-like dress so totally drowned her body that it was impossible to determine how small she actually was. It was obvious, however, that she was at least a few sizes too small for the worn-out, lace-less shoes on her feet.

She started yakking before I got the door fully open. Her words, jumbled together without pauses, sounded almost like a foreign language. I asked her repeatedly to slow down until it occurred to me that I was hearing the universal ring of retardation and ignorance. Her gestures, however, were entirely sufficient to communicate her need.

I invited her to bring her children inside and led them into the kitchen. It took only a moment for me to fix up a batch of my special grilled cheese sandwiches. The four-year-old boy and three-year-old girl hunkered greedily over their plates, chomping like starved puppies. When the last crust disappeared, they scuttled out the door behind their mom without a word.

After that initial meal, the family stopped by regularly, and I welcomed them. I had always planned to save the world or at least ease the pain of those who were hurting. Helping Teresa seemed constantly out of my grasp, but aiding this family was not. For the first time, I had the chance to see the positive effects of my efforts in someone else's life. I gave the children rides on my horses, showed them how to climb trees, and read to them. They soaked up the attention more voraciously than they consumed my sandwiches.

The woman kept nagging me for money, cigarettes, and beer. Instead, I drove the family to the local market and purchased soap, toothpaste, and toothbrushes. When we got back to the house, I lined them up beside me in front of our bathroom mirror. We took turns generously applying toothpaste and prepared to brush. I don't know how it happened, but suddenly every one of them had foaming toothpaste dripping off their chins and splattering their shirts and faces. In the end, however, their smiles were huge and clean.

As the summer wore on, the mother's skills deteriorated. On her rounds begging house to house, she took to squatting wherever she was to relieve herself. She left the children alone in the hollow while she wandered around the downtown streets. The townsfolk eventually called social services, and the social workers placed the mother in an adult living facility and the children in foster homes in Nashville.

I visited each of them a couple of times. The woman had become more frantic in her demands for cigarettes. Fortunately, she exhibited no heartache about the separation from her children because the state had determined that it would be impossible to reunite them. I never bought her anything to smoke, but

I did bring her a comb and brush in case she ever noticed that her hair could use a little attention.

Unfortunately, the children were separated from each other as well. The little girl was considered adoptable once she learned more appropriate social skills. The little boy required a more rehabilitative environment. I just felt relieved that they would all be cared for after I left for Georgia.

By the end of summer, I had saved enough money to purchase our horse trailer from Mom. I hitched it behind the fifteen-year-old Rambler sedan that my grandfather had given me. Then I packed up my stuff, loaded my horses, and hit the road. The time to join Bunny's gospel band was at hand.

Even in its heyday, my Rambler was no towing vehicle. I, however, was clueless about its limitations. Worse yet, I had never in my life pulled a horse trailer. On the highway, the trailer swayed repeatedly, fishtailing behind the car because of its excessive weight. Each time the trailer shifted from one side of the road to the other, the rambler shifted with it. To maintain control, I gripped the steering wheel so hard that my hands began cramping. I looked down at them and gritted my teeth, realizing how accurately "white-knuckled" described great fear.

When tractor-trailers sped by, their crosswinds nearly swept me off the road. I braked to about twenty miles an hour and kept my eyes glued ahead. At this rate, the trip was going to take forever. I could not get it out of my mind that my best friends were traveling behind me, and it would be my fault if anything happened to them.

Thankfully, we all survived. Following Bunny's instructions, I settled my horses at a farm owned by a friend of hers who had offered to care for them in exchange for being able to ride them occasionally. Thereafter, I rarely saw my horses because Bunny required each member of her band to commit a great deal of time to practicing for singing engagements in addition to holding a full-time job. Had I known I would not see my horses, I would have kissed them goodbye, but at that moment, it was the gospel group that filled my thoughts.

I detached the trailer, jumped back into the car, and reached over to the passenger seat for the scrap of paper on which I had scribbled directions to the Milledgeville Motel. Milledgeville sounded like a pretty Podunk place. Although it had been the original state capitol, the town now had only one remaining claim to fame—the state hospital for the insane. As optimistic as I was about the gospel band, I entertained doubts that our music was going to put the town back on the map.

The motel was easy to locate and I parked directly in front of Room 13. Even without checking in at the office, I felt certain I had found the correct room because I could hear the chords of a familiar song behind the door. The group was practicing *Keep on Walking*. Their playing sounded a bit rougher than on the tape Bunny had sent me. I paused for a moment to let my nerves calm down, quite thankful that I wouldn't have to be perfect to fit in. But I couldn't get my hands to quit shaking. I wished I had had a chance to shower before I made my grand entry. A strong aroma of horses, nerves, and sweat lingered on my clothes. It was too late to care. I knocked.

Bunny herself opened the door and hugged me warmly. "Praise God, you got here safely. Come meet the rest of the girls."

Three girls were spread out around the rather bleak, cheaply paneled motel room. For lack of chairs, each one sat on a corner of the two double beds. Almost in unison, they declared, "Praise God you are here."

Their chorus set the room spinning around me. I had never felt comfortable with Pentecostal dialogue. Even knowing they expected me to affirm their greeting by repeating, "Praise God," I choked. They stared at me, awaiting my response before any conversational exchange could begin. A prolonged silence ensured that my first words would sound awkward and foreign.

For once Bunny's take-charge personality came to my rescue. She tightened her arm around me and turned me toward the closest girl, a tall blonde girl with a guitar propped in her lap. "This is Lennie. I discovered her right here in a Milledgeville Church. She made the rest of the choir sound like first graders. She sings harmony."

Lennie made a concerted effort to be more polite than I had been. "Glad y'all made it."

I had lived in Tennessee and perhaps retained a bit of a southern accent myself, but I had never, ever before heard a thicker, more sugary drawl. Lennie managed to give the word y'all at least three syllables while her inflection covered nearly an entire octave. She responded to my unmistakable surprise with a smile that showed unnaturally straight teeth, big dimples, and a good heart.

Bunny turned me a quarter of a turn to another tall girl holding a guitar. "This is Darlene, but we call her Gumdrop because she's sooo sweet."

There is a good chance that my mouth dropped when I faced Gumdrop. She was so very lovely; she made the rest of us appear oversized, awkward, and dumpy. She had huge brown eyes and dark curly eyelashes, the likes of which I had never before seen except on a hand-painted China doll. Her natural beauty resounded with the innocence of childhood, perhaps because she had short little pigtails sticking out above her ears, and her skin was as dark as night.

As far as I could remember, this was the first time I had ever been in the same room with a black person, much less spoken with one. My mind flashed back to my brother and I, ending our petty, childhood standoffs with the rhyme, "Eeny meeny miney moe, catch a nigger by the toe, if he hollers let him go, out goes y-o-u."

My grandfather, hearing our exchange, had pulled his car over on the shoulder of the road, turned back toward us, and while wagging his finger, yelled, "Don't you ever say that again, you could be shot!"

We had no idea who was going to shoot at us, but from then on we ended our spats by catching a tiger. I never forgot Grandpa's warning that I had better be careful how I spoke about black people, and I wasn't at all sure what to say to one, especially one named Gumdrop.

Gumdrop seemed equally shy and barely spoke above a whisper. It wasn't until later that I realized what a sharp, sarcastic, and delightful sense of humor she possessed.

Another quarter turn and I faced the biggest girl in the room. Lots of light brown wavy hair and a full face made her features appear tiny and sharp. She seemed rather closed, like no matter what she said, she would not reveal much about herself.

"This is Beverly. She has the voice of an angel. I picked her out of the spring revival in Atlanta where she was singing with Gumdrop."

Beverly just nodded. "Where's that new guitar of yours? Let's get down to some music." With that, Bunny dismissed me from the room. I retraced my steps to the parking lot and retrieved my twelve-string from the back seat of the Rambler. I thought again, as I retraced my steps, how much I needed a shower.

Back in the room, I sat down on the only vacant corner at the end of the beds. Bunny was already waiting at the keyboard. The tension in the room was thick enough to cut with a butter knife, but holding my guitar in my lap made me feel better. The weight of it was familiar and my fingers knew exactly where to go. I would have been petrified to stand up and audition with voice alone, but once Bunny chose a song and I strummed a few chords, I relaxed into the music. We were all relieved to find that we sounded tolerably good together, and the need for small talk evaporated. We played and sang until well past the hour when the other motel guests would have wanted to sleep.

Before we could turn in for the night we had to pack up an amplifier, drum set, keyboard, and three guitars. The duffle bags and suitcases that were piled in the center of the beds while we practiced were shifted to the table and the corners of the room. Once the luggage opened up, female apparel materialized everywhere.

Privacy and modesty, especially important to Pentecostal people, dictated that the bathroom be used by only one person at a time. Being new, I went last. The relief I felt to use the toilet and the shower was overwhelming. When I stepped out of the bathroom, the girls were still milling around. I suspected that they were waiting to be sure that I got rid of the equine aroma before any of them agreed to sleep next to me.

Once it was resolved that I would bunk with Gumdrop and Lennie, I quickly homesteaded an outside slot on the mattress. We were all relieved that Gumdrop didn't seem to mind getting stuck in the middle. I made myself as small and straight as I could and worked so hard to adhere to the edge of the mattress that I could not fall asleep.

Besides, the drapes in the room were rather inadequate so the light from the red and blue neon motel sign permeated the room with a purplish hue that changed every few seconds when the yellow color of the "Vacancy" sign was added to the palate.

As I lay on the edge of the bed, my body was still vibrating from the long drive and the tension of arriving. I had finally come to a haven where I felt wanted. Talking to Bunny no longer had to be a secret.

Once the sound of heavy breathing assured me that everyone was asleep, I propped myself on my elbow, intending to get a better look at the band. My gaze stopped abruptly with Gumdrop. Her mouth was open slightly so her white teeth reflected the weird array of colors that invaded our room. Far more surprising, however, were two crescent-shaped mirrors created by the failure of her eyelids to fully cover the whites of her eyes. Gumdrop herself had disappeared in the shadows, leaving only three eerie little kaleidoscopes of changing color.

It was too much. I rolled back and stared at the ceiling. It took a moment for my breathing to settle back down. I would wait until morning to get a better feel for my fellow musicians.

I awoke just in time to see the bathroom procession getting back into full swing. It went without saying that I would slip back into the new-man-is-last-man position. While I brushed my teeth, I could hear the girls dragging our instruments and the amplifier out of the corners. I groaned to myself, as my stomach growled out loud. I had never stopped to eat during yesterday's odyssey from Tennessee, and I was starving. Evidently, however, we practiced before breakfast. By the time I exited the bathroom, all our suitcases were back on the beds and the girls were resuming their same stations on the bed corners.

I sat down on my bed corner, picked up my guitar, and checked its tuning. Unlike our initial, impromptu jam session, this practice resounded with the all-to-familiar ring of Bunny's insults and putdowns.

"Can't you remember anything? Haven't we gone over that chord progression at least four times? What in God's name is wrong with you?" Bunny snarled as she glared at Lennie.

Bunny's gaze then toured the rest of us, shaking her head, and pursing her lips in a manner intended to include us all in shaming Lennie. She sighed and muttered with disgust in her tone, "Again, and let's see if you can manage to get it right."

Almost instinctively, I rose to Lennie's defense. I had never mustered the courage to defend my own family when Bunny had degraded them, but after all the intervening years, all the Epistles, and all the calls, I was certain things had changed. I protested, "She almost has it."

Bunny rose from her keyboard, walked over to my bed corner, looked me right in the eye, and slapped my face with a full-armed swing. When Bunny's hand smacked my cheek, reality struck.

During the past years, I had rationalized Bunny as two entirely different people, and I had convinced myself that the kind and wonderful Bunny had triumphed over the cruel one. Now I finally understood that the two bunnies were one and the same.

I crumpled in stunned silence as tears once again welled up in my eyes. My former stoicism was no match for my surprise, heartache, and shame. I set my guitar down, gingerly lifted myself off the bed corner and exited the motel room. Finding the Rambler, I leaned against its hood and cried until I ran out of tears.

As I stood there with my head in my arms, I wasn't sure whether I just couldn't let my dream of belonging and being loved die or whether I had nowhere else to go. But as I straightened up, I knew I would return to the motel room. I fully accepted that I was not Bunny's chosen one and I felt certain that the rest of the group would know it too.

Prior to Bunny's slap, I had an inkling that the girls seemed unjustifiably suspicious of me. It turned out that prior to my arrival, whenever Bunny humiliated any of them, she built me up as the long-awaited prospect to salvage the band. After the slap, the group accepted me as just one more person that Bunny felt entitled to fix. Beverly was too heavy, Gumdrop was too shy, Lennie didn't have enough faith, and everything was wrong with me. Bunny, of course, was perfect.

Although that practice seemed eternal, it actually ended rather quickly so that everyone could get to work. Bunny and Lennie worked at a dry cleaner where a job awaited me. Gumdrop and Beverly were employed at our motel as maids.

All of us turned our paychecks over to Bunny. Our money enabled her to purchase a slightly used VW camper for the band, a pearl inlaid guitar, and a purple hot rod car, all in the name of glorifying God. That we could swallow God's need for a GTX sports car says much more about us than about deity. Bunny's peculiar charisma turned us into spineless sheep that followed her more blindly than the converts who martyred themselves for Jim Jones in Jonestown, Guyana.

Bunny took more than our money. She deftly robbed us of our sense of self and even our rational thought. Lennie had grown up in abject poverty, one result of which was deplorable dental hygiene. To avoid paying for fillings, her parents ordered the dentist to pull all her teeth and fit her with dentures before she was twenty. One night as she prepared to remove her dentures, poor mortified Lennie explained to me, "Bunny tells me that if I have enough faith and ask God, He will make my teeth grow back. She says that wearing my dentures proves my lack of faith."

Lennie burst into tears. She was caught between wanting to demonstrate her faith and the utter humiliation of removing her teeth around the rest of us. I hugged her close and tried to reassure her, "Just wear the false teeth. God loves you without any teeth and even if He is a miracle worker, He is not a dentist. It's not your teeth that matter to Him."

Lennie sobbed on. She could not be consoled or persuaded out of her misery. She perceived my words as Satan talking, Satan trying to dissuade her from what was right.

Lennie carried one other enormous burden. She loved a musical group known as "The Grassroots." After Lennie bought every one of their albums, Bunny labeled their music as worldly, not-of-God. So Lennie burned all her records to show her commitment to God. Within a few months, Lennie's reserve weakened, and she re-purchased all the Grassroots' albums. Several months later, a second set of albums, were burned. This outward display of Lennie's inner struggle repeated itself for the duration of our time together. I suspect that Lennie purchased enough albums to singlehandedly boost The Grassroots record sales to the top of the charts.

I for one should have seen through Bunny's ruse. During my summer alone on the farm, I had rummaged through boxes of things Bunny had left stored in our barn. I found books on brainwashing techniques, the *Satanic Bible,* and various pamphlets on communism. Unfortunately, it was years before I understood how well she had mastered all this material.

In the middle of one of our practice sessions, we heard a loud knocking on our motel room door. A man in a suit asked for me and handed me an official-looking envelope. The subpoena he delivered ordered me back to Nashville for three days to testify for the FBI in an upcoming criminal trial against my former telemarketing employer. Accompanying the letter was a check to cover expenses.

I packed quickly because all I ever wore were ankle-length skirts, button-down collared shirts, and tennis shoes, my courtroom wardrobe selection was limited. I folded up three clean shirts and three skirts in a paper grocery sack and headed out.

The day I arrived in Nashville, an FBI agent interviewed me extensively, asking me to describe all the details about how my coworker and I had become aware that our employer was defrauding hundreds of businesses. I outlined our efforts proudly. Then the agent prepped me on what to expect on the witness stand. Exhausted at the end of his inquisition, I drove to the record pressing plant where I had worked the previous summer. On my drive to Nashville, I had remembered that there was an abandoned room above the plant. I had decided to stay there in order to save money.

The next evening after I had testified for several hours, the agent was walking with me from the courthouse. He thanked me for my work and applauded my honesty and composure, then he added one last question, "Are you a virgin?" I was speechless—as shocked by his audacity as I was by his inquiry.

Eventually, however, I answered, "Yes."

"Well, if you want, I am a good gentleman, I would be willing to be your first, and then you don't ever have to worry about it again."

I reacted to his remark with consternation. "Do people worry about this?" But what I said was, "Thanks anyway." Then I walked away as quickly as I could without actually breaking into a run. I steered clear of him for the rest of the trial.

Across the street from the record plant where I was holed up like a transient, there was a Christian bookstore and coffee house featuring folk-type gospel music. The local Jesus-freak hippies crowded the place. Bunny loved it. We had been there together the summer I turned sixteen during several of my secret visits with her.

Each evening that I was in Nashville for the trial, I sat cross-legged on the floor of the coffee house listening to the harmonies and songs of *Dogwood,* the live band regularly featured there.

My last night in Nashville, after the coffee house closed, an older man whom I had seen in the book section approached me as I walked across the street. He spoke of his relationship with God. I listened. When we reached the sidewalk on the opposite side, he grabbed my hands and pushed my back against the wall, thrusting himself against me until I couldn't breathe. His words were harsh and low, "I can make you feel good."

With all my strength, I attempted to push him away. He pressed me harder against the wall, shoving his crotch against mine. Terrified but adrenaline-charged, I jerked both of my hands down, ducked under his armpit then sprinted to the doorway. I ran up the entire flight of stairs without ever looking back. Once inside the room where I camped, I curled up on my makeshift bed with all my clothes on. When my heartbeat finally quieted, I felt around in the semi-darkness for a cassette of James Taylor that my brother had sent me. I slipped it into my portable tape player and played the tape over and over. Finally, I fell asleep.

It was an enormous relief to be on the road to Georgia the next morning. The Nashville experience had turned into a nightmare. What had happened? What were they thinking? Why me? A young woman subpoenaed to the federal court, proud to be doing her civic duty. A woman alone—a teenager without a chaperone for protection became the victim of the dregs of manhood—within the space of twenty-four hours, propositioned and molested by men of authority in the law or the church. Men who should have known better, who should have behaved better. Men who should have protected the vulnerable young woman, but who failed her.

The journey to Nashville was supposed to be about justice, but where was mine? Two unjust men had suffered no consequences, and they left me feeling overwhelmed by guilt and shame. I wanted comfort, I needed to cry, but I couldn't think of anyone to comfort me. I couldn't think of anyone who would care.

Bunny smiled when I handed her the money I had saved by staying in the abandoned record plant. Though the price of that smile had been far too great, I was still proud to have earned it. The nightmare receded into my subconscious.

Soon after, I returned to Georgia, Bunny determined that the motel room was too expensive and too crowded. Bunny instructed Lennie to convince her mother to allow the band to move into their house to live with her mom and her ailing father. What Bunny had requested was no small undertaking for Lennie. Before I had arrived, Bunny and Lennie's mom had not seen eye-to-eye—not even close. Lennie's mom had blamed Bunny for her daughter's religious fanaticism and for her decision to leave her family.

In light of the constraints that lack of funds had imposed on us, we felt quite fortunate when Lennie's mother relented and agreed to take us all in. Lennie's home reminded me of the place where we first lived when we had arrived in Nashville in the Big Blue Monster. It was one more wood-plank shack camouflaged in a grid-like pattern to form the wrong side of town. It was the kind of neighborhood where mothers sent their kids out to beg for food or money, the kind of neighborhood that inspired the words to *Welfare Cadillac* describing people who lived in condemned shacks because they spent their welfare checks on fancy cars that adorned their driveways.

Several undernourished, mongrel dogs already resided in the house. They had defecated and urinated all over the bare wood floors for so many years that the corners of each room had rotted. The stench overwhelmed me, resurrecting my worst memory of our farmhouse in Vermont—that of cleaning cat feces out of the tub before I could bathe. I marveled that I could ever have acclimated to such a repulsive odor, and though I tried not to embarrass our hostess, I sometimes gagged.

We four girls crowded into one room with two sets of bunk beds separated by two cheap, identical dressers that were already full. The window and the walls were bare. Lennie's parents kept their room, and Bunny requisitioned the largest bedroom for herself. In no time at all, Bunny ruled the roost, such as it was.

Gospel gigs around Milledgeville were hard to come by. We played at any church that invited us and often our pay came straight out of the plate that was passed around to collect the week's tithing. I remember one time when payment came in the form of dinner at an upscale restaurant. Knowing there were no funds with which to pay us, a parishioner approached us after our performance. She invited us to dinner after she told us how our songs touched her.

On the drive to the restaurant, where we would meet up with our hostess,

Bunny emphatically instructed all of the band members to order one meal between two of us. I didn't consider this a strange request because obtaining food at a minimal cost had seemed one of the themes of life with Bunny. No one else said a word either. After we were seated at the table, our hostess smiled and chatted about our performance then graciously looked at each one of us as she declared, "Go ahead and order whatever you would like."

Bunny's stern glare reminded us to remain silent. Then she told this woman which two dinners we would have and announced that we were happy to share. When our hostess began to protest, Bunny flatly refused and ordered for all of us. She asked for extra plates and told the waitress that the five of us would divide two dinners. The minimal conversation that followed was awkward. We were all thankful when our meals arrived. Then we separated the food among us and ate in silence.

One church that hired us had a large Negro woman for a preacher and an all-Negro congregation. We arrived early and set up our instruments on a worn-out wooden platform behind the pulpit that resembled many of the other stages on which we had played. As the church members filed into the pews I noted the animation of their conversations.

"How you been, Mattie? Girl, you be lookin' good! Can you believe this heat?"

"Oh, girl, it be so hot I can boil grits on the sidewalk. You got yo fan?" Little by little, the church filled to capacity. The crowd only quieted when the pastor began to sway up the aisle on her way to the pulpit. Her bright purple robe swished around her ankles with each step. As she strolled through the church, I heard a wave of "A-A-mens" ripple along in her wake.

When she reached the pulpit, the preacher's hands started quivering at her side. In one smooth movement, her arms raised above her head, and she turned slowly around to face the congregation. She took one deep audible breath as her arms lowered, then burst out preaching. From the minute she first opened her mouth this woman did not standstill. Every inch of her body trembled and gestured as she shouted about Hellfire and Damnation. A continuous chorus of "Amens" and "Hallelujahs" affirmed her every word. She paced across the stage in front of us, then up and down each aisle. Sweat poured off her forehead and soaked her purple armpits. I had never witnessed anything like it.

The opening sermon lasted about fifteen minutes after which the pastor introduced us without even pausing to catch her breath. We had planned to run through our usual repertoire, but when we began, this congregation joined in with so many chants of "Praise Him, Glory to God, and Amen" that they drowned out the lesser-known verses of each hymn. We completed our last set then rested along with the congregation as their preacher resumed her station at the pulpit.

Immediately animated, she paced, rocked on her heels, and then threw her hands upward toward the ceiling, shouting, "Praise God!" This time, the congregation responded by flailing their arms toward Heaven along with her. I looked to each side and saw that my fellow band members had also raised their arms. Not knowing what else to do, I slowly pushed my hands up out of my lap, but even after I reached full extension, my arms lacked the enthusiastic conviction demonstrated by the rest. I did, however, feel a little less conspicuous with my hands aloft.

As the traditional call to be saved went up, a particularly large woman stood up in the back and approached the preacher. Her raised arms still swayed side to side as she came forward. Her eyes appeared peacefully closed, but she managed to locate the pulpit without any interruption in her chanting and weeping.

I jumped in my seat when I heard a hollow thud. The woman had collapsed flat on her back. As she hit the wooden floor, she began shaking. Her arms remained stiffly extended above her head, palms toward Heaven. The congregation rose and gathered close around the pulpit, rhythmically joining in the chanting and swaying.

They were all so close that I found myself having difficulty breathing. I could feel the very walls vibrating. I expected an ambulance to burst in any second to revive the poor woman on the floor. The congregation's voices grew to a crescendo. I could no longer stay in my seat. Terrified, I jumped up and charged out the front doors then fled to the safety of our van. It took the whole rest of the service for me to regain my breath and my sanity. I watched from the parking lot as my fellow band members filed out behind the congregation. The woman I had watched writhing on the floor, seemed to have survived the group effort to save her.

Donations for our performances paid for gas, but they didn't often cover our bills. Money became so tight that Bunny ordered Gumdrop, Lennie, and me to Nashville to search for more lucrative jobs. We intended to stay at my house in Fairview. Our farm was vacant for the summer because it had not yet sold.

We packed up the GTX with a minimal amount of necessities for the trip north. Bunny preferred to keep the VW bus with pop-top and my Rambler had died a natural death soon after my return from testifying in Nashville.

It was dusk by the time we reached the farm. We had to carry our own bedding into the house because Mom was still in the process of moving and had moved most of my family's furniture.

We had just arranged our blankets on the living room carpet and finished our prayers when the phone rang. I picked it up and wearily muttered, "Hello?"

"Hi," came the reply, "What are you doing back in town?"

I recognized the voice of the neighbor who lived in the house trailer kitty-corner to our farmhouse. It was not that surprising to hear from her. She was a notorious busybody who closely watched all the comings and goings in our neck of the woods.

"I'm here with some new friends. We're going to look for work."

"Who are your friends?" She inquired with a bit of an edge creeping into her voice.

"They are the girls who sing in a band with me."

Her congeniality ceased. "It seems to me that one of your friends is black. You may have noticed, we don't have Blacks in this town. The fact is, we don't want any. So, if you don't get her out of here by morning, your house could be burned down. I thought I should warn you."

I still held the receiver by my ear but no words would come. I had never suspected such malice in my neighbor. She had long professed that her Mormon religion made her purer than the rest of the Christian world. Evidently, because at this time fellowship within the Latter-day Saints didn't include Blacks, she felt free to let her racial prejudice run wild. Any remaining vestiges of loyalty to the Mormon Church evaporated as I hung up the phone and turned toward Gumdrop. "We have to get out of here. They threatened to burn down my house."

Lennie and Gumdrop had lived in the Deep South all their lives. They accepted my directive without a word. I fumed under my breath about the injustice of it all while we repacked the car. Why should I be forced to flee my own house like a thief in the night? It was I who was being robbed, robbed of my housing, my haven, my home.

We headed for Nashville in silence. The twenty-five-mile drive took me less than twenty minutes. I fired into a gas station and parked in front of its phone booth. Fortunately, a tattered phone book still dangled from a chain below the payphone, and the pages listing "Good Will" and "Salvation Army" had not been torn out. I remembered these establishments because years ago Mom and Bunny had shopped at them for our clothes. The Salvation Army provided a twenty-four-hour number. A volunteer gave us information about a woman's shelter where we could stay for the night.

In the morning, we called the Pentecostal Church. Gumdrop and Lennie accepted a room offered them by a church member who later helped them get on with a temp agency. I declined the generous offer because I knew I would overdose on the perpetual salutations of "Praise God," the casting out of demons, and the speaking in tongues. Besides, I managed to secure a higher paying job a bit further from town.

An upscale restaurant that was associated with a popular amusement park just off the freeway had hired me to cook during the graveyard shift. After my first shift ended, I was walking back to the car when it hit me that I had nowhere to go and once again, no one cared.

Inertia kept me moving across the parking lot, I opened the car door and slid in behind the wheel. Then I just sat in the purple hot rod for a minute or two with the keys in my hand. Eventually, I put the key in the ignition, started the car, and headed out. I entered the freeway via the closest entry ramp without consciously choosing one direction or the other. Then I turned off at the first exit and stopped under the next freeway bridge. After surveying the area for hobos, hoodlums or ghosts, I shifted into park. I was staking my claim. I locked the doors, climbed into the back seat, and rolled the windows partway down to get some air. I just sat there staring into the dawn until I was so exhausted that I nodded off. Then I lay down and drifted off. I slept through most of the day curled up like a dog. I awoke once and moved the car forward to take advantage of the shade provided by the bridge.

Having grown up in small towns, it never crossed my mind to worry about personal safety. In fact, after a few nights, the traffic sounds no longer kept me awake, and I learned just where to park to avoid the early morning sun. Eventually, however, the summer heat became unbearable. I would often wake up with my bare skin stuck to the vinyl seat and the underside of my clothes drenched with sweat.

Occasionally, during the month that I lived like a troll under the bridge, sleep would not come. On those nights, I got out of the car, rolled up the windows, and locked up the car to make sure no random passerby would abscond with my precious possessions while I wandered around. I discovered a polluted, little stream nearby which sufficed as a destination and a refuge where I could cool off by dangling my feet in the water.

On my nights off, I drove into Nashville and toured the center-city streets. Having spent so little time in urban environments, I found them fascinating. I watched girls who wore makeup and fancy dresses, girls who were going dancing with their boyfriends. Contrary to Bunny's indoctrination, which associated such actions with sin and degradation, these young women looked happy and healthy. However, carefully I observed them, I never saw the devil lurking in their shadows.

I, on the other hand, wore no makeup and owned only the long, full skirts dictated by our religious sect. I had never had a boyfriend, never danced, and I was unhappy. I always sensed demons following my footsteps. Something about this picture felt wrong.

One of those steamy, sleepless afternoons, during which I had driven into town, was a payday. I had already cashed my check, and my pockets were flush with cash. The subconscious part of my mind, having planned this venture for weeks, dragged my feet into a department store and straight to the cosmetic counter. The rest of me started in complete surprise when the attendant inquired in her professionally pleasant voice, "May I help you?"

"No thanks." My mouth quickly uttered as I drove my sinful feet away from the counter. Before I had gone too far, however, a new voice spoke inside me, "Do you want to feel guilty forever?"

Hearing that voice stopped me in my tracks, I took a deep breath and returned to the counter, "Maybe you can help me after all."

"Sure, honey."

I checked behind me before I actually looked at the attendant. "Can you help me with some makeup? I don't know anything about it." I felt quite certain that my second sentence was sufficiently obvious, but the voice inside me said it anyway.

The attendant smiled politely and nodded, then she selected some blush, lipstick, and eye shadow that she said would match my natural coloring. I hope she realized that the flushed face she was addressing bore little resemblance to whatever my natural coloring might be, but I said nothing because I was certain she knew better than I. Fact was, it really did not matter to me what colors I was purchasing. I simply loved how small and feminine the containers were. The attendant offered to demonstrate how to apply each product, but a demonstration was too much for even my new voice, which politely declined.

My feet then headed to the dress department. Not skirts, dresses. I selected a silky black item with a full skirt that was obviously designed to twirl elegantly if one was to dance in it. The saleswoman folded the dress and placed it in a paper bag with a crisp piece of tissue. I tucked the sack of contraband makeup in the dress bag and headed out, unsure about whether I felt more pride or more shame. Then I headed home to my bridge.

After I parked at the shady end of the bridge, I transferred the dress and makeup into one of my old paper bags, carefully hiding them between articles of acceptable clothing. There was every reason to believe I was hiding them from myself. It would be months before I would use any of my purchases.

A couple of weeks later, when the bills were caught up, Bunny summoned us home. Lennie, Gumdrop, and I moved back into the bedroom with Beverly at Lennie's house. We resumed our former routine of practicing gospel music, studying the *Bible* under Bunny's tutelage, and praying aloud. It felt as if no interlude had ever occurred.

In addition to leading our gospel band, Bunny periodically adopted a Mother Superior role, counseling her charges on topics associated with the evils of worldly living and the opposite sex. We knew a sermon was in the offing when Bunny assumed her unnaturally pious tone and diction. "God has made manifest that I talk to you about a matter that you might think is private, but remember, God sees everything."

We thought there was nothing in the world about which we had not been lectured, but we were wrong. "Masturbation is a manifestation of demon possession so if you are in need of help to cast out those demons, we can do that now."

All four of us stared at her incredulously, absolutely stunned. We were so prudish and naïve that the mere word masturbation turned our faces cherry red. If Bunny thought any of us would admit to such behavior, even to avoid eternal damnation, she must have been crazy.

In light of the absolute silence that followed, Bunny evidently felt reassured that we were demon-free, at least for the moment.

Mixed with our religious training or perhaps to enhance it, Bunny insisted on compulsory fasting. She designed an extensive assortment of deprivations. The most severe fast prohibited both food and drink for up to three, maybe four days at a time. Just doing without food could continue longer. Our typical fast lasted three days during which time our bodies and minds were supposedly rejuvenated and spiritually cleansed.

One time, however, Bunny had a revelation that Beverly should fast for thirty days. Beverly was strong. The longest I ever fasted was two weeks. Beverly ate nothing for the full thirty days. When she finally did eat, she threw up all day long.

During one less remarkable fast, I walked into the kitchen to find Bunny scooping apple pie straight from the pie tin into her mouth. She glanced up, acknowledged my presence with a nod, and just kept chewing.

Bunny could have blurted out the *Bible* verse about the spirit being willing when the flesh was weak, but she didn't bother to say anything. Had she any inkling that this particular indiscretion would become the chink in the armor through which I would finally began to see the light, I'm sure she would have quoted Matthew 26:41 for all she was worth.

It was Bunny who had convinced me that life should be defined in terms of good or bad, black or white. Here in the kitchen, I watched her, pie tin in hand, nibbling in the grey area. How could someone whom God had used to perform miracles, speak in tongues, and cast out demons, sneak food?

Bunny's presence had controlled my life for six years. I had placed her on such a pedestal that when she had beaten and belittled me I had believed her and belittled myself. But when she cheated on our divine fast, when she sneaked apple pie, she toppled from grace forever. All my emotional ties to Bunny began to unravel.

Out of defeat or perhaps defiance, I secured a new job on the graveyard shift at a local Milledgeville Cafe. I still drove the hot rod to work, but no longer gave all my wages to Bunny. I developed a friendship with the waitress, Sharon, who bussed tables in the other half of the restaurant. The world outside my tiny sphere no longer seemed so foreign.

While Sharon worked, she often chatted with a tall, thin, young man who was her fiancé's best friend. He would pay for a cup of coffee in exchange for the right to hang out with her at the counter. Whenever I passed by, he greeted me with a smile and a wink. At first, I ignored him. I had lived for too long under the "Men-are-dogs" umbrella. Eventually, however, I noticed that when he smiled, one corner of his mouth rose higher than the other and wonderful dimples appeared. His disheveled bad-boy appearance perfectly reflected his bad-boy reputation.

After a while, I picked up on his deliberate migration toward my section of the counter. He wrote notes to me on napkins and left them under his coffee mug. I smiled to myself as I read his quips and pocketed his tip, but I refused to acknowledge his efforts. No question though, I was flattered. No man had ever flirted with me, or rather, if one had, I had not noticed.

One night, he left a napkin stating that he wanted my phone number and would call me. This napkin gave me pause—I was as intrigued with him as I was disillusioned with Bunny and her religion. I had yet to see a miracle and the foreign tongues sounded more and more like fakes. I sensed that my demons were still dancing around and that "casting out" was not an effective way to get rid of them. The next evening, I gave this stranger my phone number, on a napkin, of course.

By the time I got back to Lennie's house that night the full impact of my impetuousness hit me. What would the girls say if they answered his call? What would Bunny do? What would God think? To keep from having to answer such terrifying questions, I employed every possible excuse to hover around the area of the phone. I snatched it up the next evening and sighed audibly upon hearing his voice, far more relieved that no one else answered his call than that he followed through with his promise. His banter began, "I told ya I'd call."

I had little experience with small talk and had never before conversed with a man my age so our conversation proceeded awkwardly at best. I struggled to come up with even a few bungling words. Then I heard him say, "I love you." Three words were all it took. Even though I was too embarrassed to tell him then, I decided I loved him, too.

He invited me to accompany him to the hospital the next evening. We would be going with Sharon to visit her fiancé, who had been stabbed in a fight. My first date. I hung up the phone and retrieved my make-up from its hiding place among my skirts. I wrapped it in my work uniform along with a pair of jeans and a shirt.

When our shift ended the following afternoon, Sharon helped me apply my makeup for the first time. Each beautiful container was set out on the shelf in front of us. I picked up the blush first and turned it over in my hand a couple of times. Appreciating the weight and shape of it. Magic dust or contraband? *Maybe both*, I thought. Then I handed the container to Sharon and watched my reflection as she brushed a pinkish highlight onto my cheeks. My features were coming to life. Artificially, of course, but it didn't matter. By the time our makeup ceremony was complete, my eyes had more sparkle and my lips were more inviting. I thought that I might even look a bit pretty.

In his friend's hospital room, my date stood behind me and rubbed my shoulders. Even though the others were looking, he kissed me.

Shortly thereafter, Sharon invited me to move in with her. Her parents had given her a trailer-home and she needed a roommate to share expenses until her wedding. Without a second thought, I accepted.

The summer was coming to an end, Gumdrop was leaving the group to go to college, Beverly's parents insisted she return home, and we had only a few remaining engagements. Above all, Bunny had eaten apple pie. At the beginning of time, one bite of an apple had justified Eve's eviction from the Garden of Eden. How could I possibly trust a person who had shoveled the forbidden fruit in by the handful?

I told Bunny I was leaving, then I packed all my possessions in cardboard boxes. Sharon's fiancé and I moved my horses to his father's ranch. I had not seen them for several months but now that I controlled my own life, I could ride daily. From the safe distance of Sharon's trailer-house, I mustered up the courage to confront Bunny about the purple muscle car. I had decided to ask her to sign it over to me. I called her and got straight to the point, not willing to risk the strength of my resolve against inane small talk. "I am working until three today. I wonder if you would please sign the car title over to me since I have been making the payments. I really need the car."

Fifteen minutes later, Bunny arrived at the diner. We sat across from each other in a booth. Bunny dug the title out of her pocket, flattened it out on the tabletop, and signed it. I couldn't believe it was that easy. We had not even spoken when she rose and walked away. She glanced back once as she left. It was the last time, I saw Bunny. After six years of cowing before her tirades, I had had the last word, and it was about the title to a muscle car we had purchased in the name of God.

I followed Bunny out, but only after allowing enough time for her to drive away. I walked over to the car, my car. Before I opened the driver's side door of my car, I paused for a moment to slide my fingers gently across its hood. It was an unconscious gesture similar to the stroke I gave my favorite horses before I mounted. When I realized what I had done, I chuckled.

For the first time in my very controlled life, I would answer only to myself. I stood alone, on the brink of a world, I could not begin to comprehend. I fully intended to jump feet first into an entirely different life, but what a rabbit hole that opening turned out to be. I had never worn my black dress, gone to a dance, or used any drugs. My new friends introduced me to all these things. But that was in the future. I turned the ignition of my car and struck out on my own.

Innocence Lost

An innocent, yes
Unsure and naïve
So unaware of the real world
But—not for long.

Released into reality
With no guiding hand to stay my course
No word to advise me
No moral compass to uplift me

Sex, drugs and uncensored speed
Quickly tainted what once was pure.

I was free. Free of Bunny, free to make choices, free to suffer the consequences of the real world.

Not long after moving in with Sharon, a salesman came into the café and offered Sharon and me a real deal, an affordable way to save money through life insurance. It sounded like a sure winner to us, so we agreed to meet with him. We made an appointment for him to come to our trailer-home in two days.

That afternoon, I was just finishing showering when the doorbell rang. It was more than an hour before we expected our salesman. Wrapping myself in a robe, I answered the door. There stood Mr. Insurance. I told him Sharon wasn't yet home, and I instructed him to wait in the living room while I got dressed. As I turned away, I felt him grab at my robe, tearing at it as he snarled, "You are going to like this."

I clutched my robe as I ran for my room, hoping to shut the door before he could follow. He pushed the door harder than I could and when he got into the bedroom, he threw me down on the bed. I struggled in frenzy, pounding and kicking at his body as he frantically held me with one hand while he removed his shirt. I scratched my fingernails deep into the flesh of his back.

He stopped cold and stood up. Then he backed up to the mirror and craned his neck over his shoulder to get a good look at the damage. He retrieved his shirt from the floor and fumbled with the buttons. The look on his face had transformed from conquest hunger to fury. But I sensed another emotion as he coldly growled, "My wife is going to kill me."

The door slammed as I wrapped myself back up in my robe. Shocked and terrified, I sat on the edge of my bed. Angry tears flowed. I was stunned by the fact that this man had walked into my home clean-shaven and dressed in a suit and tie. So quickly, he had reduced himself to the worst of animal behavior. I accepted no responsibility for his choice as his behavior was so deplorable there was no blame other than his own, but I told no one, not even Sharon. When she commented that we had been stood up by the handsome salesman, I just shrugged and told her I had changed my mind about buying insurance.

Soon after I turned nineteen and not long after our first date at the hospital, I experienced sex, consensual sex, for the first time. My new boyfriend told me he loved me, he held me and touched me. The way two bodies felt, skin-to-skin, amazed me. And, I didn't go straight to Hell, not that night.

Of course, he didn't love me; he just wanted to have sex. He was such a flirt that it shouldn't have surprised me a month later to hear that he was seeing other girls. Rumors abounded at Milledgeville's top teen hangout, the local Pizza Hut where I now worked a second job. I was so naïve that, at first, I refused to believe such stories. I had no experience with the chase and the heartache that make up the Game of Love.

Not being one to wait around for answers, I called from my day job and asked him to see me that night. I tried not to sound too serious in my request. He chose not to hear any anxiety at all.

"Sorry, I'll be hanging out with the guys, we are going to a party in Atlanta."

I tried another angle. "Why don't y'all come down and have Pizza before you go? I get to work at five. I'll buy." I hadn't planned those last words but an answer was worth more to my subconscious mind than the price of a pizza, so out they popped.

He allowed that his buddies would kill him if he refused my offer and showed up with the gang within an hour of the start of my Pizza Hut shift. I wrote down the orders for my guests then served their pizza. I fussed at myself about mustering the courage to confront my boyfriend. I might never have made it but for the fact that I had to pay a full pizza price for the opportunity.

As the boys were finishing up the last slice of pepperoni, my boyfriend patted his leg. And he told me to come, sit on his lap. "Let me show you how much we appreciate this fine meal."

As his unsuspecting face puckered near mine, I ducked around the kiss and put my lips up to his ear. "I've heard that you're seeing other girls," I whispered. "I want to know if it's true."

It didn't occur to me that he might lie. It didn't occur to him that he needed to. His crooked smile and dimples danced in front of me as he said, "So, I love the girls, what can I say? I have a reputation to uphold."

Oh, the cost I paid for his reputation. So, my first foray into sexuality had wasted what should have been nature's most beautiful and intimate gift.

My body shut down. Nothing felt normal. I slowly stood up and, without a word, stacked up a pile of plates. I stumbled slightly then stepped off in a drunk-like stupor. Thanks to long-ingrained habits, I managed to survive the rest of my shift, get to my car, and turn on the radio. The second I recognized the tune of a familiar love song I began sobbing uncontrollably.

No wonder there are so many ballads about breaking up. A broken heart had to be the worst pain in the whole world. Only the accompaniment of sad, sad music made it possible for words to even begin to capture such pain.

After three days of crying and finally resolving not to kill myself, I began to hope for a new love to fill the enormous void that kept resurfacing in my life. My search was random. It was easy to find men who would be with me. A part of me actually believed that sex served as an indication of love. No doubt that part was blinded by the same gullibility and naivety that had enabled me to idolize Bunny when all I experienced should have warned me otherwise.

As a means to escape myself, I developed quite a passion for speed. I found it harder and harder to resist testing the power of my very own purple hot-rod. In time I became something of a celebrity at the local police department. The fastest time at which an officer clocked me on a city street was a hundred and ten miles per hour. Not surprisingly, the police awarded me a number of speeding tickets that were followed by warrants for failure to pay my fines or show up in court.

When the enormity of my transgressions finally registered, I called my father from the police station and asked for his help. He ordered me to slow down with the very same tone he used when he had forbidden rafter running. It was a relief to hear such concern in his voice. His promise to send a check to cover my tickets was secondary. I handed the receiver to the officer. My father assured the officer that he would take care of everything.

The police chief's patience ran out after two weeks of waiting for "The check that was in the mail." The chief summoned me back to the station.

My father, my childhood hero, had disappeared again and left me to fend for myself. Why couldn't Dad see that I was spiraling downward? Why couldn't he understand how much I needed a hero again? I was headed for the Big House.

With my one free phone call, I swallowed my dignity and called my ex-boyfriend. He had bragged to me in the past about his prowess as a narcotics agent. It didn't take long for him to convince his friends at the station to offer me a deal. The court would drop my speeding tickets if I would work undercover for the law. My ex would show me the ropes. I had no money, and jail time sounded less than appealing, so I figured, *Why not?* Thus began my short-lived career as a small town "narc."

Only a backwoods, southern, redneck town would consider enlisting a naïve, out of control, nineteen-year-old girl as an undercover agent. Drugs had never been a part of my life. As a matter of fact, my life had been so controlled that I had never even seen an illegal substance. How bizarre that circumstances now made it my job to smoke pot. After all, it took a user to make connections with users.

My new role gave me a better perspective on why the Pizza Hut was so well known as the hub of after-hours action. Once I tuned in, it was easy to eavesdrop on our young, rowdy customers as they bragged about getting high at someone's party. I became adept at flirting with the braggers and fished for an invitation to join in the fun. I took pride in my knack for convincing any guy to come back and pick me up when my shift ended.

The moment my target left the Pizza Hut, I phoned the police station and described the vehicle that would be returning for me. Shortly after my shift ended, I hopped in that car and drove off with my ride. An undercover officer would pick up our tail and flash his lights. My poor, new, unsuspecting friends would pull over, then be ordered out of their car and slapped in handcuffs. I was handcuffed right along with them.

The officer would separate his victims and interrogate each one separately. Of course, his object was to speak to me so that I could spill the beans about where he should search for the pot. To complete the charade, the officer stuffed all of us into the backseat of the squad car and escorted us to jail cells.

When the paperwork was completed, I was released. Each time I walked out of my cell, I had kind of a creepy, guilty feeling about my complicity. I had to remind myself that I was doing something good for society, not to mention keeping myself out of jail. But a second voice kept nagging that my false friendship had put some poor sucker behind bars. Ah well, the pile of my old traffic tickets was shrinking away and none of the officers gave me any new ones as I sped through life.

I was aware that I made a goodly number of busts, but I didn't realize that I was also making a lot of dangerous enemies. Those involved in the drug world don't take kindly to jail, and given time, they would find a way to express their displeasure.

Meanwhile, my living situation changed when my roommate married. I sang and played guitar at her wedding. Then she sold her trailer and moved in with her new husband. I rented a small frame house, a classic slumlord offering.

The dinginess of my abode faded at twilight when I lit the candles and oil lamps I had strategically placed in every room. In truth, I had no money for deposits so I didn't have the utilities connected. Besides, it was summer, and electricity was hardly essential in a haunt where druggies and sex partners crashed.

On the nights when my buddies poured in to hang out, I played guitar while the guys drank beer and regaled their girlfriends with wildly exaggerated tales of their hormone-charged youth. Random, illicit sex outwardly manifested the deep emptiness I felt. Men used me; I used them. In the mornings, I stepped over the carcasses of drunken partiers on my way to work. The group slept off their booze, ate my food, and waited for me to return from one of my two jobs. Not once did any of them offer to assist me with food, beer or living expenses.

My drug-sex-and-alcohol lifestyle was not anything I had anticipated even in my wildest nightmares. Many were the nights that, as friends partied at my house, I cruised up and down Main Street just to avoid going home. I might make the loop five or ten times, checking out the same groups of guys each time. I was trolling for the fellow who would check out my car expecting to see a fellow hot-rodder. When his gaze met mine, I would smile, wink, and punch the gas, dusting him. Then I would circle back. There was a part of me that never gave up the quest for romance, or at least a bit of cavalier, suggestive conversation.

After the street loiterers gave up the ghost and headed home, I drove the back roads and threw "Little Miller" bottles at street signs, all the while belting out harmony with the hit tunes playing on the radio. Music kept me tumbling along, but only for the moment. My heart knew I was alone—alone in my house, at my job, in my car—alone with only my thoughts. I had become everything that Bunny said God condemned. I had lost touch with everything that I had once believed mattered.

The Opposite of Heaven

now i'm sitting in the waiting room
playing with the toys
i am here to exercise my freedom of choice…

as far as i can tell
the world isn't perfect yet…

i am growing older waiting in this line
but some of life's best lessons
are learned at the worst times
under the fierce fluorescent
she offered her hand for me to hold
she offered stability and calm
and i was crushing her palm

~ani difranco

It was inevitable that all the afternoon delight would catch up with me.

The Pizza Hut had just hired a new manager, named Charlotte. This comely and graceful young woman had, until recently, been training to become a prima ballerina. While we cleaned up the restaurant after closing, she would punch a few buttons on the jukebox, selecting music that would invite her feet to spin and twirl over the crumbs and trash scattered on the floor. Her arms extended, her hands floated and her face glowed with the ecstasy of one doing what she was born to do. Though her movements were lovely to watch, chronically swollen knees dictated that her dancing career had ended.

Because of her loss, or in spite of it, Charlotte took me under her wing. One night, she invited me to her favorite bar and ordered Brandy Alexanders for us. As we sat across from each other in the dimly lit booth she chuckled, "You have to try one. These drinks are so delicious you won't even know you are drinking alcohol."

She was right. After drinking several of the sweet, creamy concoctions, I discovered myself hunched over the outside curb, barfing up my guts. Charlotte helped me up and shepherded me to her car as she teased, "I told you to try one. All those refills were your dumb idea."

When I could no longer slice onions for the daily pizza preparation without running to the bathroom to throw up, Charlotte began to suspect that my real dilemma had little to do with the overdose of Brandy Alexanders. "Could you be pregnant?" she asked as she gently stroked my back while I bent over the john with beads of sweat forming on my forehead.

When I stood up, she put her arm around my shoulders and turned me to face her. "Could you be pregnant?" she repeated.

I was so naïve that I had not entertained the idea even for a moment. Her question, however, shocked me into the realization that, yes, it could happen. In fact, I was sure it must be so.

At that moment, Charlotte was the closest person in the world to someone who gave a damn about me, which is to say I didn't give a damn about myself. She was adamant that I abort the baby. She had had an abortion once and listed for me her complete litany of justifications. "You are young, and you have your whole life ahead of you. How do you think you would care for a child?"

I never verbalized an answer, but when she brought up the life ahead of me, all that came to my mind was, "So what, who cares."

To her question about how to care for a child, I admitted to myself, "I have absolutely no idea."

After a moment of silence, I said to myself, as much as to Charlotte, "All right, let's get it the Hell over with."

As my boss, Charlotte wrote a note guaranteeing payment to the Atlanta Abortion Clinic. The clinic accepted her commitment for the purpose of scheduling my next appointment, but a note would not pay the bill. I needed to arrive with cash in hand when the time came for the procedure.

Desperate situations give rise to unexpected courage. I called my mother, who still lived in Reno with her fiddle player and my little sister. We had a short conversation. Mom agreed to loan me the money with strict payback instructions. I heard no concern for my situation, only for the repayment of the loan. I hung up the phone and scribbled,

I'm sorry (I'm in trouble here)
Of course, I'll pay you back (tell me you care)
I'm sorry to disappoint you (how could I)
I get paid the first of the month (come hold my hand)
I'm sorry (tell me I don't have to do this)
I'm sorry (Mostly sorry for me)

I drove the forty-five-minute route to the clinic alone. Actually, I drove past the clinic a couple of times because it was so poorly marked, I did not notice it. Eventually, I parked across the street, walked up to the lobby door, and entered into a pale blue waiting room where well-worn Naugahyde sofas lined the walls. I gave my name to the receptionist then sat down to wait, holding tightly to myself with both arms as if the room were very, very cold.

In the weeks since I accepted the reality that I was pregnant, I had thought about nothing but this baby. I believed she was a girl. I would have named her Beth. I would have shown her daisies and horses and fields of new-mown hay. I would have sung songs for her. During this time, my soul had played word games with me, "You would or you should?"

I squeezed myself harder to expel such thoughts. Finally, I accepted the reality I had created. I would have, yes I would have done these things, but I won't, and Beth won't.

Having resolved at least this portion of my future, I became aware of the other people in the room. On both sides of me sat young girls in various stages of my same circumstance. One of them had brought her boyfriend with her; the others were alone like me.

Once our eyes met, we moved closer to each other—an offer of silent support. My hand released its death grip on my shoulders and reached out to the young woman on my right. Pain-filled tears ran down each of our faces while "Boulder to Birmingham" drifted through the overhead speakers. My insides turned inside out.

The receptionist called my name. I approached the counter, then she asked for my money. Pay first. I handed her the bills, and she counted them before she sent me to the procedure room where a young nurse instructed me to undress and lie down on a narrow table covered with a white sheet.

Having never had a real physical exam before, I had no clue why the table had metal cups projecting from its end. I was still crying quietly as I lowered myself in between them then lay back and stared at the tiles on the ceiling.

When the nurse returned, she spoke to me kindly, "Slide back, honey, and put your feet in the stirrups." I was so dumbstruck that I didn't move. How could these cold, abominable metal appendages be called stirrups? I just stared at them. Ever so gently, she picked up each foot and placed it in the cup so that my legs stuck up and exposed my private areas. I couldn't believe it.

The nurse explained every step of the procedure as the doctor performed. He never actually looked at me. Neither of us ever spoke. The room was so quiet that the sound of suction branded my hearing forever. The nurse held my hand and I squeezed as if life depended on it. Mine did.

My eyes remained glued to the ceiling as I attempted to memorize its pattern, but my mind kept returning to reality. This could be a piece of Hell, and I deserved it. I pictured my last great heartache and realized that losing a lover was not the worst pain in the world. People wrote songs about lost love because it possessed a poetic kind of sadness. Abortion was an unspeakable tragedy. It was a horror that words could not capture and music should not lighten.

When it was over, I drove myself home where I wallowed in self-pity. I felt overwhelmingly alone and sad. When I returned to work, Charlotte avoided the subject. My mother never called, and no one else knew. I wrote my baby a letter and placed it in a special box where I saved my Pony Club ribbons, my underlined Bible, and my ticket from the John Denver concert. I penned, "Dear Beth."

Then I cried continuously as I wrote about how sorry I was, how I loved her, and how I knew she was being cared for in heaven by those better than I. I promised her she would be with me always, but I knew better—all I would really possess was my own empty sorrow and a simple written letter.

Lost

I've got a fast car
But is it fast enough so I can fly away
I've gotta make a decision
I leave tonight or live and die this way.

~ Tracy Chapman

One night not long after the abortion, the engine of my car quit running while I sped along the highway. I coasted on to the shoulder, braked to a complete stop, then got out. Having no clue what else to do, I locked the doors, walked to a gas station, and called a friend for a ride home.

The next morning I returned to my precious car and stared at it in shock. There was glass everywhere. At least a dozen bullet holes had pierced the roof and exploded in the backseat. Of course, I knew that being a narc would not make me popular, but I never considered it life-threatening. Now I was scared. Bullets kill, and I did not want to die.

I had two options. I needed a car, so I either needed to buy a new car or fix mine. I decided to explore the possibility of a new car first as my hot rod was so totally destroyed.

A robust salesman directed me to a shiny silver car and opened the passenger door inviting me in. He shuffled around to the driver's side and settled in behind the wheel, then started the car.

As we motored along the back road behind the used-car lot, he regaled me with the wonderful features included in the vehicle. I explained my limited financial position. He smiled at me as he pulled over and put the car into park. Leaning over into my side, he said, "There are ways I can help you if you care to help me."

As he reached for my breast, I caught his arm in midflight. "I am on my period."

"Well, come back in a few days, darlin', I am sure we can work out a deal that will work for both of us."

I got out of the car and slammed the passenger door. Without looking back, I bypassed the car lot and kept walking until I found a payphone. I thumbed through the yellow pages, selected an auto shop whose name suggested it might be cheap and dialed. I told the garage attendant to tow my car in and rebuild it.

During the two weeks, while I waited for the repair, I hiked to and from the Pizza Hut and my grocery store job. Not one of the crowd who regularly crashed at my house ever offered me a ride even though they drove past me as I walked.

The attack on my car told me something big had gone down. It made me paranoid that bad guys were after me. I checked constantly over my shoulder and paused to inspect every alley before I passed. At night I slept in a booth at the Pizza Hut, too scared to return home.

One night, my leg swelled up, infected and fiery red because of a gash in my calf muscle. I had cut my leg a couple of days earlier, carelessly climbing over a barbed-wire fence while taking a short cut across the field when I visited my horses. All night, I soaked my leg in an empty pizza sauce bucket as I sat on the corner of a red, vinyl-covered bench of a four-man booth that I had chosen because it could not be seen from the road. My body was alternating between shivering and sweating, chills, and fever. Exhausted, I slid the bucket under the table so I could rest my head on the Formica tabletop where I finally fell asleep, using a bunched-up, checkered tablecloth as my pillow.

In the morning, I got a message to come to the station to see the police chief. He was a large man with a deep Southern accent and grammar befitting his good-old-boy swagger. As I entered his office, he smiled and stretched out a big, beefy hand. He gripped my hand with unnecessary firmness as he held up a newspaper article about the biggest marijuana bust in the history of his precinct. The article credited an anonymous tip as the key to the bust. That tip had come from me.

That particular night, I had been cruising with a group of known dealers, smoking weed, and shooting the breeze with them. They mentioned several acres of land they had planted in premium marijuana. I made the call to my usual contact then thought no more about it.

The chief complimented me, but in the same breath, made it clear that this bust was big enough that he was genuinely worried about me. "Little lady, I'm gonna lock you up for your own good or you better get outta town. And I mean right now."

The chief's warning was perfectly timed. My car's repairs had just been completed. I headed straight for the body shop, picked up my car, drove to the house, and packed whatever would fit, leaving space for my cat and my new Alaskan malamute puppy. I didn't even bother to lock the front door when I carried them to the car. I stopped by the Pizza Hut to say good-bye to Charlotte and pick up my final check and left Milledgeville. Forever.

After listening to the chief's lecture, I had called my brother who was living in Tennessee. He and I had remained in touch, getting together a couple of times during my stint in Nashville. My scrawny, little, tag-along brother had grown into a strapping handsome young man who stood about six feet tall. Ted and his best friend dropped everything to borrow a truck capable of pulling my horse trailer. They located a woman who owned a pasture and wanted the horses. Then they picked up Chenaniah and Outlaw. Best of all, they provided me a safe place to stay for a couple of days.

I called Ann. She now lived in Utah and said I was welcome to come and stay with her. I had left all my possessions in the hot rod while I camped out at my brother's, so I just reloaded the cat and the puppy. I hugged Ted tightly and hit the road.

My second exodus west of the Rockies was another late summer journey. The weather was just as hot and humid as it had been during the Greyhound bus voyage. This time, however, I was the one behind the wheel, and the further I drove from Georgia, the better I felt. I rolled down the windows, let my hair hang loose, turned up the music, and kicked off my shoes. One foot pressed heavily on the gas, the other hung out the window.

For three days, I drove all night and into the early afternoon. The midday heat was too much for my animals, forcing me to seek refuge at some cheap roadside motel. Since most motels would not accept pets, I paid for a room then drove around to the parking lot. I unlocked my room and picked up a couple of towels from the bathroom. I left my door open while I returned to the car where I covered the puppy and cat in the towels so I could smuggle them into the cool of the air-conditioned room. We slept through the heat of the day. I awoke at midnight and slipped out with my pets to continue west.

An incredible sense of freedom came to me. I was leaving Bunny behind. It was also my plan to distance myself from the bottomless pit of need—perpetually needing someone who would love me. I didn't know anything about Utah, but I did know Ann cared about me. I willed it to be okay.

Searching For Love

Loneliness haunts me
Brief moments
I pretend to be loved Endless hours
Knowing—I am not

The next morning, I stopped at a roadside rest stop. I changed from my short-shorts and tank top into something more modest before driving the rest of the way to Ann's. Her new house immediately felt like home. All the right pictures hung in all the right places. Ann had the same lovely horses and the same, albeit older, wonderful little girl. Their valley in Utah was pristinely beautiful, but it was the fresh start, not the fresh air that invigorated me.

My new life, however, was not much of a change from my former routine. I accepted a job volunteering at Ann's Montessori school, then picked up a waitress job at the local Pizza Hut. Working with the children and living with Ann kept me grounded for a couple of months, but then my craving for acceptance and unconditional love began to resurface.

Ann was a generous woman, but her natural demeanor was aloof and businesslike. Because I needed overt affection and praise, I felt shunned. I remained convinced that I was incapable of earning the respect of the important people in my life.

There were certain things, I knew I did well. I could ride a horse, connect with young children, make pizza, wait tables, give a man pleasure, and make narcotics busts. It took the combination of all these things to afford me any sense of competence and connectedness. It wasn't long before I contacted the local police department and told them I had experience with narcotics work.

The head of the local narcotics department soon contacted me. He assigned me to work with a big Mexican officer, a nice man who spoke kindly to me. But the drug laws were far more complicated in Utah, and I didn't know anyone at all, much less local drug users.

At about this same time, Ann had a talk with me. What she said was that it was important for me to become more independent so, I should consider moving into my own place. What I heard was that she wanted me out. I felt totally rejected.

If only Ann had known how much I needed her guidance and direction, how her home and family promised the single lifeline that was keeping me from drowning in self-destructiveness. But Ann knew nothing of the darker side of my life. She saw a twenty-year-old woman who wasn't making any friends. She had no clue about the promiscuous drug abuser who would risk her life as a narc to justify her existence.

Within a few days of our talk, I located a little house in town where I could have my animals, and I moved in. Mr. Policeman came by to "check up on me." He was amorous and sweet. He touched me because he seemed to care. He never asked me about undercover work, instead, he invited me under the covers. I never saw that officer again and did no police work. I took a good hard look at myself and wasn't happy with what I saw.

With Ann's guidance, I settled on a way to improve. Years ago, a great-aunt on my father's side had set up a trust fund to assist any of us kids who chose to attend college. I decided to follow in Ann's footsteps and seek a degree in educating young children. College might be scary, but it offered a welcome change in my daily routine.

My nights, however, still felt empty. I started searching without the slightest idea about what I was seeking. I drove aimlessly up and down Main Street and then wandered restlessly around my house in the dark, while I listened to music.

I flirted from the safety of my car but refused to go home with anyone. For the moment, it was satisfying enough if men indicated a spark of interest in me as I cruised past. It gave me a sense of power to speed off when I knew I could have any one of them I wanted. If I wanted.

About two months into the first quarter of school, I returned to my car after class to find a note on the windshield under the driver's side wiper blade. Some guy, who liked my hot rod, wanted to meet its owner. He signed the note including his phone number. Eventually, I called him and we talked about cars. He collected GTXs and drove a '68. My GTX was a '70, a model he didn't own.

I fear that my side of our conversation was a bit of a letdown. He already knew my car had an oversized engine and that it had a posi-trac rear end for racing. I knew it drove fast, but that was all. We agreed to meet on the boulevard to race.

I drove to the appointed intersection at the appointed time. I had no idea who I was looking for, but he recognized my car and pulled up beside me. His first words challenged me to a light-to-light race. The light ahead of us was still red. I pressed down the gas pedal and revved the engine to the critical point at which it could only be held back by my standing on the brake. I briefly glanced at him and winked as the light turned green. Then I jerked my foot off the brake. Our tires screamed and we flew. My car crossed first under the next traffic light.

I pulled over, grinning with a smile I hadn't used for as long as I could remember. He pulled abreast, shaking his head and wagging his finger at me. He tried the excuse that he had to shift while my car was an automatic. It was my turn to wag a finger and shake my head. I couldn't stop grinning.

Winning the race afforded me sufficient confidence to inspect the defeated driver more closely. He had blue eyes and short, wavy blond hair with just a tint of strawberry. Once he stepped out of his car, I realized that he was also quite tall and thin. He was impressed with my car; I was impressed with him. I invited him to my house. He told me he was a virgin, I told him the same.

About a month after our race, we began living together. He wanted steady sex and an escape from his aunt's house. I wanted the illusion of Prince Charming. No matter what experience should have taught me, I still clung to the dream of that royal personage charging up on a white horse and inviting me to live "happily ever after." For the sake of this dream, I devoted myself to a man, I barely knew.

In all fairness, I did suspect that he never wanted to take responsibility for my eternal happiness. He didn't even want to be responsible for himself. He did not get himself to work on time and could not make himself attend classes regularly. The college eventually kicked him out, suggesting military service or a Mormon mission. Still, I loved him or at least I loved the idea that we could be in love.

The fact that he did not return my dedication, did not deter me. I had always believed that my hard work, sheer will, and dogged determination could change my life, and I had repeatedly deceived myself into thinking that these same efforts could change others. I focused on anything important that needed to be done. I didn't return to college but held the regular job and paid the bills. I cooked, cleaned, took out the garbage, and dealt with landlords.

He would stay out late and sleep in all morning. Getting him out of bed was worse than prying rocks out of fence postholes at the Fairview farm—and far less rewarding. So, despite my nagging, he was late for work or just did not go. He left me alone at night while he drove around with friends. If he was away on weekends he often did not return until he had missed a day or two of work.

The illusion of love, to which I desperately clung, was slowly slipping away, but I could not make myself let it go. This sad, shallow experience was the closest I had come to knowing romance. I wanted to die when I couldn't make it work.

Knowing this relationship would never last, I stubbornly promised myself that I would not leave without someone whom I could love forever. I had my painful IUD removed and a few weeks later became pregnant. This baby would not care if my nose were too big, if I dressed poorly, if I left a light on, or if I was too tired to wash the dishes. This baby would love the essence of me. I ate healthy food, took vitamins, and swore off alcohol. I did not even drink soda.

Upon hearing about my situation, my father showed up. He took my boyfriend for a drive and gave him the age-old lecture that repeatedly accompanied a shotgun pointed in a reluctant suitor's backside, "This baby will either be yours to raise or it will be mine. If you want to be a dad, you need to marry my daughter and accept the responsibility of being a husband and father." Part of me appreciated my dad's intervention. I was long overdue for a champion. But once again Dad showed up after years of absence. I had really needed for him to help me with my speeding tickets, not to determine the course of the rest of my life.

Against our better judgment, we were married. We met at the courthouse downtown. His mother attended the ceremony to sign as our witness then took us to a salad buffet for supper. My baby was due a couple of months later.

About that time, I received a collect phone call from my little sister. In a trembling voice, she said, "I'm staying at a friend's until the end of school, and I won't go back to Mom's house."

"What happened? Are you okay?"

"Mom started punching my head, and Ted had to pull her off of me. I don't even know what I did! I will not go back again. Her man and her music are more important to her than I ever have been. I won't go back!"

"You won't have to," I promised.

Teresa came to live with us for her senior year of high school. I couldn't allow her to have nowhere to go. She had become impossibly inconvenient for my mother, her fiddle player, and her music. Mom could not handle the distraction of a teen-aged girl who needed help growing up.

I loved having Teresa with me again. Long after I had left Tennessee, I continued to harbor such guilt over my inability to stop the beatings that Bunny regularly dealt her. Maybe I could make it up to her. Maybe.

Unconditional
Love

I'll walk in the rain by your side
I'll cling to the warmth of your tiny hand
I'll do anything to help you understand
I'll love you more than anybody can

John Denver

How can anyone fully comprehend the phrase, unconditional love? How could I? I had not had it, not from my parents, as I knew them, not from the men with whom I spent my late teens and early twenties, and not from God, at least the way Bunny had described Him. Still, when I held my first child, I knew that I could give love unconditionally.

My baby boy arrived on a snowy spring evening in April. Because my obstetrician was going out of town for the weekend, he induced my baby the Wednesday before. I lay on my back with all kinds of monitors attached to my abdomen and tubes inserted in my arm. My husband was so freaked out by the epidural that he had to leave long before the birth. The medication took away the pain but added to my sense that the whole procedure was mechanical, clinical, and unnatural.

At heart, I was a farm girl. I had seen the miracle of new life and wanted to experience it, even the painful part. Here in the delivery room, my body was so numb, I could not even tell if I responded appropriately to the doctor's call to "Push, push hard."

As a result, it took a set of forceps to drag my baby into the world. When the nurse laid him in my arms, however, my life changed. Forevermore, time would be measured in terms of him.

While I recovered in the hospital the next day, my little sister brought me flowers, kissed my cheek, and told me how much she loved me. My husband followed her into the room. He brought me a Pyrex measuring cup and muttered with a good deal of embarrassment, "You did good." Heaven knows what he thought I would measure in the hospital. Horrified, I stared at him. The last thing I wanted was an object so utterly useful.

My son and I, went home that evening. I was fully committed to being the best mother that all the advice articles in *Mothering* magazine and *Mother Earth News* could nurture. *Mothering* focused on back-to-nature parenting. It's not all that newsworthy that babies will ingest green beans more successfully if they are cooked forever then blended, but in an era of Gerber, Huggies, and Enfamil, it was reassuring to read that some experts approved of my desire to give my son fresh food, cloth diapers, and breast milk.

There was no way I would let anyone else raise my child. So to finance my staying home, I cared for six other children in our house. My experience, at the Montessori school, made it possible for me to do more than just cope with all those kids. The Montessori Method allows children to explore their environment and control their own learning. Students work independently while a teacher directs their discoveries.

The end result of applying the Montessori Method in my yard was the total destruction of my flowerbeds. My paying charges explored dirt, bugs, and leaves, while I cared for my six-week-old baby. It was the perfect trade-off for the kids, their parents, my son, and me.

It's not that six part-time kids and my own son weren't enough. But my husband and I really wanted a little girl. So, eighteen months later, a second miracle came into my life this time, following the guidelines of *Mother Earth News*, which introduced me to home birthing under the direction of a midwife.

The midwife I selected, had followed my pregnancy through appointments in her home. Like the physician, she listened to the fetal heartbeat and measured its growth. Unlike the physician, she also became my friend. She made me the same spicy snacks that had helped her overcome morning sickness. Her thoughtfulness warmed my heart even though her remedy proved ineffective. More importantly, she included my son in his sibling's birth. She sat him by my shoulder while she discreetly examined me.

My second child arrived on the last day of the World Series. My dad had come to Utah for the event, but while I was in labor, he remained glued to the television set with my husband. They felt as if they were participating in the birth by offering to bring up chips and Coke during intermissions.

Thanks again to my *Motherhood* subscriptions, I had learned about natural childbirth. I had, however, very limited experience with female discomforts, so labor pains came as a great shock. The articles I read, indicated that birth contractions progressed into an incredible urge to push, but I felt no such motivation. All I could think was that I hurt so badly I wasn't going to do anything that might make me feel worse. My good-buddy midwife turned into a demanding general, ordering me to get to work. Once I snapped out of my stupor, the baby came quickly.

My midwife knew how badly we wanted a daughter. She laid the baby on my stomach and allowed my husband to tell me that we had a girl. I would not take anyone's word for something so important and made him hold the baby up so I could see for myself. In fact, I checked a couple of times although I don't know what I thought could have changed during the previous minutes.

I lay back on my pillows and sighed in relief. This was the experience I had wanted. It was so peaceful. I could feel it all, all the pain and all the joy. Mother Nature indeed knows best.

Teresa was not with me for this birth, so no one brought me flowers. My husband, however, had his gift, ready. On the morning of our daughter's birth, he had gone shopping by himself and purchased a dustpan. It was no cheap knockoff. It was the real thing, a brown Rubbermaid dustpan. He handed it to me with pride, saying, "You've been wanting one of these."

I didn't respond out loud but I thought to myself, *You've got to be kidding*, or maybe I thought, *If this is the best you can do, then no more kids for you, and no more practice at making kids either.*

My second baby had colic. When I called my mother to tell her about my daughter, I described the birth and the joy and the exhaustion and the crying. She responded, "It's payback time, I had to deal with you—you had colic."

Come on, Mom, it's not about you this time, I thought to myself. *Don't you dare compare yourself to me as a parent.* But I said nothing. Instead, I carried my daughter all day and rocked her all night for six weeks. My son, the day-care kids, and I went on with our lives, adjusting to crying as background noise. My husband spent most of his free time somewhere else.

Illusive Dreams

I imagined my life as a fairytale,
Believed I could will it so
I desired to be in love with you
In my mind, I created it all.

But, in the end, a bitter fallacy
Far removed from my fairytale dream.
Your shining armor grew rusty,
Your gallant steed, a broken down hot-rod car.

Does love have to be so needy?
Is there an endless hole which
Only being in love can fill—or leave empty?

Should being in love feel so fatal?
Are we supposed to trade life for love,
Or just say we would?

The following summer, my husband made up for the mundane gifts he had given me. He offered me something far more useful than the measuring cup and something I wanted far more than the genuine Rubbermaid dustpan. He borrowed a horse trailer from a neighbor, hitched it to his old truck, and drove to Tennessee to pick up Chenaniah and Outlaw. My horses had never been far from my thoughts and he knew it.

Recently I had been able to buy both horses back with money I set aside from babysitting. My husband's mother loaned him money for the trip. My little sister, who had apprenticed at a horse farm in Kentucky after high school graduation, drove back with him to Utah to help with the animals. My husband was not a horse person.

He and I had purchased a house at a state auction. We first noticed the house a couple of months earlier when we drove to my appointments at the midwife's home. It was completely boarded up and deserted, like something a person could buy cheaply. We stopped and pulled the plywood away from the windows far enough to peek in and see a fair amount of broken glass scattered over the torn-up carpets. The house had been used as a youth correction facility and apparently, the youth had not been corrected often enough.

We contacted the city office to find out how to bid on the house and submitted our offer. After the highest bidder rejected the property, it became ours, and we borrowed money from both our families to fix it up.

The house came with one acre of land, but it was surrounded by another hundred acres situated at the base of the Wasatch Mountains. The state had agreed to our pasturing horses on the hundred acres if we would put up a fence and maintain it. So, while my husband was on his way to Tennessee to pick up my horses, I put up a fence. What a labor of love. My children would be raised in the country with open fields, fresh air, and access to mountain trails. Paradise regained.

Believing that I had to earn such good fortune, I committed myself to being the perfect wife, mother, and housekeeper. I would have given anything for my husband to commit, at the very least, to a job that paid our bills. It seemed possible that we could create the idyllic life described in John Denver's songs.

He spoke of country living, families who laughed together, the sweetness of children, and love. I knew we could create that in our home as well.

My part in our perfect life began with the most basic tasks. I made breakfast while he dressed. I packed my husband's lunch and included notes that wished him a good day and said, "I love you." When he got home, I had dinner on the table. Okay, so the bed was not always made, and the house was not always picked up, but the clothes were clean when they were needed.

Living for the dream, kept me so busy that I was able to put our miserable marital relationship on the back burner for a while. In time though, it began to matter a lot. We both knew that I shouldered all the burdens and that the arrangement worked far too well for my husband. Because we never talked about serious issues, when they got out of hand we fought the kind of fights that never resolved anything. He stormed out to sulk with his friends and came home ready to make up by making love. I was hurt when he left, and by the time he returned, I was twice as mad and resentful. The only thing I was ready to make was his bed in the doghouse.

We went through a brief stint of counseling. Following our usual pattern, I made a committed effort and he remained distracted or did not show up. After a while, the nightly worrying when he didn't come home just wore me down or the illusion of Prince Charming fizzled out. Either way, I could no longer face the agony on our children's faces as they watched us fight.

The day he forgot my 27th birthday and had not returned home hours after his workday ended. I packed his belongings in black plastic garbage bags and set them out in the driveway. When he eventually drove up and came in the house, he said not a word about the garbage sacks. I walked past him and headed for the truck in the driveway where I removed the distributor cap and hid it in a bush before returning inside. Then I told my husband he had better call a friend to come and pick him up. That was it. After all the misery, he just left. It was that simple and we were probably both relieved.

Ironically, that very night, my former neighbor came over to wish me a happy birthday. When I told him my husband had just left me, he responded by shaking his head and expressing his own longstanding admiration for me, "He must be crazy. I've never known anyone as talented as you with a guitar and crafts and horses. I was always so jealous when I worked with him and saw the lunches you had packed for him with notes saying how you loved him. Sometimes, I'd pick one out of the trash and read it, pretending it was for me. It's funny, but I was the one who felt guilty when I knew he wasn't going home after work."

That easily, he swept me away. Yes, it was the rebound phenomenon, in fact, instant rebound. He spoke to me at a moment when I desperately needed someone who saw value in me.

I had good reason to believe this was a good man. He was the one who had loaned us the horse trailer to pick up my horses. He had understood my longing for Chenaniah and Outlaw because he loved his own horses. We had ridden in the mountains together, gone on family hikes and picnics, and laughed together.

He was a self-declared mountain man, part of the loose brotherhood of avid outdoorsmen who gather at Rendezvous to resurrect and honor the life of the west's earliest explorers. He had once commissioned me to make him a few articles of traditional gear. I had sewn a coat called a capote made of striped wool trade blankets and a fringed leather belt with beaded thunderbirds. I had great respect for his reverence for self-sufficiency and his vital connection with nature. All these things I knew about him, but his adoration of me came as a complete surprise.

Over the next several weeks, he bought me simple but meaningful gifts, things I would have bought myself if I had the money or the chance. He gave me a necklace with a silver horse and a book about training horses. He made me a leather belt and even named his new puppy after me.

In the five years of our marriage, my husband had given me only the dustpan, the Pyrex measuring cup, and a couple other equally useful items. My new admirer said all the things I had longed to hear from my husband and did all the things I wished he had done.

We had a torrid three-month affair, made more intense by my deep longing for love. He talked about a future with me, like it would be cool to have a child together. He wrote long letters declaring his love for me and offering to pay for my divorce. He asked me to marry him, although he was still married with four children.

By early fall, I knew I was pregnant. I wanted this baby as a token of the desperate love I felt for this man. The keyword here was desperate. I needed this man. I would die for him and believed I would surely die without him.

During the time when our attachment raged with passion uncontrolled, I justified the whole affair by believing my lover's protests that his marriage was over. But a part of me knew better. That part could only hope that his wife remained ignorant of our liaison because she, too, had been my neighbor and friend. On a woman-to-woman basis, I considered my actions deplorable, but at least for a while, passion outweighed reason and guilt. When I eventually had to own up to the affair and I heard myself say, "I never meant to hurt you." The words rang shallowly even in my own ears.

Ironically, once my husband found out that another man desired me, he showed up with roses. Perhaps, he meant this traditional token of love as a conciliatory gesture, but I interpreted the flowers as proof positive of how little he knew me. During the five years of our marriage, he had never noticed how much I disliked roses. So, to me, the long-stemmed, red flowers looked more funereal than romantic. Our marriage had ended, and its death knell was rung with roses.

As surely as I knew my marriage was over, I also knew my affair had to end. Becoming pregnant brought me to my senses or at least part way there. I had lived next door to this man. There were some ugly truths, I needed to face. I had heard him yell at his family with inappropriate crudeness. I remembered how he cruelly mistreated the family dog. I did not want a man who kicked his dog to raise my kids. I could not possibly marry this man.

When the bubble burst, I needed both friendship and advice. I contacted the midwife who had delivered my daughter. We had remained close during the two years since then. I wanted her to deliver my next child in a few months and right away I needed her to deliver me from the overwhelming sadness that had displaced my blind elation. She intervened without moralizing or judging.

When my lover contacted her to explain that he intended to pay for her services, she responded by requesting that he give me space to sort out my life. He rose to the occasion by sending me a long letter and strictly adhering to the midwife's instruction that he contact her instead of me to check the status of our baby.

In a follow-up conversation with my midwife, I expressed concern about the lack of religion in my children's lives. Having found no personal satisfaction in organized religion, I had steered far away from any regular church involvement. As a result, my children knew little of Moses floating in the bulrushes, David felling Goliath, or Jesus feeding so many with so few fish.

My friend responded with a challenge, "Shouldn't you be as conscientious about their religion as you have been about selecting the method of your children's births?"

Once again, seeking approval from someone I admired, I did a stint in a new church, this time in the Jehovah's Witness faith. I received Witnesses into my home, studied with them, and attended their services. These efforts gave me some hope that I had found the true religion, the answer to my prayers.

But Jehovah's Witnesses offered no programs for children. All of the kids sat beside their parents throughout the services. If they fidgeted or made noise, their parents escorted them outside and spanked them. The Witnesses apparently believed that kids came into the world with an obligation to focus on the Lord in a silent and reverent manner. When my own children acted like children, the parishioners suggested I not spare the rod as I was spoiling my kids.

I did not believe for one second that Jesus would spank little kids for their natural exuberance about life. As a matter of fact, I remembered that He expressed great reverence for childhood, instructing grown men and women to believe in Him with the innocent faith of children. The Jesus I sought, would have laughed and rolled in the grass with my kids. So, I left another church I had joined for all the wrong reasons.

I had strongly desired spiritual relief because I longed to assuage the guilt I felt toward my lover's family. I also sought to resolve a nagging question about whether I could love the baby I was carrying as much as the two children I already had. I conceived this child in desperation and carried it with guilt. I had been able to distance myself from my lover. Would I be equally distant from his child?

To keep my mind off such a frightening dilemma, I made each day so busy that I would be exhausted every night. Fatigue sufficient to engender sleep came naturally as the result of days filled with my own two children, six or eight day-care kids, the dogs, and the horses.

My five-year-old son and two-and-a-half-year-old daughter adored the horses, but before they could ride, they had to agree to take turns with all the other children in the house. I could fit two kids at a time in a western saddle on Chenaniah, and I lead him around while the other kids played nearby.

Everyone loved Chenaniah the best except my son, Bobby, whose loyalty was pledged to Outlaw. After fifteen years of a cranky disposition that kept adults at bay, the mare quietly and carefully toted my little boy around. And he loved her in the same manner that another kid would adore a huge stuffed toy.

Chenaniah accepted all the kids' petting and treats, but he saved his heart for my daughter, Anna. Here was the horse who was so tense and anxious if an adult mounted him, he might rear over backward or run away as he had done with my brother during our album-cover photo shoot. With Anna, however, he was the soul of kindness, utterly aware of how small she was and how big he was. If she approached him in the pasture while he was lying down, he would rest there quietly while she climbed on him or kissed his face. If she arrived when he was standing up, he followed her around like a puppy. Theirs was a beautiful friendship.

Anna loved Chenaniah so much that she wanted him to sleep in her bedroom at night. I stood firm in insisting that Chenaniah was not a house pet. Though so young, she was already clever enough to modify her questions when they engendered an answer that didn't suit her. So, when I told her for the hundredth time that she absolutely could not bring a horse in the house, she looked up at me with a twinkling in her blue eyes and asked, "Could Chenaniah come inside if he walked in by himself?"

Surprised by her question but, of course, thrilled by her precocious reasoning, I answered, "Well, he wouldn't come in by himself, would he?" Then I thought no more about it.

A bit later, I saw Chenaniah en route to the front door. My daughter had enticed him from the pasture, through the gate, up the driveway, and on to the stoop with a trail of carrots. His progress was slow but steady as he sauntered from vegetable to vegetable.

I could scarcely believe my eyes, but I had to intervene most carefully. The horse was roaming freely in the front yard and could choose to escape in any direction whenever he desired. I grabbed a nearby hay rope in one hand and my daughter in the other. We slowly approached the fugitive. It became immediately obvious that he had no intention of straying from Anna. He walked right up to her and rested his head against her chest. I slipped the twine around his neck, and together we led Chenaniah back where he belonged. How could another child bring me this much joy?

Well, that other child was due any time, so I would soon find out. Four days before my twenty-eighth birthday, I called my midwife and asked her to come over. The intensity of my labor had already revived so many memories of pain that I began to question whether I really wanted to birth another child. Such doubt came a bit late.

The midwife arrived and watched me pace around. Finally, she insisted I get upstairs so she could check my cervical status. By this time Anna had fallen asleep in the new baby's downstairs cradle, so only Bobby accompanied us to my bedroom. He sat quietly on a pillow by my shoulder and asked an endless stream of pressing questions about the delivery. "What will the baby eat? How will it get out of your stomach? Can I bring you some juice? Can I bring the baby some juice?"

I was past the point of answering, I tried to tone down my cries, but as the labor pains intensified, he could see that I was in real pain. His questioning became more intense. "Are you okay? Do you want juice now? It would make you feel better."

My oldest son, ever the helper, ever sensitive to the needs of others believed that a cup of apple juice could cure anything. He would have brought me gallons if I had hinted it could help. It was, however, his presence not his juice remedy that softened my pain. So I asked him to just stay beside me and assured him in-between my labor pains, that I was okay.

Bobby had never experienced birth before. His inquiries and anxieties were only dispelled with the arrival of his baby brother. He entered the world crying but quieted himself as soon as the midwife placed him on my chest. When first I put my arms around my new baby, he was still tied to me through the umbilical cord. He lay peacefully in my embrace and I sighed, overwhelmingly relieved that my nagging fears were unwarranted. From the moment I touched him, I loved this child, too.

My daughter awoke, climbed upstairs, and peeked into my bedroom. She arrived in time to witness her older brother cutting the umbilical cord. Her eyes nearly popped out of her head at the sight of the curly pink connection between her new baby brother and me. With her "Blankie" in hand, she hurried past the foot of the bed and climbed up to snuggle in by me. Like her brother, she could have taken an active role in the initial baby care, but she was too busy sucking her thumb to participate. Thirty minutes later the whole family headed downstairs together.

The next morning at six A.M., the first of the eight children that I tended showed up. Thank heavens for Sesame Street, a program brought to us that day by the number nine and the letters B and C. Public television provided such healthy entertainment for the older kids while I cared for the new baby that by the end of the week I considered Bert and Ernie my new best friends.

If I had had the luxury of personal time, I might have contemplated how overwhelmed I was. But, I had no energy to spare on negative feelings. Even my previous depression subsided as I helped my children grow together.

Time passed quickly. A few months before my baby boy turned one, my divorce was finalized. The court-ordered child support, but it never came, never ever. Nevertheless, no matter how difficult our lives might become, I elected not to involve the state in prosecuting my claim for child support. I did not want my children's father to end up in jail for his refusal to support them. What chance would these kids have to grow up proud of their father if he lived in jail? So welfare became my only option.

Once I applied, the state would garnish my ex-husband's wages on our behalf. Knowing what lay ahead, he quit his job to work for a relative who agreed to pay him under the table. I wrote him once begging for money to help his kids. In response, he arrived at the house with his mother. She stormed in and ordered him to sit next to her on the couch. She carried my letter in her hand and shook it at me as she called me a miserable ingrate for seeking support when I was the lucky one who got to live in her house.

As part of the divorce settlement, we had transferred the title to our house to her. The court then awarded me the right to live in the marital home. My ex-mother-in-law became my landlord. Because I qualified for welfare, the state made rent payments to her.

The whole time that his mother ranted and raved, vowing that her son need not pay anything as the father, my ex-husband said nothing. He just stared at his feet. He never raised his eyes, even when his mother announced that he was leaving and he walked out behind her.

What the Hell was so important about his shoes? If he had looked around him, he would have to see that we were barely surviving, that his children were growing up in poverty. I was so humiliated, it took at least five years before I sought any further financial assistance from him. In all that time, he offered nothing and made no arrangements to see his children.

The absence of his father was particularly difficult for Bobby. In a subconscious attempt to demonstrate the depth of his despair and his need for paternal attention, Bobby looked for ways to injure himself. He would pinch his fingers in the door or hit himself with a stick. I begged my ex-husband to visit with his children and provide some solace to them. When he refused, I set up counseling sessions with a well-reputed child psychologist who helped my son work through his sense of loss.

Making It
Work

Too many unpaid bills
Too many "What's for dinner" dilemmas
How could I feed another?
My heart is far too heavy,
I'm so, very, very sorry

How could I give to you
All the everything you would deserve?
How can I give to those already mine
All the everything that should be theirs?

The easy way out
Is never truly easy

It meant everything to me to remain at home while my three children were young and I intended to make the most of our time together. Unfortunately, my years as a stay-at-home mom passed prior to the time when Martha Stewart elevated homemaking into an art form. Still, the country girl in me honored traditional handicrafts, and it was a joy for me to share them with all of the children in my care.

I wanted my kids to experience the taste and aroma of fresh food that they helped raise. Each spring I tilled a garden and let the children take turns placing seeds in the rows I spaded. They spent the summer helping me weed, water, pick, and eat our produce.

We also prepared homemade bread, but only on the weekends when the day-care gang was absent and I only had my own children in the kitchen with me. My kids loved to punch and knead the dough even more than they loved the aroma of fresh bread that soon filled the house. I did my best to sanitize the six small hands that measured, mixed ingredients and dipped into the bowl for taste testing. I'm certain, however, that our loaves were not fit for public consumption.

Although home cooking and welfare kept us from starving, it provided no discretionary funds. Being cash poor forced me to turn every other aspect of our lives into a moneymaking venture. The state had previously agreed to let me use the entire one-hundred acres surrounding the house in exchange for my keeping up the fences. This arrangement allowed me to board eight to ten horses, which grazed along with cattle belonging to the other farmers who had acquired pasturing rights. I also bred my Alaskan malamute so that I could sell her offspring. All the kids helped raise the puppies, who flourished in spite of the occasional peril of being carried around by the neck. By the time the pups were old enough to be sold, the entire litter was childproof.

Not every investment succeeded. I was given four baby chicks and thought it would be lovely and healthy to have fresh eggs. The children loved the birds and carried them around like they did the puppies. My plan for fresh eggs went out the window when the chicks all turned out to be roosters. We drove the roosters to a nearby chicken farm and said goodbye.

It was impossible for me to purchase many toys. I felt certain, however, that my time and inspiration offered the kids far more than Toys-R-Us. It didn't take long for the children to adapt to my philosophy that kids get more satisfaction out of playing a small part in the real work of life than they do out of working at playing.

On arriving one morning for their first session of daycare in our home, two new preschoolers looked at me and demanded, "Where are the toys?"

I put my hands on my hips, bent down to their level, and smiled. "Let's meet the other kids and they will show you."

During the course of the day, the children cooked their own scrambled eggs, measured dirt in the sandpile, had sword fights with sticks, used their lunch bananas for phone conversations, rode horses, and stretched out all over the living room carpet while I read them books. They took turns using the real vacuum and cleaned windows with Windex spray. At the end of the day, I asked the newcomers, "What did you think of the toys?"

The two looked at each other and giggled. "They're the best and they're everywhere."

To maintain the children's interest in the daily chores required a great deal of energy, combined with the "Mary Poppins" touch. Each little duty became a game. So when the fence needed repair, we carried a portable radio with us into the field and cranked up the volume. I dug postholes while the kids took turns pouring water in the hole to soften the dirt. When a good song came on, all work stopped, and each child had a turn in my arms while we waltzed, spun or invented steps for a pseudo tango. Arthur Murray might have questioned our technique, but no one could question our enthusiasm.

The problem, of course, was that there was not enough of me to go around and not enough money to finance our basic needs. I had become an expert at concoctions featuring the bean-and-rice diet of third-world countries. I disguised that magic combo in soup, tacos, vegetables, and pasta. We had no such thing as leftovers. Everything in the refrigerator became stew.

But eating beans did not pay the utility bills. We ran out of money. When forced to prioritize, I let the natural gas bill go unpaid until the utility company turned off the gas. I figured we could survive without heat because it was summer. I could improvise without a water heater by filling canning kettles on the electric stove, then boiling water to warm my children's bath.

One evening while carrying about three gallons of near-boiling water to the tub, I slipped because I was wearing only socks. I managed to duck away from most of the steaming water that splashed in my direction, but a goodly amount still doused my feet. The knit material of my socks soaked up the boiling water like a sponge. Immediately the heat scorched my skin. I had to set the kettle down before I could rip off the socks. By then, the water had burned deeper.

The skin on the tops of my feet erupted in yellow, fluid-filled blisters with bright red skin surrounding them. I was in agony as I ran back to the kitchen sink and soaked towels in cold water to wrap around my feet. When I could move, I returned to the kettle, picked it back up, and used the remaining hot water to warm the tub. As I lifted my waiting children into the bath, they asked me why I was wearing towels instead of shoes.

All that night I sat up, dangling my feet in buckets of ice. Memories of the night when I had soaked my infected leg at the Pizza Hut flooded my mind. I had felt desperate and alone then; I was alone and desperate now.

Each time I had to change the water, the burning sensation drove me crazy, but it went without saying that if I didn't have money for the gas bill, I couldn't afford emergency room medical care. So, I doctored myself the best I could, wrapping the burns with gauze soaked in the liquid I obtained by cutting open the leaves of my aloe plant. Days passed before all the blisters broke and the oozing subsided. It was impossible to wear shoes, so my chores had to be done barefoot. My burns slowly healed, but time provided no cure for our financial woes.

Fortunately, for our increasingly limited budget, I had learned a good deal about automobiles from my ex-husband. During the five years of our marriage, he had indulged his passion for GTXs by purchasing whatever models he could afford. Given a price range that low, it was not surprising that we ended up with a front-yard full of broken-down hot rods in need of repair. Many evenings, we spent time together under one or another of these vehicles.

Once he was gone, my ex-husband towed several of these treasures to his new home. I had all the remaining carcasses hauled away. I kept a Jeep because it seemed a reliable enough vehicle. I knew how to maintain it by tuning the engine, replacing the hoses, and changing the oil.

The Jeep kept running through the summer and fall, but during the coldest part of winter, my limited mechanical expertise proved insufficient. One early evening, after dropping off the last of my daycare kids, I was driving home with my own three when the engine died. Without power steering, I struggled to maneuver over to the shoulder where snowplows had built up a significant snowbank during the previous week. As the momentum of the car slowed, the right fender buried itself in the slush and we stopped.

After savoring a moment's relief that we were safely out of the traffic, I popped open the hood, stepped out the driver's side door, and stood on the edge of the tarmac. I had to stand in the slush to get a look under the hood. In between stomping my bootless feet and blowing on my gloveless hands, I adjusted all the engine parts that I knew to check. Then I reopened the car door and asked my six-year-old son to slide over behind the wheel. I propped him up, placed his small fingers on the key, and showed him how to push it forward when I gave the signal.

I waved at him and he turned the key in the ignition, but nothing happened, not even a click. Again, I checked the battery cables, distributor cap, and spark plugs. My hands ached as I banged on every part I could identify. Still nothing. My heart sank. I stared up at the darkening sky and cursed the world. Then I closed the hood and stood in front of the car—frozen for a moment by the bitterly cold air and by the enormity of the unfairness of it all.

I stepped through the snowbank to reach the backdoor on the passenger side. I unbuckled the baby from his car seat and lifted him out. I helped the older kids out on the sidewalk and buttoned up everyone's coats, locked up the car and headed for help. I carried the baby, Phillip and held Anna's hand. Bobby clutched my coat. The weight of all the kids hanging on me felt like the weight of the world. I had bitten the bullet before and swore to myself that I could do it now, but at what cost?

As we trudged further along the roadside, a horrific vision crossed my mind's eye. I saw refugees, social outcasts, the bottom rung of the ladder. I could not shelter my children from the reality of our poverty. In fact, I could not even shelter them from the winter wind.

I thought about the saying that God won't give you more than you can handle. I had plenty of time to concoct my retort as we trudged in the slush. God has no idea what he has given me because I cannot continue to handle this. In my bitterness, I cursed the God that I thought must have hated me. How did I get here?

But we weren't anywhere yet. We were still on the shoulder of a road, slogging through the snow. As I commanded myself to put one foot in front of the other, my thoughts finally took a different turn. I remembered another expression—defining craziness as doing the same thing over and over but expecting a different result.

It was time to do something different. Even if I saw no light at the end of the tunnel, I was determined to start looking for one. It was time to go back to school. I would have to give up home-schooling both my older children. They could already read well, print, and compute simple math. They could be enrolled in public school. My two-year-old son would have to go to some type of child-care facility. All these things I resolved before we reached the gas station and got a ride home.

The next day, I began my action plan. A few phone calls demonstrated unanimous agreement that the elementary school with the highest overall academic record was located near the local college. Our house, however, was situated at the other end of town.

Because I was still receiving welfare, the state wrote a letter to the school district advising them of my situation and requesting a hardship transfer. If my children could attend the elementary school nearest the college, I could transport my kids to school, attend classes, and then pick them up. The transfer was approved.

Phillip was even more fortunate than his siblings. The college had a well-reputed pre-school affiliated with its early childhood program. I immediately put him on the waiting list and signed him up at a local daycare in the interim.

After I made arrangements for my children, I requested an appointment with an advisor at the college. A faculty member in the education department told me it would take four years to complete a teaching degree. I shook my head as I answered, "I absolutely must be done in three."

My tone surprised my advisor far more than my declaration. He recognized desperation when he heard it. Although he gestured to indicate little confidence in the achievability of my goal, he responded with genuine thoughtfulness. "I will do whatever I can to help."

Then he informed me of CLEP tests that I could take in general education subjects, which, if passed, counted for college credits. As I rose to leave his office, he extended his hand and with his handshake, offered a most sincere, "Good luck."

Funded by welfare, grants, and student loans, I enrolled for the next fall's classes. I had passed all the available CLEP tests, thereby eliminating a full quarter's worth of hours. In my first quarter, I signed up for eighteen credits. Classes were interesting, but mostly I saw each one as bringing me one step closer to being able to raise my children in the manner they deserved.

My early morning class was titled Interpersonal Skills for Prospective Teachers. During one otherwise uneventful class session, the professor instructed us to write down the name of the single most influential person in our lives.

My hands turned cold. I couldn't move. For the past eight years I had thought little of Bunny, but here was the moment of truth. Bunny had been the most influential person in my life, and it made me sick. I rose from my seat and left class. I was still in a stupor when I reached my car. When I sat down behind the wheel, my hands started shaking and sobs welled up in my throat. Tears were still running down my cheeks when I regained enough composure to drive home.

To suppress the negative memories of my past, I concentrated on my children's future. Their elementary school was living up to its reputation. Though public, it had all the advantages of a private school—small classes, a professional atmosphere, and skilled, enthusiastic teachers. The principal knew every child by name and treated her students with dignity and respect. The teachers considered themselves the premier faculty in the district. My children were flourishing. Their behavior and grades remained exemplary.

Almost three years later, during my student teaching, I worked under a woman who had often complained to me that the teachers from my children's school behaved as if they were superior to the staff of any other elementary school.

One afternoon as she and I sat together during our students' recess, she put her hand on my arm to get my full attention, then said, "I think you need to know something I overheard last night at a district meeting."

I was a bit surprised at her tone but looked up, quizzically. She continued, "One of the teachers from your children's school complained that she didn't know what things were coming to now that kids like yours were attending her school. She expressed a fear that her elite school was in danger of losing its status."

I was shocked and appalled. It was true that the other kids attending my children's elementary school came from the families of doctors, lawyers, and other professionals. My children were perhaps the only ones who qualified for free lunch. Tears of shame welled up. I had no reply.

For years I had worked to ensure that my children would never be disadvantaged because I was their mother. No matter what the cost. I bought them the trendy jeans and the *in* shoes when they became aware of the difference. There were even times when I knew I was paying for their status symbols with bad checks, but I also knew I would pay the store back as soon as I had money. I could never forget what it felt like to be in sixth grade and be dressed like an outcast. My credit rating was a small price to pay to keep that heartache out of their lives.

Obviously, however, a child's school status isn't just about looking the same and acting better than the rest of the class. It is also about intangible things that money can buy, and lack of money can make impossible—things like the right parents and good prospects.

The complaining teacher had never had my children in her class. Her words may have broken my heart, but my dander was up. I made an appointment to speak with my children's principal. I entered her office with a chip on my shoulder the size of the Titanic, and even before sitting in the seat she offered, I demanded, "What exactly does it take for a kid to be considered elite?"

The principle stiffened and rose from her desk upon hearing my challenge. I didn't give her a chance to respond. Instead, I blurted out, "My children earn straight As and have never been in your office except to receive praise. How can they possibly put the reputation of this precious school in jeopardy?"

She stared at me and I could see that she was struggling to catch up with the tone of this conversation. A part of her may have bristled at my attack on her school, but a much larger part rose to the defense of my children. Her demeanor helped calm me, and I answered less emotionally when she asked for the details supporting my allegations. When I finished my story, she assured me that she would look into the situation, and I believed her.

The next day, the principal summoned the offending teacher into her office to meet with me. Quietly and deliberately, that teacher stated, "I was out of line and would like to apologize."

Her words were few, but her body language spoke volumes. She sat down with her arms folded and her legs crossed. She would never understand that her brand of concern for the school's reputation taught the wrong lesson to all of its students. Still, I did allow myself a small sense of self-satisfaction: My children had finally given me the courage to stick up for someone I loved.

On the other hand, I still lacked backbone and moral fortitude in situations concerning myself. My younger son's father phoned me periodically. He and his wife had divorced about a year after our son was born. My former lover now lived alone in town and he usually saw his son on holidays.

On one such occasion, before Phillip climbed into his dad's car, he turned to me and said, "Mom, if I miss you, I will just look in the mirror. I will see you 'cause we have the same eyes."

Both parents swelled with pride. We each hugged him and then we hugged each other. The father carefully examined the mother's eyes, then said, "I love those eyes, I love them in both of you."

I looked away, but not quickly enough.

When he called again, it was almost midnight. The kids were all asleep. A close friend from the college was spending the night after having come over to play cards. I woke her to explain that I was leaving for a while, and out I went.

My son's father, my former lover, was drunk, pitiful, and flatteringly pushy. His speech was slightly slurred as he told me how much I still meant to him. He continued murmuring sweet nothings as he leaned heavily against me. I had lived without the affection or touch of a man for a very long time. I didn't refuse him even though I knew I should.

I soon became nauseous and confirmed my worst fears with a home pregnancy test. I could not do this to the children I already had. I had to get through school to provide some kind of future for us. I could barely keep my head above water as it was. I told no one. I was too humiliated and disgusted by what I had done.

The moment my pregnancy was terminated, I lectured myself harshly, *I will never need anyone again. Need makes one vulnerable. If I am ever with another man, I will be with him because I want to, not because I need to.*

I was bitter. I wanted someone or something to blame instead of myself, but I found no one. Then I addressed my spiritual side and acknowledged that I no longer believed in God or in destiny.

From here on in, my life would be controlled by my own conscious decisions combined with hard work. As I condemned my deplorable choices, I found myself inadequate. I had my tubes tied a couple of months later.

Saving Children

How sad you are, little girl
Somewhere behind those eyes
Lies the truth
Can you just be well enough to
Tell, someone, anyone?
Your mother left you, and your dad,
Well, I don't know about him You pay the price
With tears, with angst, with craziness
Anything to make the days go by Out
of control, no longer with anyone An
imagined mother,
Takes the place of the one who left you.
Someone to love you A
way to be nurtured You
must do it yourself So
very, very lost
Little girl

I finished my second required student-teaching session at the end of my third year at the college and was hired a month later. Thus, began my career as a teacher of children with disabilities.

From the beginning, I found myself drawn to those marvelous little people, children whom others had branded "behavior disordered." They have little experience with academic success because of their lack of meaningful connections and appropriate social skills, or perhaps because their emotional turmoil runs too deep. Many are so distracted by simply trying to survive that they have little energy left for absorbing math and history. Every year they touch my soul—they teach me. I am determined to connect with them, and I believe I teach them.

Once I came to honor the defiance, audacity, and anger through which they survived, I had the key to assist them in developing self-control. I could help them to live with the hand they had been dealt until they could change it. In the interim, I showed them they mattered, that they had choices, and that it was important to seek out joy.

On a typical day as the classroom desks filled, I looked out at "my kids." At the desk closest to mine sat a thirteen-year-old Hispanic girl whose lovely dark tresses presented quite a contrast to her tired expression. She had endured years of sexual and physical abuse from her father. Her mother turned a blind eye to the abuse to preserve her marriage and neighbors refused to take the poor child in. So, before her situation was brought to the attention of Social Services, she spent her nights under a bridge. She now lived in foster care.

In a row to my left, a twelve-year-old boy slouched in his chair. With skin the color of polished oak, deep brown eyes, and black hair, he was one of the most physically beautiful children I have known. He had dedicated his entire life to caring for his drug-addicted mom. He never knew his Native American dad. He recently fathered a baby girl with a young girl he had loved since he was ten. He adored his daughter and brought her to school to meet me. Cradling the baby in his arms and rocking her gently, he told me, "She is the only thing I have ever had in my life that has been truly mine."

Two seats further back—an empty desk. My heart felt a sense of emptiness and loss as I looked at that desk. Six months earlier, my administrator had brought a sixth-grade boy to my attention. The principal requested that I observe the boy's reading class and introduce myself. Approaching his desk, which was set apart from the rest of the students, I became aware of a terrible stench.

He glanced up as I pulled up a chair beside him and I smiled. His thick, dark, hair lay plastered in dirty waves around his round face. His shirt barely covered his round frame and his pants were ragged on the bottom because they fit him so poorly that they dragged on the floor as he walked. His big toe had worn holes through his tennis shoes when his feet outgrew them. He returned a reserved smile, then looked back down at his work.

After class, I invited him to a private area where we could talk. I was specific and blunt. Hygiene issues had to be addressed immediately. We discussed the fact that many children struggle with bed-wetting and how the daily shower then needs to be in the morning before school.

I obtained shampoo, bar soap, and toothpaste from the school counselor. The principal, being a man, took the boy to the locker room to shower. Thereafter we kept a change of clothes in the office for him, and he began attending my class.

As I gained his trust and we built a relationship, I learned about the hell in which this kid lived. He was beaten by his stepfather, and his mother suffered with schizophrenia. He didn't know who his real father was. As the school administration waded through the process of obtaining aid for this boy, his family moved. For other teachers it had been agony to have him in their class, it was agony for me to no longer have him in mine. I never heard from him again, but I often wondered how his story turned out.

My moment of reflection ended when the bell rang. I took a quick attendance tally. I saw children who are gang-involved, sexually involved, and court-involved. Some had been or were being sexually, emotionally, and physically abused. There were children who hungered both for food and for connections with people who would care about them. I understood them.

It's hard to teach curriculum and prepare for state testing when such turmoil remains unresolved. I first heard it in tidbits of conversation, offhand comments, sarcastic remarks, and physical outbursts. Then I taught my kids to speak up, speak out, and speak honestly when I asked them to explain their behavior.

Whatever their responses, however, it breaks my heart, I tell them, "It doesn't have to be this way forever. You have options and can make choices for yourselves. But you must remember, there is more to life than just putting one foot in front of the other. Make it a good thing that you exist. You are the author of your own stories. Live with a purpose."

My students come to expect these weighty words from me; I think because they realize how committed I am to what I am saying. Perhaps, they also understand how committed I am to them. I play with them, share my life, and do my best to give them joy. They are some of the bravest human beings I know.

I have no tolerance or understanding for the adults who ignorantly visit their "sins" on their children. Even those parents leading desperate lives in silence only perpetuate their problems when they raise their children to do the same. They use their own stories as an excuse to fail. "I beat my children because I was beaten, I can't help doing drugs because my parents did drugs." Their children end up like balls in a pinball machine; their families pull the pin that shoots them bouncing here and there until they find a way to stop.

I believe that once we become responsible for another, we become responsible to make their stories better. We can begin to right the wrongs. We can make responsible choices based on what we know and have figured out. There is help available, we can seek it out and gain the knowledge we need in order to help ourselves overcome any obstacle. We have the answers inside us, but we sometimes could use some help getting to them.

Rescuing Horses

Photo used by permission from
Pro Photo and Pam Olsen

I hear in my heart
I hear in its ominous pulses,
All day, on the road, the hooves of invisible horses.

Louise Imogen Guiney, from *Wild Ride*

At about the same time, I discovered my talent for rescuing school children with problems, I found a way to rescue condemned horses. My two older children, now seven and eight, had become quite capable riders on the ponies my mother gave them after Outlaw and Chenaniah passed away. To be able to ride with them, I was seeking a horse cheap enough for me to afford.

One of my students told me about a young Thoroughbred horse who was owned by her math teacher. This man moonlighted as a horse trader. The horse had proven ill-suited to barrel racing so he was to be sent to the local auction. I contacted the teacher and he agreed to let me try the horse before he shipped him off.

It was mid-winter, and the snow was knee-deep the day I first rode the reject. Perhaps because the snow slowed him down, the horse behaved acceptably enough for me to see some potential for training and selling him. I could make money while I rode with my kids. This convenient strategy justified a purchase price of one hundred dollars over meat price, paid in installments, of course.

My new horse was a four-year-old, dark-dappled grey gelding. His shaggy winter coat camouflaged what an elegant animal he would soon become. My new horse's registered name was Banjo Rocket, we called him Banjo.

Banjo was as brave as Dusty had been. He would jump ditches, water, poles or banks with enthusiasm, all the while focusing on his next challenge. His attitude gave me such confidence and he trusted me so implicitly that little by little my investment strategy fizzled. I would never let anyone tell me I had to sell Banjo. I would never outgrow him. With the exception of my children's needs, no financial need could be so great that I would sacrifice my friend.

Banjo became the best competitive horse I would ever own. His performances afforded me the credibility to launch a second career as a rider, instructor, and horse trainer. My investment plan had to be revamped, however, to incorporate my commitment to keep Banjo. I contacted his former owner to ask about the auction process. He described year-round, bimonthly sales. Better yet, he informed me that I lived up the road from the most notorious horse trader in our locality, and he told me where to find the killer pens.

A couple of days later, I headed out to meet the infamous horse trader and check out his stock. Nothing could have prepared me for the heartache that clutched at me as I drove past his dust-filled corrals. Metal panels tied together with hay rope and chains confined dozens of the most pitiful animals I had ever seen. They were young, old, skinny, fat, tame, wild, healthy, sickly, hurt or scared. There were Quarter Horses, Arabians, draft horses, Thoroughbreds, and everything in-between.

Whatever the breed or condition, they all had acquired the same attitude once they entered the killer pens. They milled around with their heads hanging low, nibbling non-committedly on the yellow, moldy hay that was scattered around in the dirt. They walked through mounds of manure as tall as their knees.

Some say that animals have no emotions, but I would swear these horses knew they had been cast away; they knew this was the end of the line. I only prayed they were not aware of the fact that they were destined to become French hamburgers and dog food.

My initial reaction was anger toward the S.O.B. who made a living buying and selling these horses. Just as I was working myself into a fury, the horse trader himself sauntered up to me—a beer in one hand, the other extended to shake mine. He spoke his standard greeting, "Denny here, want a beer?"

Denny's drawl perfectly suited his battered cowboy hat and tight jeans. I became aware that a belt was buried under his belly because of the sterling-silver, saddle-bronc championship buckle that authenticated its owner.

Realizing that the negativity of my personal judgment would be counterproductive, I introduced myself rather formally and explained the type of riding I did.

In classic horse-trader fashion, Denny drawled again, "I might could supply some Thoroughbred-type animals if I thought you could get a decent price for 'em. Darn near every other week I ship the packers a semi-truck loaded to the hilt, but I suspect we could make a little extra from a riding-type horse."

It was hard to maintain a good mad when listening to Denny. By the time he finished expounding on his personal philosophy, politics, and economics, I couldn't avoid the sensation that I was chatting with a color-character from an old western movie. He concluded, "A man like me can't, hardly, make a dime with all the taxes and regulations Uncle Sam slaps on a guy these days."

When my anger subsided and Denny finally paused for a sip of his beer we worked out the details of an arrangement. Denny would select an appropriate animal and let me work with it without paying any money upfront. If I could

turn it around and sell it, then Denny made money, I satisfied my yearning to save the world or at least a tiny part of it, and some horse got a new lease on life. We struck a deal.

I appreciated that Denny took this chance when there was absolutely no reason for him to trust me. It was possible, he didn't have a more lucrative market for Thoroughbred horses. But it was also possible that under all the bravado beat a pretty decent heart.

It wasn't long before, genuine respect evolved between the horse trader and me. Even if recycling pets into meat was a horrible profession, it was not his fault that so many animals were discarded. I once showed up on shipping day and saw the way the horses were crammed into semi-trailers. The injured, panicked, and hesitant ones were prodded with electric shocking sticks until they gave up the fight and loaded. Worse yet, I knew they were fated to ride a thousand miles to the slaughterhouses in Middle America without food or water. Some would die in transit; all would die eventually.

Theirs would not be a foolproof, humane death. One after another, they would be prodded into a narrow chute from which there was no escape. Then, in assembly-line fashion, they would be killed by a blow to the head with a mechanized stun gun. They would not all die with the first impact.

I hated to be involved so closely with this reality, but Denny's cooperation enabled me to save some from this peril. I had to concentrate on them and be thankful that when Denny bought a horse at auction that he figured would work for me, he called.

My pasture was only a couple of miles from the killer pens, I could lead or ride the horses home and work with them for a week or two. I put each one through an intensive training course. They had to walk, trot, and canter correctly, and perhaps jump small jumps. More importantly, they had to stand quietly and respect humans.

If the animal showed promise, I would pay Denny whatever price he asked. When I wanted a horse of Denny's for my children, he allowed me a year or more to repay him.

In the years before I arrived on the scene, Denny had his rodeo buddies ride most of the horses that passed through his pens. Given enough beer, those cowboys would get on anything, and it didn't take them long to separate the wheat from the chaff. Denny could make a better deal on a riding horse, leasing the animal to a movie set or a dude ranch. If the horse bucked, it was potential rodeo stock.

Shame on Denny and his pals, but they used electric cattle prods to assess a prospect's bucking action. If it showed real power and natural prowess, Denny fed it up and contacted the rodeo-circuit supplier. Some of the animals, that didn't make the cut, suffered lasting physical or mental scars; a few developed a fear of men or confinement that no amount of kindness could ever overcome. It was my greatest fear that those innocent creatures would cycle back to the killer pens, and no third chance would come their way.

To maintain emotional distance from the animals in the pens, Denny called each one of them, "Son-of-a-buck." Once a horse had a name, not even a seasoned trader could ignore the tragedy of its fate.

Denny adored his personal mounts and spoke of them as his partners. I think he hung as many snapshots of his horses on the walls of his house as photographs of his children, and I'm certain that Kitty, K-bar, and Tinky outnumbered pictures of his mother-in-law.

I, too, avoided naming the undesirable horses, but I never adjusted to leaving them behind. Many times, I wished for a syringe with an overdose of sedative to put down an injured or old horse that I could not market—to spare its otherwise horrible, painful ending. The old ones were the worst. They had served people well, only to be auctioned off when they were no longer of service.

There was one exception. On my weekly stroll through the killer pens, an old grey gelding kept following me. His nose almost constantly rested on my shoulder as I walked. I had to push him away to inspect the other animals. When I finished, he hurried to push through the gate with me. I shoved him back, stroking his nose while telling him how sorry I was he must remain.

That night, I couldn't sleep. Denny thought I was crazy when I called in the early morning to ask the old horse's price. I picked up the old boy before breakfast. Even before I finished opening the back of my horse trailer, he jumped in.

During the day, I made a few calls and that very evening a family with four young children phoned, asking to see him. They were so excited they couldn't wait until morning and arrived that night, after dark. All four children clamored around as he stood patiently munching on the carrots they had brought. Two at a time they rode bareback around my front yard. They had a short dispute about his name, but they settled on

"Snowball" before they left. Within an hour they returned with their horse trailer, and tears ran down my cheeks as I waved them off.

Another of the improbable resale horses was so thin that I did not know if he could live through another week of wasting away. Open sores, akin to the bedsores I remembered on the geriatric patients at Pine Forest Academy, covered the angles of his frame where skin stretched over bone. As I approached the pens, he raised his dark bayhead. A wide forehead and dished face caught my attention. Large, liquid eyes gazed not exactly at me, but through me. This bag of bones with a tangled, shaggy mane still had sufficient pride in himself to look at a human with that special countenance that horsemen call, "the look of eagles."

Having memorized Walter Farley's book, I remembered that he described The Black Stallion the same way. How ironic that the first living, breathing creature I saw who could match The Black Stallion was starving in a killer pen.

Financially, I couldn't afford the horse but emotionally, I could not leave him. I paid a hundred dollars a month until he was mine. When he became healthy enough to ride, I discovered that he was a roarer. This breathing defect can limit the potential of any horse. It causes a roaring sound when the horse is exercised at a gallop. To sell my new prospect as a competition horse, he would need surgery to open his airway mechanically. I decided to invest in the surgery.

Once the horse recovered, I paired him with a young teenage girl. I selected her because I thought her peaceful spirit would calm him but still leave his proud nature intact. In time, they were lovely together and competed successfully against far more seasoned performers. She asked for, rather than demanded his best effort; he gave his all freely. Their high scores reflected the suspension and animation of joyful cooperation.

My daughter often joined me at the pens to select prospects. She also ventured out on her own years before I would have given her permission. One weekend when I had to be out of town, I hired one of the older girls in Pony Club to stay with my children. It turned out that my sitter was less responsible than I had hoped. My eleven-year-old daughter talked her into going down to the killer pens to choose horses they could turn for a profit.

It was January, the ground was covered with snow, and it was late. By the time they walked the mile to Denny's pens, it was past dusk. The place was deserted, of humans, that is. No one actually lived at the pens. Anna knew where the tack was kept, so she and her babysitter grabbed halters and started trying out mounts. Eventually, they each selected a pony and rode home in the dark.

By the time I returned a couple of days later, the girls had ridden the ponies everywhere, named them, and located prospective buyers. It never crossed Anna's mind that I would be less than pleased.

In retrospect, what good was my fear? She had already survived. My reaction switched to disbelief—what audacity. How could I disbelieve the obvious? My daughter exuded such confidence and pride. I did allow myself to give her a short lecture on safety, and I announced that I would never leave her under the care of a fellow horse person. My daughter was too persuasive, too fearless, and too proud for my own good if not for hers.

I called Denny immediately to explain why two of his ponies had disappeared. He laughed, drawling, "That paint mare was just an old Injun pony off the reservation, probably caught to trade for drinking money. The other son-of-a-buck was some fool's spoiled-rotten pet that rears up all the time. They brought him to me 'cause they didn't think it was right to sell him to some other fool."

In spite of such dire information, we sold both ponies to good homes where they performed admirably.

Over time, my family developed an efficient routine with our sales prospects. We visited Denny's pens weekly. I selected horses with athletic conformation and became quite an expert at looking past bony frames to search out quality. I often thought, how inappropriately the expression "quality horseflesh" described my choices. Often these animals had no flesh on them at all.

I dewormed every horse we took home on trial. Worming served three purposes: first, it allowed the new horse to recover their health; second, it kept the new horse from infecting my herd; and third, it bought the horse a month's leeway. Denny couldn't send an animal to slaughter within thirty days of deworming.

Some of the most athletic prospects carried a bucking-horse brand, which indicated they were raised on a farm that bred rodeo stock. These animals, like the ones Denny tested and rejected, evidently lacked some quality that rodeos were seeking, but it didn't mean they didn't have some buck in them.

The re-education of these horses was best suited to Bobby. His were the gifts of bravery, balance, and a strong pair of long legs. He loved to tackle these tough mounts, and would ride anything. There were times when "Anything" protested energetically enough to buck him off, but I don't remember a single instance when he didn't land on his feet and get right back on. "Anything" always gave in, eventually. Especially once the poor animal realized that its submission was instantly rewarded with fair treatment and kindness.

My daughter's specialty was cosmetics. She took great pride in eradicating all vestiges of the killer-horse look and replacing it with proper show horse grooming. Most of the time she could bathe the horse, pull its mane, detangle its tail, and clip its whiskers in a matter of hours—hours of hard work.

But one poor little mare took much longer. Hundreds of ticks coursed the underside of her belly, her chest, and the area between her front legs. We felt so repulsed and sorry for her that we started picking off ticks before we had even decided whether to take her. She was only three years old, but she stood quietly for over an hour while my three kids and I removed the engorged bloodsuckers. As we picked, we concluded unanimously that this appreciative little mare deserved a second chance. We raked up the ticks, dug a little pit, and burned them, then led the mare home.

In the end, my little family team managed to rescue and retrain over a hundred and thirty horses of every size, shape, breed, and color. I just wish we could have saved more.

Rescuing Me

How could I have arrived here without you?
Your support has been so pure
No judgment ever bestowed
I could be honest, I could cry
You would listen, and allow me silence
Silence in which to find answers,
Answers that had always been within me
You waited for me to find them

The Pony Club had hired a traveling instructor from back east to manage its summer program. Sondra was a single, twenty-eight-year-old woman with a Masters in counseling and an honorary "doctoral" degree in making the most out of life. Pony Club was her ticket west. She had picked the West over the rest of the country, thinking she could get a regular job and still teach riding in the summer and skiing in the winter.

Sondra taught my children about horse care and riding in much the same manner that Ann had taught me. She taught by example, motivated by pride in her work and respect for the animals.

She also understood the partnership aspect of horse sports. Riding brings out the best and the worst of the rider. Not just the rider's ability, but also his or her character. Many times I heard Sondra tell her students, "A good ride is like a dance whether you are roping, reining, jumping or riding dressage. A bad ride can only be improved by changing you. Your horse is absolutely immune to reason or discussion. But if you improve your balance, strength, and feel, you can mold his energy and give him confidence to overcome his fear. Your horse will try harder, and stretch and exert more, if you ask correctly and fairly within the scope of his ability."

When a problem arose, Sondra addressed the situation calmly, "What do you see going on here?" At first, the whole group responded with the universal gestures of problem avoidance—almost in unison, lowering their eyes, shaking their heads, shrugging their shoulders and mumbling, "I don't know."

"Not acceptable. Own your problem. Mistakes are good; they mean you challenged yourself. Repeating mistakes, however, is foolish, it means you failed to assess, evaluate, and fix."

Little by little each of the kids rose to Sondra's challenge. Her tone, as well as her demeanor, assured them that she was correcting them as riders without criticizing them as people. As their responses became proactive, their riding ability increased, but not as rapidly as their sense of self-worth. What a bargain our Pony Club had made. For the price of a riding instructor, each child received a new way of looking at himself or herself and at life.

The essence of Sondra spilled over into my life as well. Initially, our common ground was the horses. Like me, Sondra had grown up in the Pony Club. Despite the fact that she had never owned her own horse, she had graduated at the National Pony Club's highest level. In her personal experience, the inability to afford her own mount had proved no deterrent, but to the rest of the horse world, her accomplishment was as remarkable as a ballerina learning to dance in tennis shoes.

Our first interaction began with casual conversation about my two older children's lesson. As we walked along, I carried my youngest son. My experiences as a struggling single mother gradually leaked into our dialogue.

A typical New Englander, Sondra was as blunt as she was self-assured. The longer I talked, the more bitter I became. She listened respectfully then she called me on it. "That sounds like a victim talking."

No one in my whole life had ever called me a victim. The word stopped me cold. I fell silent and Sondra respected my silence.

I fumed all the way home. The more I thought about it the angrier I became. *She was only my kids' riding teacher, what right did she have to judge me? My penchant for self-justification kicked in, too. I saw myself as a rescuer, not a victim. Just look at all I suffered trying to save my little sister. Hadn't I gone back to college to redeem my family? Who else went to the killer pens to ransom starving horses? Wasn't it enough to give so much of myself to help others? Who wouldn't be bitter after all the lousy things all the lousy people in my life had done to me? Who had ever pitched in to deliver me from my heartaches?*

That sounds like a victim talking, I finally admitted. Sondra's words set me squarely at a major life crossing. Stop, look, and listen. Did I really want each day of my future to mirror the existence I had suffered in the past? If I had been a victim, it was time for a change. It was time for me to rescue myself.

A few weeks later, I mustered the courage to mention my first tentative step to Sondra, "I'd like to get in better shape; maybe I'll join Weight Watchers."

Sondra answered carefully, "There's no need for you to spend your money on a program if you are willing to make the commitment to do it on your own. If you have some time tonight, I'll come by and we can talk about it."

That evening Sondra and I sat down at my dining room table. We did not bother with small talk about foods or calories. Instead, Sondra politely asked my permission to share with me a bit of her personal philosophy on life.

"I believe there is a thought behind every action that people take, and I mean life-altering actions as well as insignificant, everyday ones. The key to changing action is to identify the thought that motivated it. To do that, you have to listen to the conversations going on within yourself. Once you honestly identify the motivating thought, you can change the behavior."

"It's like with food. You go to the refrigerator and open the door. In all honesty, is your thought, 'I'm hungry or I'm bored?' If you're bored, calories won't solve your problem, but admitting to your boredom can motivate you to get your act together and do something."

Our conversation was unnervingly heavy, but I respected Sondra's credibility. "You have to take charge of the small things to make bigger changes happen" was exactly what I heard her tell my kids when they rode. I could picture in my mind how she would help a frightened child make a stubborn horse jump a formidable obstacle by breaking the task into bite-sized pieces. The child must control herself first, then evaluate the jump and assess whether the risk was appropriate for her skill level. Most importantly, she must commit: Every rider knows, "Your horse will follow where your heart goes."

Sondra picked up a napkin and sketched balancing scales. "It's all about equalizing the basic human needs for fun, freedom, power, and belonging." She didn't expound. She made a statement for me to ponder, then handed me the napkin. The rest of our conversation lasted no more than fifteen minutes, most of which we spent discussing the hike we could take in the mountains near her home. But her words had introduced me to a power that intrigued me, the deeper power some people call "inner strength."

As Sondra left, she embraced me. I returned to the dining room table. I sat back down, retrieved the napkin with her sketch, and held it in front of me. As a follow up to Sondra's conversation, I began to lecture myself, *Okay, I have options. Life is not controlled by fate and it's not controlled by circumstances. If it's controlled by me, then I'd better start figuring out how to take charge. It's time to dump the bitterness and self-pity.*

Blaming others had come naturally to me. My dad blamed his debt on the bank. My mom blamed her lack of stardom on the music industry. I blamed the hard moments of my past on God and life itself. The idea of taking responsibility for my future felt terrifying, but at the same time, liberating and empowering.

I narrowed my focus to two things, *First, I will dream my own dreams and it will be my effort, not fate, which determines whether these dreams come true. Second, I will eliminate the word "Try" from my vocabulary.* In this moment of self-honesty, I recognized that each time I approached a situation saying, "I will try," my soul was giving me permission to fail if I just put forth a modicum of effort. Each time I had concluded my effort with, "I tried," I was excusing that failure and at the same time expecting a pat on the back for whatever effort I had made. Now was the time to invent a new way of being: Welfare had been a handout; Sondra's strength would be a hand up.

Sondra was no flash-in-the-pan psychologist. Without saying as much, she offered herself as my mentor, role model, cheerleader, and friend. She would stand beside me for the long haul. Beside me, not behind me. I had to take responsibility for making life changes; I began jogging, biking, hiking, and going to the gym. In no time, I was in the best physical shape of my life. I loved looking in the mirror as I brushed my teeth. *So long mousy, overweight housewife and pitiful single mother.*

As our friendship blossomed, Sondra and I eased into an unwritten partnership on several of the horses I rescued from the pens. I either called her when I thought I found a horse she would like or she called me when she felt she had clients who might be interested. For herself, Sondra could afford to buy one animal at a time. She put months of effort into training each horse and several of the animals Sondra bought through me competed successfully at national eventing competitions.

One of these horses was a rather small black horse that I found standing in the pen for animals that were too sick to ship. He stood apart even from the infirm because the ravages of his illness left him at the very bottom of their pecking order. When I called Denny to get some history on the animal, he said, "I think that sorry son-of-a-buck wants to die."

The horse had strangles—a bacterial infection that causes a horse to spike high fevers while the lymph nodes under its jaw swell to the size of tennis balls. These abscesses rupture and release copious amounts of yellow puss that drains for days.

When I first inspected the little black horse, the nodes under his jawbone had burst, leaving gaping holes from which a thick, yellow, discharge continuously dripped. His head hung low, his nose and eyes were caked with a thick layer of mucous.

Each time his fever raged, he sweated profusely. It was winter and he lacked the normal body mass to protect him from heat loss. As a result, when his fever subsided, the sweat froze all over his body. Frosty white crystals created an eerie contrast with his shaggy black coat.

I can't imagine why, but I called Sondra and told her about the horse. I explained that I thought he would make it and that he was a special little animal. Because he was so sick, he lacked the energy to move around, but he stayed on his feet. Intuition told me that if he lay down, he would never get up. Perhaps he knew it, too.

I checked on the little guy several times a week. Because his infection was highly contagious, I would not touch him, but I spoke to him and he lifted his head to gaze at me. The first few weeks I'd say things like, "Hang in there, buddy, you can make it."

By the time I'd been conversing with him for a couple of months, I found myself promising, "If you just hold on, I will get you out of here." By the end of three months, I was committed to my promise.

It was early spring when he started to perk up. He recognized my voice and came to the fence to meet me. As soon as the fissures sealed over, I brought him home.

He had surprising spunk when I rode him. More importantly, he moved, even in the spring mud, as gracefully as a gazelle. I called Sondra to come try him and she, too, fell in love. She returned the next day to take him home and told me she had laid awake most of the night, puzzling about a name and settled on L'Chiam, the Hebrew toast that translates, "To Life." L'Chiam went on to compete at top-level event competitions all over the United States and was resold for forty times his meat price.

Sondra also told me about a girl's camp in Vermont where she had taught riding for several years. The camp needed a director for its riding program, and she was willing to put me in touch with the couple who ran the camp. Based on Sondra's recommendation, I was hired after a phone interview. The camp directors were also interested in leasing my children's ponies.

As soon as school was out, I headed cross-country with my three children, pulling our horse trailer behind us. Unlike my first trip to Georgia years ago, I had become proficient at hauling horses.

Generations ago, Brown Ledge Camp had begun as a summer haven for the daughters of Northeastern socialites. Its primitive, rough-hewn cabins overlooked Lake Champlain's tree-covered hillsides. As pleasant as these structures were, their most charming feature was a legacy from past campers. Each girl was encouraged to leave her mark for posterity by writing with permanent marker on the walls, ceilings, boathouse or barn. Grandchildren wrote their names next to their grandparents, and bunkmates signed together, dating their experience. The younger girls wrote unabashed love notes to the horses, even to the ones that had bucked them off. The older girls' love notes often focused on the dashing male counselors, even the ones who had never spoken to them.

I had two days before the campers arrived to get acquainted with the four instructors, five stable girls, and fifty horses in my charge. The camp kept a string of about ten animals; the rest were shipped in from the Midwest under contract with a local horse wrangler.

The wrangler, a testy middle-aged woman from a nearby village arrived with the first truckload of horses. Her stock trailer held ten to twelve wide-eyed animals that stood relatively quietly because their feet were immersed in a good foot of manure.

I was stunned as I watched them jump out the back of the trailer. They had long, tangled manes, their coats had only half shed out, and they were fully caked with mud. It was apparent that any shoes they wore were left over from last season.

My title as Director of the Equine Program suddenly seemed ludicrous. I called my crew together and they approached with big smiles. A couple of the instructors and most of the stable girls had come from England and Scotland. Most of them had worked at the camp before, knew the routine, and were undaunted by the job ahead.

Each of us grabbed a horse or two and began scrubbing. Once the color, markings, and sex of each animal could be determined, it was given a name, ridden, and put in a stall with a flake of hay. The trick was to evaluate the first dozen horses before the next truckload arrived.

It took about five deliveries to unload all the horses the camp needed. Occasionally, when our wrangler arrived we handed her back an animal that would not work, that could not be made safe in the next forty-eight hours. Each time she shook her head in disgust and tried arguments like, "Just give it a week," or "Put one of those Scottish girls on it, they made it work last year."

Sometimes I relented, other times I turned over the lead rope and said, "Okay, you get on and ride it."

As desperate as she was for the five hundred dollars, she received for each horse she provided, she never once got on the animals we had declared too rowdy, too recalcitrant or too dangerous. She just marched them back into the manure-carpeted trailer and stuffed an extra mount into the next load.

By the end of the day, our string was complete or at least every stall was full. We had one remaining day to fit tack for each animal and get it ready for two to three class sessions each day.

The arrival of the girls was the complete antithesis of the arrival of the horses. I had heard the campers were from well-to-do families. Their parents, trunks, and belongings demonstrated that the rumor was understated.

My job included serving as a counselor for a cabin of fourteen-year-old girls.

The four bunkmates ran the gamut of personalities. One young lady's attitude supported all the stereotypes about snobby-little-rich-kids. Within her first few sentences, she made it clear that the labels on her belongings defined her. Another of the girls, whose worldly goods were indistinguishable from the first, presented herself as the most grounded young woman I had ever met. She looked twenty, had all the grace of a woman of thirty, and spoke with the wisdom of the ages. The last two were best of friends. They had bunked together for years and spent most of their time giggling about events to which no one else could relate.

My work directing the riding program featured the same range of personalities as my cabin counselor experience. Each camper approached the program differently. Tradition required that each girl brush her assigned mount, clean its feet, and tack up before her lesson. Most all the girls fell into the routine without incident. One young lady, however, firmly declared, "I am not going to put my hands anywhere near that horse's feet."

I answered her calmly, "Okay, then you won't be riding."

She looked me right in the eye and declared, "That's right, I won't," And she stormed off being very careful to avoid the pile of manure in front of the barn doorway.

That one never looked back, but almost every other girl did. They loved their horses. They smuggled in treats for them from their lunches, they kissed them and returned in their free time to write them notes or to braid flowers in their manes. Dedicated riders were permitted to adopt a horse and give it special attention. By the end of the summer, every horse in the herd was a far happier and healthier creature than when it had arrived.

It was part of my job at the end of the camp season to find winter homes for the animals who had earned a return ticket for the next summer. We matched these horses with university programs, riding schools, and individual families. The worst of our string we returned to the wrangler and then locked up the barns for the year.

My own children had the summer of their lifetimes. In addition to riding with me, they had participated in theater performances, tennis tournaments, and water sports.

Before we headed home, I wanted them to see my childhood home, my paradise. I called ahead and made arrangements. We spent the night at the home of one of the former Daredevils.

The next morning while my kids slept, I put on my running shoes and my headphones, turned on a John Denver tape, and headed out for the farm. I had to see the farm alone first. I wasn't sure how emotional it would be, or what emotion it would engender.

As I ran, the dawn light lit my way, and the mist surrounded me. When I reached our lane, the intervening years dropped away. I was going home. I jogged past the house of the woman who gave our ponies sugar cubes and the hill where we had held our swearing contest. The Milky Way Farm sign was long gone. The sadness I felt dissipated when the elm in our yard came into view. I was enveloped in a sweet aroma, not the sick-sweet perfume that drops out of the pages of women's magazines, but the deep earth scent of dirt, daisies, and dandelions—the aroma of paradise. Memories flooded in with the smell of it all.

Running became harder as I choked on the familiarity of it all. The tears running down my cheeks had blurred most of the changes that the years had wrought. It was home. I was home.

I stopped in front of the elm tree and picked up a handful of dirt. I held it tightly for a moment then opened my hand in front of my face and smelled. I had a treasure, which I saved in my pocket. Once I had savored my moment, I could not wait to share this place with my children.

I drove back to the farm and took the kids with me to meet its current owners. They gave us permission to explore my childhood. The stream I had remembered as quite mighty was a mere trickle, but the rest of the farm looked the same. I had heard that we store our history through sense of smell, and indeed it was the barn aroma, like the subtle odor of the moist dirt, that triggered the memories. There, I described my life to my children. I showed them the rafters I had run, but refused to let them attempt my feat. Although the stall where Dusty was born remained unchanged, they were unimpressed. I led them to my pond and watched my kids catch frogs and salamanders— lovely creatures who had probably descended from my former pets.

I also toured my children through our one-room schoolhouse, newly converted into a historical museum. Because the building was locked, we snuck in a window. I had to show them where I had scratched my name on my old desk and where their uncle had set the school on fire. I couldn't resist leafing through one of the old books we had used. Children no longer read these books—they just sat on the shelf to enhance the aura of historical authenticity—my history. The book contained one of the horse stories I had read so many times. I couldn't resist. Tucking the book under my arm, I helped my kids out the window and departed. I had never stolen anything before and promised a contribution to the museum fund to assuage my guilt.

The magic of camp continued for three summers. The third summer, I was completing my thesis for a Master's in School Counseling during the quiet hours in the camp routine. I stayed up late each night to study, but still rose early in the morning for jogging or biking.

Brown Ledge was molding my children, too. My daughter had moved into a cabin with three girls she had known for a couple of years and loved the independence afforded by separate sleeping quarters.

I saw a good bit of my older son, or at least I saw his name. As Bobby matured into a handsome young athlete, the older campers penned affectionate notes about him on cabin walls and barn doors. Their heartfelt inscriptions described him as "so fine" and confessed their infatuation with the enthusiasm of first love.

I suspected Bobby was aware of their praise, but he was a shy fellow and never said a word. No one ever caught him reading the notes, and no one ever saw him write back.

My youngest child was blossoming in a different way. Phillip's experience came the closest to replicating my own childhood. Because he was both younger than the campers and a boy, he did not participate in the camp routine. Phillip spent his time galloping up and down the roads, catching toads and acquiring poison ivy, all the while looking more and more like my tag-along brother.

Everyone knew Phillip and everyone loved him. They welcomed him in any activity—from riflery to arts-and-crafts. The drama department created bit parts for him in their weekly productions. This exposure instilled in him a long-lasting love for theater.

Wrap up of camp, this third summer, followed the same process as the two previous years. We tackled the hectic job of placing another fifteen to twenty good horses, packed up the saddles and tack for storage, and locked up the barn.

The finale for campers was the all-night bonfire in the grove, an annual event of incomparable emotion. Best friends sat close, holding hands and singing their favorite songs. I marveled at how camaraderie had matured them. The snobby ones acted less arrogant as they discovered more in themselves to be proud of, and the shy ones learned to speak up. They had developed friendships totally unlike anything I had experienced except with my sisters.

I had already bid farewell to my riders. Several had earned the Vanguard plaque for knowledge, horsemanship, and teaching skills. My daughter had coveted the award, but she had missed the mark because she lacked the maturity to meet the standard for teaching. Anna and several others who fell short made a pact to go for it next summer.

Many young women sought my older son for a tender or emotional adieu, but he had escaped to bed early in the evening. Bobby's absence provoked a last salvo of love notes. I had ordered Phillip to bed also. He considered himself everybody's little brother, and the emotional partings would have been quite over the top for his eight-year-old psyche, besides, we had a long ride ahead during the next few days.

Hanging On

"Once upon a time"
So your fairytale began
You cried, I handed you your "Blankie,"
Placed a Band-Aid on your knee,
Kissed your hurts away—you smiled.

"Once upon a time"
Isn't now.

You are hurt.
The damage cannot be erased.
Not with Blankie, a Band-Aid, or a hug
There is no "Once upon a time."

We had only four days to travel before I had to resume teaching in Utah. We packed our gear in the Bronco, loaded the two-horse trailer with the ponies, Beauty and Temptation, assembled our snacks and last-minute treasures, then departed in the early afternoon

Beauty had come with us for her third summer as a camp pony. She was a tiny thing, but aptly named. Her dark grey body was beautifully proportioned—like a scaled down Thoroughbred, and her attitude demonstrated all the cockiness of one who assumed the world's admiration. A chronic Houdini, she became a real pain for my instructor team each summer—regularly escaping her stall, carousing around, and heading for the athletic fields to graze. The smallest campers, however, adored her, so her stall walls were covered with inscriptions. Beauty's accolades lacked the sophistication, vocabulary, and spelling accuracy of the bigger horses, but the sincerity and affection they exuded were obvious to anyone who bent low enough to read them.

Temptation was an equally refined little bay, a couple of hands taller than Beauty, but nowhere near as popular. He was too small for the older riders and too feisty for the younger ones. Because he hadn't worked well for the riding program, the camp declined to place him for the winter. I was unwilling to send him back to the wrangler where his safe passage through life was less than secure, so I offered to take him home to sell. I felt certain he would perform well in the Pony Club world.

We drove through the night until about 2 A.M. when I pulled over for a nap in a rest stop somewhere in Indiana. I awoke sufficiently refreshed to hit the road again, thankful for the opportunity to drive while the ponies were standing quietly and my kids were sleeping soundly. The first light of morning was just beginning to erase the night.

We were heading west on I-80, cruising close to the 55 mile-per-hour speed limit. I approached an eighteen-wheeler merging onto the highway and crossed into the passing lane to avoid losing momentum.

I was just pulling abreast of the semi when an explosion detonated under my vehicle, setting off shock waves that blasted my eardrums. My scream was drowned out by a deafening grind of metal against metal that electrified every hair on my body. I could still feel the scream in my throat as pandemonium broke loose. The Bronco unleashed such raw power in its bucking and twisting that I knew my steering wheel no longer dictated its course.

My eyes and energy instinctively focused on controlling our crazed vehicle. I would lose the last remnant of control if I hit the brake. Above all else, I fought to keep from sideswiping the tractor-trailer traveling beside me. With my next breath, I yelled to my kids, "Hang on!"

The safety of our very lives depended on staying within a single, narrow lane, but the Bronco paid no heed. I felt like a flea trying to hold back a charging elephant. The car jerked again, then bolted leftward onto the shoulder. It hurtled down a shallow embankment and careened across the median. Finally, the ruts created by the Bronco's assault on the earth deepened sufficiently to wrestled the car to a heaving halt.

Before the car even ceased shaking, I had jerked around, panicked about my children. Next to me, I could make out my daughter in the early dawn light. Her eyes were wide in fear, but her seatbelt had held her. She nodded when I blurted out, "Are you okay?"

As I lunged over the seatback, I caught sight of Bobby, climbing out from the floor behind my seat. "I'm fine, Mom." I heard truth in his words as I intently inspected his face, hands, and arms.

And my youngest—hours ago he had stretched out his sleeping bag in the back-back to maximize space for the night ride. Now a black hole had replaced the back door of the Bronco.

I flew out my door and glared back at our tracks. About ten feet behind the car, Phillip was gingerly standing up. The sight of him gave me back my heartbeat. He looked scraped up, but not broken, not bleeding, and not crying. As I hugged him tightly, my body began trembling.

My thoughts then jumped, *Where are my ponies?*

I could make out the trailer about twenty-five feet from where we stood. It was upright but damaged beyond belief. I approached in slow motion—the worst seemed inevitable. The absence of noise was deafening. Frightened horses stomp, snort or kick. Only death is silent.

My stomach churned as I forced myself to peer in over the tailgate. Temptation was standing almost normally. Beauty, however, was smashed into the feed compartment three feet above the trailer floor. She had been traveling with her lead rope tied behind the feeder. Evidently, the force of the crash that had propelled her to the feeder had flipped her past the knot so that her head became trapped under her front legs. She was wound up like a pretzel, and it was impossible to determine her status.

Fortunately, the semi-truck driver stopped. He had already used his CB radio to call for emergency help and an ambulance arrived quickly. Believing that Phillip was not badly hurt, I permitted the drivers to take him to the hospital in the company of his thirteen-year-old big brother while I figured out how to salvage the ponies.

Anna and I returned to the trailer. I used my pocketknife to saw apart the rope holding Beauty's head, then I hooked a lead rope to her halter. I had no idea what was going to happen when I pulled, but I had to get her out of the feeder. Although Beauty was small, she still weighed five or six hundred pounds. With the might of necessity, I managed to drag her from the feeder. Beauty popped out, landed with a thud, and scrambled to her feet. As soon as she realized she could move, Beauty shook her head and jumped out the back of the trailer. Almost instantly she started munching on the long grass in the median. A normal horse would have been terrified after being trapped in such a confined space. Beauty, however, could fall back on her long history as

Houdini, the master escape artist. She looked not only unscathed, but also rather indifferent to her ordeal.

Temptation managed to back out, but it was obvious that his back leg was badly injured. Finding Beauty, however, he, too, lowered his head and began grazing. The trucker had also called a veterinarian who arrived with a trailer to transport my ponies to his clinic. Both loaded right into his trailer and were soon on their way.

I was still holding the vet's phone number in my hand when I thanked the officer for escorting my daughter and me to the hospital. Phillip had been examined, and the emergency physicians released him after determining that he had suffered a concussion. A local hotel offered us lodging for that day and night while I made arrangements to get my family home.

I phoned my little sister and Sondra. Sondra called the camp to let them know what had happened. Teresa and her husband paid to have our belongings shipped home. We rented a car and drove to the site of the wreck to retrieve our belongings from the truck and trailer. We also located my younger son's clothes and sleeping bag scattered throughout the grass of the median. I grabbed everything as quickly as possible, hating to dwell on the damage or relive the accident. We left as a crew arrived to tow the wreckage. Driving away, the rental car stuck momentarily in one of the ruts created by our stampede across the grass. It was alarming to see how much damage we had caused. Within a few weeks, however, I was able to put quite an accurate estimate on that damage. The highway department billed me $150 to replace the grass.

Back at the hotel, I called the veterinarian. I was both relieved and devastated by his report. Beauty, our family pet, would be fine. "The larger pony will have to be put down. His hip muscle was torn from the bone and he will never be free from pain."

A local farmer stepped forward and offered to keep Beauty until arrangements could be made to bring her home. True to his word, he called a month later when he and his buddies headed west for a hunting trip. He transported her as far as Wyoming and we met him there.

The morning after the accident, we resumed our homeward odyssey. I inserted my cassette into the rental car tape player and turned up the volume so that James Taylor could sing us home. By the time we arrived our mailbox was filled with letters, cards, and donations from Brown Ledge Camp. I was dumbfounded and touched. I had not dared to dwell on how I would pay for the aftermath of our wreck. Their generosity eased that burden. School began the following day.

Just as the first bell rang, I was summoned to the office where the principal told me a call waited. I sighed as I picked up the receiver and said, "Hello."

For a brief moment the other end of the phone was silent, and then the sounds of Mariah Carey's song, "Hero," drifted through the receiver.

"There's an answer

> If you reach into your soul
> And the sorrow that you know
> Will melt away."

I knew it was my little sister. This wasn't the first time we had shared music to lend support to one another. I knew every word of the song, but I felt as if I were hearing it for the first time, like it had been written just for me. Once again, Teresa offered me a lifeline, and her timing was perfect. School was about the kids. I had no chance to grieve or even digest the past days, no time for exhaustion or pain. The treadmill had started.

Three months later, my children had dressed for school and I was serving our standard breakfast of scrambled eggs, toast and vegetarian sausage. As I sat down opposite Phillip, he stared blankly at me—eyes wide open. Then he fell off his chair. His limp body hit the floor with a thud. I flew around the table and grabbed him in my arms as his body began quivering. His trembling escalated violently. No matter how tightly I held him, I could not stop the relentless spasms. My heart was beating so hard my entire body pounded. I willed myself to breathe, then I shouted to Bobby, "Call 911."

Silently I screamed within myself, *Administer CPR, you know how to do it.* Advanced CPR training was a prerequisite for employment at Brown Ledge Camp, but no amount of training could prepare me—a mother gripped by fear that her child was dying. Administer was a classroom word—my mind was shouting, *How, How, How?* Breathe-press-press seemed hopelessly inadequate. Just as the procedure materialized through the blackness of my mind, my baby took a deep breath and his body melted in my arms. I called to my unresponsive son and rocked him as we waited for the ambulance to arrive.

The paramedics said he had suffered a seizure. They carried him to the ambulance on a stretcher and, in an act of true humanity, broke their rules and permitted my older son to accompany him to the hospital in the back of the ambulance. My daughter and I followed them.

A pediatric neurologist along with our pediatrician agreed that my son's concussion during our accident had traumatically induced epilepsy. Both physicians warned that grand mal seizures could occur many times before they stabilized his medication.

Their dire predictions proved true. Far too many times over the next several years, I sped to the hospital, pulling off the shoulder to hold my little boy when his seizures escalated then continuing to the hospital during his comatose stage. My personal fitness program and healthier mental attitude had not prepared me for such pain to be heaped upon my child.

My sense of self-reliance and inner strength did survive. I felt more confident as a teacher; I liked myself as a person; and I believed I was succeeding as a single parent. I still, however, remained obsessed with providing for my kids in a manner that forestalled their feeling disadvantaged because I was their mother.

Years earlier when Phillip had attended the preschool offered by my college, I had overheard two student teachers conversing as they observed him. One remarked with utmost concern in her voice, "I wonder what will become of him. Research says there is a significantly higher failure rate for children of single parents."

I cannot imagine why a statement of untutored, immature young women affected me so powerfully unless perhaps, it described a reality that I already feared. How could it be that love, dedication, and effort could not outweigh single parent status? What could be more unfair than perceiving my children as semi-orphans wandering inevitably down a path of failure?

Fortunately, my obsession motivated me. I knew my kids could succeed, and by their early teen years, they knew it as well. One afternoon Bobby, then in the seventh grade, brought home a slip of paper asking me to attend a special meeting because his teacher had nominated him to serve as a People to People Ambassador. If he was elected, he would travel to Europe as a special envoy, representing the United States in schools and before government officials.

The nomination was an honor, and tears filled my eyes as I sat in the auditorium listening to the experiences available through the program. If my son were selected, I would find some way to send him.

The moderator explained the trip fees—six months to raise a king's ransom. I sold extra horses, gave more lessons, wrote letters, and took a second job working a graveyard shift as a telemarketer. I organized a fundraiser we titled "Service-a-thon" through which our friends and neighbors pledged money in exchange for service hours that our family donated in a homeless shelter.

Our job at the shelter was to serve dinner to the transient population. Each of us stood behind a cafeteria counter and ladled out measured portions of dinner items. Several men toted "Will Work for Food" signs with them as they filled their plates, but none of them took me up on my offer of farm work. Our few months' effort made us more realistic about the homeless subculture and my son gained a new perspective on American life as he earned the privilege of representing his country abroad.

In the end, each of my kids had a turn as an ambassador. Bobby traveled Europe; Anna was sent to Australia, and Phillip toured New Zealand. So even if "Single-Parent" defined part of my children's reality, it did not mean "Lesser Parenting," it was just that all their support and guidance came from one person—me.

Alone

I called you today, your birthday
Such emotion I felt as I told you how my son, your grandson
Was suffering
Of course, you said, "He's okay, he'll be okay,
He's a good kid."

Easy for you—just say the right thing
Never have to act at all
Not your problem and you're right, of course
You could make a difference
But, everyone is too busy
To be an Aunt, Uncle, Grandma, Grandpa
Even friend
Alone again—MY problem

If it isn't small talk, "Everything is fine,"
"How's the weather there?"
Don't call

In your chosen space of not knowing
Ignorance is truly bliss
Not knowing means no need to act
Better for you to just believe and hope the best

But, in my space far from you
I will not turn and choose not to know.
Love is more compelling than the bliss
Love is also so alone.

The first time it happened, I was speechless. My older son and I disagreed, nothing new. But this time the venom and volume in his retort foreshadowed a distinctly different relationship. Our seventeen-year partnership had ended. Mortal combat had begun.

Having graduated a year early from high school, Bobby was thrown into the collegiate world prematurely. He was handsome enough and brilliant enough to make a success of his new surroundings, but he lacked the maturity to pull it off. It was not long before he was in over his head, skipping classes, experimenting with drugs, and terrified to tell me. So instead, he worked at keeping the tables turned by attacking me.

We had been so close, sharing the same goals and often thinking the same thoughts. It was uncanny how frequently he and I came up with the same alphabet words or guessed each other's twenty questions subject when we played family travel games. I knew my son to be sensitive, caring, and responsible. Who was this monstrous individual dressed in my son's face?

I ached deep in my bones for the loss of my companion, and I was horrified by the cold, calculating stranger who took his place. I said to Bobby, "How can you do this to me? Don't you know that I would lay down my life for you?" He shrugged and turned away. He didn't care, or couldn't care, and he said so. Of course, I knew that all of this anger wasn't about me, but emotionally, it felt like it was.

Bobby had all kinds of friends to meet. Motherly instinct warned me that his friends were up to nothing good. My idea of a reasonable curfew sounded ridiculous to him.

He yelled, shouted, and threatened to walk out. I blocked the doorway and he shoved me away. Fortunately for me, he was still seventeen, so when I phoned the police explaining how my son was intending to leave, two officers drove immediately to the house. They took my son aside and laid out the letter of the law. "Like it or not, your mom's the boss. She has a legal right to make you stay home, and we'll enforce it."

My son had never lacked respect for authority; it was respecting me that was his problem. He responded to the officer with an appropriate, "Yes, sir," then shut himself in his room, and shut me out of his life.

Confrontation interspersed with silence. My heart ached, but I held the line because I knew about druggies. They had shot up my car and threatened my life. Bobby didn't know what I knew. He cared so little, and I cared so much.

Perhaps I could have managed one rebellious son without feeling like a failure, but my younger son had begun to struggle, too. The first years after our wreck, we had worked with his physicians to titrate his medication against the challenges of his physical and mental growth. Phillip's first prescription medication controlled his seizures, but left him unable to function at school. He fell asleep during class and, when called upon to respond to a question, would lose his train of thought halfway into his answer. His teacher expressed real concern.

When he switched to a different medication, the seizures returned with a vengeance. With no apparent warning, Phillip would collapse in a heap, clutching his legs to his chest, throwing his head back, rolling his eyes, and crying out, "MOM, MOM." I talked to him as he seizured. "Listen, I'm here, it's okay. Breathe, son, breathe. I love you." I caressed his hair as the violence passed leaving a rag-doll version of my son in its wake. The following day, Phillip could scarcely walk. Thankfully he slept most of that time because I could hardly watch his staggering and stumbling without crying. When his dosage was finally balanced correctly, he tolerated the second medication much better. We all sighed with relief that he seemed to be thriving.

To the credit of his elementary school teachers, who had carefully followed his epilepsy protocols, Phillip earned good grades. He had lots of friends and liked school well enough to qualify for the gifted and talented program when he graduated into middle school for sixth grade.

The advent of hormones, however, coincided with the decrease in class structure that characterizes the middle school experience. Given the opportunity to change class every fifty minutes, Phillip would push the limits of each teacher's patience until the ringing bell allowed him to gallivant off and start the annoyance game again. Not one authority figure held him accountable for the minor misdeeds that collected themselves into a pattern of chronic behavior problems.

Phillip's bright and amiable character became prankishly manipulative. When caught overstepping, he immediately admitted the error of his ways and expressed genuine sorrow. The rest of the time he fluctuated between being a social butterfly and the class clown.

At first, respectful apologies coupled with excellent test scores camouflaged the extent of his disruptive behavior. The gifted program provided outlets for his energy, and he remained involved and learning, creative and theatrical. But his work ethic and attention span were deteriorating, records for his homework performance was deplorable, and he interfered with other students' ability to learn. By the end of the academic year, the verdict was final. No matter how gifted or talented he might be, my son could not come back.

I tried to engage Phillip in discussion about the school's decision, but he had nothing to say for himself. He acted as if it didn't matter. He had messed up, never saw the writing on the wall, and never thought about the consequences.

So, the same year Bobby started at the local university, I had enrolled Phillip in a new school on guest status. There, for better or worse, his spirit remained undaunted. Overestimating both his ability to charm people and their capacity to forgive him, he just forged ahead. I warned him, but he remained oblivious to the reality that he pushed people so far that they could not, or would not, deal with him.

About the only consequence that impacted Phillip's goofing off was my shadowing him for two full days in the new school. I sat beside him in each class. We had made a deal that he would pay me back for the wages I paid to the substitute who stayed with my students. Under my watchful eye, we staved off further disruption, for a while at least.

Then came the incident that broke the camel's back. It involved the bus driver. Like most of his cohorts, my son's driver was a retired farmer who parked his bus in his backyard and transported school kids as a second job. Tension between rowdy students and grumpy drivers was legendary.

One winter morning, when Phillip's bus pulled into the school parking lot to deliver the kids, other students were already deep into a snowball fight. My son jumped off the bus, eagerly joining in. The driver yelled to him, "You throw like a girl."

The driver's insult had thrown down the gauntlet. Phillip turned around, packed another snowball, and looked the driver in the eye. Who cared if his windup appeared feminine? His aim was as accurate as a sharpshooter's. The snowball arched through the bus door, across the aisle, and exploded in the driver's face, frosting his glasses, and drizzling down his sweater. One snowball ended the duel.

The driver had no intention of overlooking this humiliation in front of the other kids. His responsive parry would be swifter and more deadly than the snowball. He saw to it that my son would not be invited back to the school next year. Guest status left us no recourse. We survived the rest of the year, but little more could be said of it.

No matter how hard I worked, I could not meet all the needs of my sons, and I felt the condemnation of singleness in "single parent" coming back to haunt me. I felt both alone and lonely, so terribly inadequate for my boys. They were starved for a male role model, for a powerful hand to hold them in line, but neither of their fathers chose to fill that void. As my boys were spinning further out of control, I called Sondra. "I feel like I am hanging on to a cliff with bloody fingers, like I could lose my grip at any moment."

Phillip had run himself out of options. For the last year of middle school, he had to attend our neighborhood school, which was located in the district where I taught. With his transfer, the line between my professional life and my personal life blurred. Unlike his brother, Phillip was rarely confrontational, but his poor choices would now reflect directly on me.

As the school year proceeded, Phillip's minor misbehaviors escalated into serious problems. His tardiness grew into truancy. Each time the principal suspended Phillip, she called me into a special meeting to discuss his reinstatement. I sat at a conference table opposite the same professional educators with whom I otherwise worked. The questions they directed at me were the same ones I had asked the parents of other problem students. Humiliation engulfed me as my cohorts discussed my son and his problems. My hand periodically reached for a tissue from the box set in front of me by a sympathetic teacher.

Both my sons were making choices that were the antithesis of everything I had raised them to believe and everything I taught in my classroom. I had modeled values that held us to the highest standard. If Phillip didn't care about what he was doing to himself, couldn't he care about what he was doing to me?

The administrative staff wanted to place him in the "school-within-a-school" program for problem students, gang members, and drug users. I fought their decision, knowing that the slippery slope my son was riding would never reverse if he found camaraderie and support in a peer group of malcontents. In desperation I offered, "If Phillip can stay in regular school, I will take care of his disciplinary work hours." We struck a bargain.

My supervision of Phillip allowed him to avoid district-ordered, make-up hours with other problem kids. I could isolate him from the other truants already ensconced in the legal system by creating worthwhile programs at the library, the animal shelter, or the Nature Center; and I would volunteer with him.

Life on the home front no longer functioned. I clung to the illusion that maintaining our former routine would help keep my boys grounded. Each evening at dinnertime, we permitted each other a short respite. The truce began when we sat down together around the dining room table. Our family tradition required us to share our day through categories. The first to speak could choose between the best, the worst or the funniest thing, or one lesson learned that day.

Bobby went first. He sounded excited explaining a new calculus concept as his best. Anna's worst was the tragic conclusion of a book she just finished. Phillip could hardly contain his laughter describing his kitten jumping up in the air when our Doberman startled him. Left with the "Something Learned" category, I shared a new quote, "Life is not about how many breaths you take, but rather, about what takes your breath away." Then we ate together in relative harmony.

Once the dishes were cleared, however, the confrontations began again. Anna reacted to our family's chaos quietly. She despised her older brother's rudeness, but she cherished his friendship. In the past, their relationship had worked because of their common interests and their complimentary personalities. Bobby was older, bigger, and braver, but he didn't mind including his sister in his life. Anna had kept everything organized for both of them. Now the peacefulness between them that began in their earliest memories was suffering.

When the brother she admired attacked the mother she so loved, my daughter ached. At first, she began waking up early to feed the horses—anything to help me, but when her efforts changed nothing, she became angry. She was disgusted with both her brothers and believed I was too easy on them. She found no reward in remaining the good kid, the invisible kid. I may not have expressed it adequately, but I thanked God for her goodness. I don't know how I would have survived my entire brood rebelling at the same time.

As fall approached and Bobby continued to flounder, I sought options that would buy him time to grow up. Teresa and her husband, who resided in the highbrow equestrian country of Eastern Pennsylvania, offered to contact a nearby steeplechase trainer who might hire my son as an exercise rider. When Bobby responded to this prospect with a modicum of interest, I was thrilled. The trainer offered him a job, and my sister offered him a home.

Bobby and I had a wonderful three-day drive across the country. We talked, sang along with the radio, and laughed together. I hugged my son goodbye, hoping against hope that my sister's husband would be the masculine role model my son so badly needed.

But Bobby was not the model son they had hoped for. He was unmotivated and elusive. His friends wrote to him often, and my son was homesick for them. Teresa's husband phoned me weekly, calling my son a liar and a druggie. He was so derogatory and negative that I hung up in tears at the end of our conversations. The prospects for role modeling evaporated. One of Bobby's friends flew back east and drove home with him.

At the end of that summer, Phillip started his first year of high school. He and his sister would be attending the same school while Anna completed her senior year.

Truancy followed my son the way gum sticks to a shoe. This year, however, the school gave no allowance, no working off unacceptable behavior with volunteer hours. My son was creating his permanent record, and out of the palette available to him, Phillip kept choosing black.

Across the street from the high school was the hangout for kids who wanted to escape reality and check into the alternative world. The Pizza Runner featured a cheap lunch special and a well-secluded backlot. My son was drawn to that space like bees to honey. New friends introduced him to the joys of pot, which in turn introduced him to the joy of indifference.

The high school was hardly a bed of roses. Tension between races, religions, and teen cultures was palpable. Phillip hung out on the fringes of the skater crowd. He didn't care for their skateboards, he just liked their outfits. He wore the oversized baggy pants that greatly offended the jock crowd, so it was inevitable that he would become a target for confrontation on their turf, the gymnasium. One of the football players was roughing up Phillip's friend, slapping him around for the fun of it. The jock responded to my son's retort of, "Knock it off," by smacking his friend again. Phillip hauled back and socked his adversary in the face. The incident ended with a string of threats against my son and a black eye for the jock.

By afternoon, half the football team had fixated on revenge. Rumors spread so widely that even my daughter, one of the preppy kids, heard about the impending fight against her brother.

There was no realistic escape for Phillip. The team located him and escorted him forcefully back to the locker room where his archenemy, shiner and all, awaited him.

The rest of the team circled to cheer the spectacle as Phillip was thrown down and the beating began.

But the football team hadn't counted on my daughter. Anna had spent years tackling half-wild horses in the killer pens with less than half the determination she had to rescue her brother. Once she discovered where Phillip had been taken, she started running. The "Boys Only" sign above the locker room doors served no deterrent. Anna burst into the gym room like a ValKyrie with a mad on. She grabbed the kid on top of her brother, who outweighed her by a couple of stones, and threw him into the chain-link barrier separating two rows of lockers. Then she snatched her brother off the floor and marched out, closely followed by an awed entourage of her friends. They headed straight for the principal's office, the closest available substitute for protective custody. Both boys were suspended, but the animosity between them faded, as neither had any desire to relive the incident.

Phillip did not always have his sister around to watch out for him as he continued down the road to self-destruction. Having exhausted my resources, I phoned Sondra. Desperately I cried, "I don't know how to help him. How do I help my son?"

Sondra had by now earned her doctorate in neuropsychology. She suggested, "Phillip's seizures or seizure medication might contribute to his school and social problems. You should have him tested. I know a really good neuro-psychologist who taught some of my classes. I can contact him for you." A month later the test results showed my boy had profound deficiencies in abstract reasoning and impulse control. He tested so high in other areas that these deficiencies were particularly significant.

Phillip's doctor concluded that the initial head injury, followed by years of seizures and medication, had caused permanent damage in his thought process. It was virtually impossible for his mind to anticipate the consequences of his actions. We had to accept that medication would never make his life normal. From now on, we would have to make allowances, and Phillip would have to cope in a world where allowances are not always available. I could no longer pretend that my son could pull it together if he would just make the effort.

After further testing and diagnosis, the school drew up an accommodations plan, and counseling with the neuropsychologist began. Phillip's conversations with his therapist sounded positive, but his actions negated my optimism about their benefit. His drug use was becoming more than experimental and his truancy became a daily issue. He entrenched himself so deeply in a passive-aggressive attitude toward life that his responses to questions became limited to shoulder shrugs or blank stares.

Emotion had disappeared from my son's life, but it boiled over in mine. Guilt overwhelmed me. Painful themes from my childhood resurfaced as my thoughts plunged into darkness. Self-condemnation and feelings of inadequacy kept me from admitting to others that I was drowning. Connections with friends became distant, some by my choice, some by theirs. I became closed. I found refuge in a river of solitude and let it flow through me and around me.

One afternoon as I drove down the freeway to deliver a horse, the conversations were with myself. *Call Dad, maybe he would help, or your sister or brother.*

I picked up my cell phone, scrolled through their numbers, then set it back down. *No, they all have their own lives to deal with, I can't put any of my stuff out there. I can't bear to hear their ridicule and empty words of advice.*

Tears welled up in my eyes. *You got yourself into all of this. It is your fault so you are on your own. You made a choice to be with your baby's dad and you divorced your older kids' dad so you better find a way to deal.*

I was crying so hard that I could no longer see the road. I pulled over and lay my head on the steering wheel. During the eight years since the wreck, I had often berated myself, *Maybe you didn't have the Bronco serviced right. Maybe there were signs of mechanical failure that you missed. Why did you have to go to the camp anyway? You were responsible to keep your son safe and you failed. You deserve the pain, humiliation, and guilt. You got yourself into this and dragged your baby with you.*

I lifted my head from the steering wheel when I heard a familiar melody. Music provided solace, escape, and the feeling of resting with an old friend. Alone with the music, my soul quieted. Alone in my truck, I had time to drown and cry when no one would know. Alone on the shoulder of the road, I found a scrap of paper and scribbled through my troubled tears:

It's an empty place
This space where I now reside
Room enough for my thoughts and for self-pity
Feels like dying inside

What happened to the joy?
To "Carpe Diem," to the always smile?

My life's blood pours from my eyes as I cry
I'm lost
I'm coming apart
My bones no longer holding my skin to form

My life, my thoughts, ME
It all lies behind the green of my eyes,
Swimming in my tears

Can you look deep enough to find
ME

When an opportunity came to move to a small family horse farm in our area, I jumped at the chance. The move would solve three issues. My older son, now nineteen could rent our old house and share expenses with his buddies. He was no longer a minor so I could no longer intervene between him and the choices he was making. Whatever his future held, the angst between us would diminish. Phillip, who continued to struggle academically, could attend a well-funded county school instead of the inner-city senior high. I could regain space for my horses—a subdivision was eating up the land that used to be their pasture.

In exchange for rent and my horses' board, I would care for the owners' horses and the farm. They offered me access to their arenas and jumps, a tradeoff which enabled me to continue giving riding lessons and training horses.

About a month following our move to the farm, I received a phone call from one of Phillip's half-sisters, "My dad shot and killed himself last night."

What does one say upon hearing such news? My thoughts turned immediately to my son. I had to find a way to tell him and the strength to deal with his reaction. Because Phillip was continuing in a counseling program, I contacted his therapist to give him a heads up. I knew it was my responsibility to tell Phillip about this tragedy, but I was terrified it would make him suicidal. I asked the counselor for advice, but he had none. When he responded with, "Call if you need me." I sensed that he hoped I wouldn't.

That afternoon, I asked Phillip to accompany me on the daily run to the county compost facility to dump the farm's manure. As I drove the tractor slowly down the road, he stood on the running board. I looked into his eyes and said with a voice intended to express an appropriate balance of sympathy and reality, "I have something I have to tell you that is very difficult for me to tell and horrible for you to hear."

Poignant pauses interrupting my sentence alarmed him more than I had hoped. He stared at me and indicated by nodding that he was ready for me to go on. "Your father shot and killed himself early this morning."

The words hung heavily in the hot July air—as heavily as my heart. When he spoke, his words carried no emotion. He stated it simply, "It's the final way for my dad to let me know I didn't matter to him."

Outwardly, my little boy continued to show no emotion, but inwardly he fell apart. Drugs became his regular escape, lying was routine, and the trust between us ended.

The destructive theme in my life was repeating itself—the shame that I couldn't hold it all together, the feeling that I couldn't be good enough. I saw once again the specter of bloody fingers losing their grip on the cliff's edge.

We would get through it, if I could just figure out the right things to say and do for him. This commitment to Phillip left me no time to dwell on how my ex-lover's death affected me.

My son's counselor felt that Phillip was using drugs to mask the pain and confusion he felt. How does one stop another's downward spiral when it is fueled by unspeakable loss and illegal substances? We did survive the summer, but little more can be said of the weeks prior to the start of his sophomore year.

My son's records from the city school district transferred with him to the county high school. His transcripts showed that he had accumulated almost no credits. The combination of disruptiveness, truancy, and failure to turn in homework outweighed his passing test scores and left him with failing grades in almost every subject.

The records of his neuropsychological tests indicating traumatic brain injury also transferred to the new school. They qualified him for an individualized education program under the Individuals with Disabilities Education Act. But no customized education program could outweigh his choice of friends. My son immediately gravitated toward the same drug involved, unmotivated crowd he had just left.

The new school administration had zero tolerance for "safe school" violations. Because intolerance had never served as a deterrent for my son, trouble inevitably crossed his path. Phillip got caught for smoking, truancy, and finally marijuana paraphernalia. When the drug charge triggered random testing by the juvenile court system, I sighed with relief. I would finally have some backing in disciplining my son. I knew he had wandered astray, he knew I knew, but I had lacked proof.

The court system filled that gap. When a urine analysis tested positive for marijuana, the court ordered my son into a drug-counseling program. This required me to pay six thousand dollars, attend classes with him every Wednesday night, and take him to drug court every other Wednesday afternoon. I needed the program to help me get by son back on track, but I felt as if I were the one being punished. I didn't have the time or the money, but I also didn't have the choice.

At the bi-monthly drug court, a judge doled out rewards or punishments to the various participants in the drug program. One at a time each teen stood while his or her counselor, probation officer, and a prosecutor discussed that individual's progress. Once again, my son charmed them all. He said all the right things, made all the right apologies, and did it all with a subtle humor that provided a welcome relief in the somber court routine. I had to bring the group back to reality. As the parent, I had the final voice to speak of my son's progress. He was not progressing.

The kids in the Drug Court program were never permitted to miss a group counseling session. My son, however, a huge fan of Spiderman, wanted permission to miss a session to attend the opening of the new Spiderman movie. Neither the counselors nor I agreed, however, we encouraged him to make the "right" choice.

From Phillip's perspective, the right choice was all about the movie premiere, so the incident was brought before the judge. His Honor granted permission—conditional permission. If Phillip missed a session to attend the movie, he had to appear for the following court session in his Spiderman outfit. Two weeks later, after the discussion concerning Phillip's progress ended, the judge had his picture taken with "Spiderman." Again, I had to be heavy. I was the one to stand and express concern about my son's decision and his recovery. I was so tired of being the tough one, of feeling devastated, humiliated, and guilty.

Phillip and I viewed his life differently. After all, he had been through, after all, he had put me through, the truth came out one evening as we did chores together at the farm. Phillip walked up and put his arm around me. Smiling his big smile he said, "Mom, in my whole life, I've never really been unhappy." Then he walked off.

I was shocked. One part of me wanted to drag him back and show him something that would make him unhappy. The other side of me was thrilled to have raised such a resilient person. For years I feared that the trauma in his life would build-up to the point where he might take his life. In fact, it hadn't much registered at all. It wasn't just the brain injury that had insulated my son, it was his personality as well. He was born a child of joy—demanding and impulsive came after the injury, but these negative traits never eclipsed the positive one.

Astrolabe

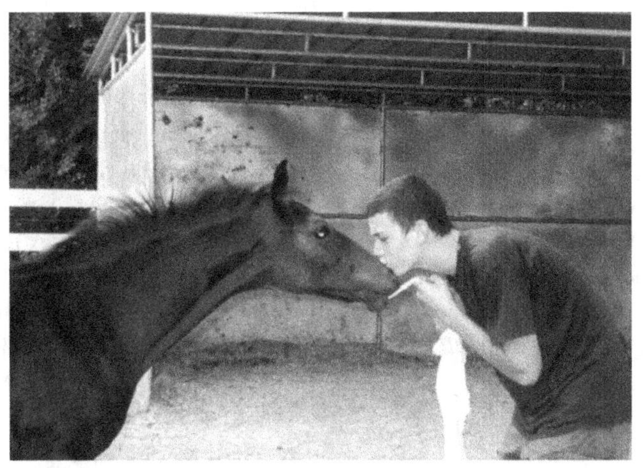

Perfect Start
17 days, left side
Gonna be a colt! Already, a
place in my heart

Into the world
Summer baby colt
Up before mamma
Declaring your right to be

Swirls on your cheeks
White heel for speed
Liquid purple eyes
Toothpicks for legs

My astrolabe
A way to measure my bit of heaven
Years of waiting come together
A bundle of equine attitude

Never back down little man Rule
your corner of the world Swiftly eat
up the ground, as you run
Away with my heart

Even during the most painful times, one can find moments of respite or even a few bright spots. So it was during the moments when I struggled with my youngest son preceding his father's death. The time had come when I could fulfill one of my long-standing personal dreams. I was awaiting the birth of a foal that I had bred to be my future partner, my future friend. I had to pinch myself to believe it had all come together.

I had chosen the name for this foal five years before its conception. The name came from a movie titled *Stealing Heaven*. I had selected this particular video because its jacket described the movie as a tale of medieval history and forbidden love, two of my favorite themes.

The movie was based on the true story of Abelard and Heloise, two twelfth-century lovers who now lie buried together in France. Because Abelard taught religious philosophy to parishioners in the Catholic Church, he was required to remain celibate. His vow, however, never anticipated a student like Heloise, the brilliant, educated niece of a higher church official. Their love affair was searing.

When Heloise became pregnant, Abelard was terrified for her safety. He secreted Heloise away to his sister's chateau in the country where their child was born. When Abelard returned alone to his teaching post in Paris, Heloise's uncle had him castrated as punishment.

The tragic romance brought tears to my eyes, but what touched my soul was witnessing the thought and love that Heloise invested in selecting a name for their son. She chose Astrolabe, the name of the instrument used by mariners to measure the heavens. Her choice symbolized her belief that a mother's love for her child could only be measured by an instrument designed to encompass the heavens. Like the heroine, I considered my children the immeasurable embodiment of heaven.

By the end of the video, I had resolved to name my next horse Astrolabe. It didn't matter that the name would confound most of the equine world; it would mean everything to me.

Once I had the name fixed in mind, I began daydreaming about Astrolabe's parentage. Banjo was the finest horse I had owned. The closest I could get to reproducing his lineage was to breed his sister, Jazmin, who belonged to a friend. My children had borrowed Jazmin for numerous Pony Club activities, including a national championship in Lexington, Kentucky. Jazmin was brave, dignified, and as aloof as a true lady.

The other bloodline necessary for my perfect foal would come from Secretariat. He had long been my hero, the most incredible racehorse ever, winning the Triple Crown and shattering records that had stood for over twenty-five years. I met him once on the farm where he was retired to stud. His presence was overwhelming. Words cannot do him justice.

When the year came that I was able to lease Jazmin, I located a son of Secretariat in Montana. My eighteen-year-old daughter and I loaded Jazmin in our horse trailer and headed North to Big Sky country.

The Montana stallion had inherited the essence of his father. I recognized Secretariat's eyes. Anna and I scrutinized the rest of him and then we looked at each other and grinned—huge grins. He would do just fine. For three days and nights, we lived in the tack room of our horse trailer, then returned home, hoping Jazmin was pregnant. I was incredulous to think I might realize my dream. Seventeen days after returning from Montana, the vet checked Jazmin. The ultrasound clearly showed a pregnancy in the left horn of her uterus. An old wives tale dictates that a left-sided pregnancy foretells a colt. I was ecstatic.

On the second of June, one month before Phillip's father died, my foal arrived. In spite of careful nightly monitoring of the mare in her foaling stall, Jazmin birthed Astrolabe in the pasture after I went to work. He was picture perfect, dark bay with the touch of white on his left hind heel that Arabic legend describes as a mark of speed. From the moment of his birth, my little Astrolabe announced his presence boldly. He never backed down to the adult horses, never showed the respect demanded in a herd.

When he met the big Dutch Warmblood horses at the farm, he marched up to them like the general in charge, then spun around, flicking his spindly legs with childlike disdain.

When troubles with my boys threatened to engulf me, I would walk out to the pasture and lean on the fence to watch Astrolabe. Swift and fearless, he galloped around the farm as if ready to take flight. No wonder it has been said, "When God announced his gifts to the animals, He gave to the horse 'that man will find you beautiful.'" But part of me feared getting too close to Astrolabe—like he was too good to be true, a dream that couldn't last. There is no instrument that can truly measure heaven. The optimistic side of me thought maybe there was a god; maybe some higher power was smiling down on me after all, saying I deserved this gift. But, too much of my emotional self was wrapped around this little colt.

The day Astrolabe died, he died running with wild abandon, with the confidence and assurance of the king of the world. But, he cut a corner too close and was gone from me.

It happened in August, shortly after Phillip had lost his father. I was at school late for a faculty meeting. Phillip was home and wanted to help me by turning Astrolabe and his mother out to pasture. While Astrolabe dallied and played along the way, my son led Jazmin on ahead. As he continued around a corner, the distance between the mare and her baby grew.

When Astrolabe realized he had been left behind, the colt panicked and bolted toward his mom—without calculating for the corner. He missed the alley and slammed into the threaded end of a metal bolt protruding from the fence post.

Phillip phoned me at work. Absolute panic in his voice told me that my colt's injury must be critical. I called the vet from my cell phone as I rushed home, letting him know

I would get the horses to the clinic immediately. I roared down the farm drive, jumped from the truck, and ran to the pasture with Phillip. The sight of Astrolabe drained every ounce of blood from my face, but I could not lose control in front of my son.

My perfect baby was standing in the middle of the paddock, utterly broken. He had sideswiped the corner post so hard that the bolt had snapped his ribs and filleted the flesh off his side, exposing broken bones and punctured lungs. With every breath, foaming blood sprayed through the holes in his lungs. He would have to be humanely destroyed.

I wrapped my arms around Astrolabe's broken, bloody body and hugged him to me as I half carried, half dragged him behind Phillip, who was leading Jazmin to the trailer. I kissed Astrolabe goodbye as I lifted him into the trailer beside his mother. He was put down shortly after arriving at the veterinarian's clinic.

Phillip had loved Astrolabe, too, and I knew he felt responsible. This second unnecessary death could only compound the confusion and pain he already felt. I had to bury my own grief again.

I was so concerned about sparing Phillip's sense of guilt that I felt guilty when he found me clutching the pasture fence and sobbing. I had just finished cleaning Astrolabe's blood out of the horse trailer. It was so much blood, so much tragedy. My son gave me a sad and knowing look and walked away. There was nothing to be said. Words could not describe our grief. Not even silence captured it, but silence was more profound.

My first impulse was to call Teresa for comfort. Because she was not home, I spoke with her husband. He responded with a litany of criticism, what should have and could have been done to prevent the accident. His voice on the other end of the line sounded cold and indifferent as he quipped, "Ah well, you can get another horse."

I did not need to hear how Astrolabe's death could have been prevented. The tragedy was real, and I had wanted someone to care about what it meant to me, to understand that my heartache penetrated far deeper than another horse could heal.

Was it asking too much to want another person to comprehend such a private place in my soul? My friends' outpouring of sympathy eased my immediate pain over the loss of the foal, but they could not understand that what I really mourned was the death of my dream. It was the illusion that I had the power and the right to create the perfect animal for myself as a reward for surviving my past as a person with dignity. The dream was snatched away, leaving me as dry and as desolate as the desert in which I live.

No God, no saving grace
No reward for goodness
All that fulfilled the dream
Violently gone with blood and broken bones
Go ahead, make sense of it
You can't, there isn't any
Dreams shot to hell
Keep it all inside
Others are hurting

Old Souls

A word, a thought
Tears and smiles
Subtle familiarities
Forever present in space and time

A couple of years later, a gift of wonder came into my life. A new pebble dropped into the pool of my existence. The ripples emanating from this one would bring new perspective to many lives.

Bobby, then twenty-two, called to invite me to dinner. He phoned fairly often so there was nothing unusual about his call, but an invitation for dinner together suggested a new twist. Something was up. As his mother, I had a feeling I knew and was not the least surprised when he informed me that he was to become a father.

This was not what I had wanted for my son or for my first grandchild. He needed time to figure out his own life before he brought a child into the world. He needed to graduate from college, to have the chance to stretch his wings, and to experience adulthood before the next generation tied him down.

In spite of my disappointment, I knew Bobby would be a good father. On the other hand, I was still drowning as Phillip's parent and was not at all sure I wanted to rise to the responsibility of grand-parenting this prematurely conceived baby.

Bobby's girlfriend already had a five-year-old daughter named Alex. This pregnancy meant we would inherit her whole family, so I committed myself to a dry run at being Grandma. Alex was standoffish at first and rather intimidated by the animals at the farm. Before long, however, she and I established a bond through which she discovered the joy of including a bit of country in her life.

Of course, I introduced her to riding. While she showed herself to be athletically adept, Alex never developed any allegiance to the horses. She did, however, admit that swinging on a rope tied to the old barn rafters and landing in a pile of soft hay was more entertaining than watching yet another cartoon show. Alex's excitement about becoming a big sister began to rub off on me.

When my son finally told the rest of my family about the pregnancy, my sister, Teresa and her husband called Bobby and me to offer to adopt the baby. They took great care to couch their proposal in terms of a solution to a "less-than-perfect" situation. But I heard their ostensibly generous offer as selfish and judgmental.

My offspring had spent their entire lives in less-than-perfect situations. Instead of helping the children in my family, Teresa wanted to adopt a baby out of my family. I was hurt. How could she and her husband think we would not take care of this child?

Recent years had already strained the bond between my little sister and me. As we developed differences of opinion, I withdrew from her. To avoid her censure, I would sacrifice a lifetime of companionship.

From the perspective of this growing distance, Teresa's life had come to look like the life I had coveted for myself. Teresa had become an equine veterinarian and married comfortably. "Happily-ever-after" seemed within her grasp. I saw myself, by contrast, as settling with less and struggling more. But, even if the disparity in our lives contributed to making the circumstances around this new child's birth "less than perfect," I would never relinquish my life's blood as long as I could contribute to her well-being.

By the end of our conversation, a chill had eased over my sister's and my relationship. Bobby and his girlfriend politely thanked Teresa for her offer and declined it.

For the next several months, Bobby phoned often to keep me updated about the pregnancy, and he brought me the latest ultrasound pictures. He called to tell me his daughter's name would be Elyssa, a word that meant "sweet blissful dwelling place of happy souls." It touched me that such thought was going onto her being, and I felt a growing sense of peace.

My friends in the equestrian community gave Bobby's girlfriend a Martha-Stewart-style baby shower. She loved their gifts for her baby; I cherished their support for me. I had, at times, felt socially inept among this dignified, educated, and elegant crowd. This celebration came as an unexpected surprise.

Bobby's girlfriend invited me to attend the birth. It was awkward, but I was honored. I knew she had wanted her own mother with her. When her mother was unavailable, she even asked me to come into the delivery room.

My granddaughter came into the world on a late fall morning. Because she was small and her temperature was low, the nurse wrapped her in blankets and placed her under heat lamps. I hated to see Elyssa spending her first hours in this world in a bassinet alone, so I moved a chair over and sat beside her, resting my hand on her back. My palm and fingers covered so much of her tiny body that my conscience rested. She must feel secure.

When my turn came to hold Elyssa, I placed her in my lap so that she faced me and I could study her, every inch of her. I sensed in her being a part of me, two generations removed. But the sensation went deeper than I could explain through a blood relationship. I had heard that the eyes are the window to the soul. Elyssa's eyes, not yet clouded by earthly focus, gazed into mine and seemed content to absorb the intensity of my emotions.

Once again, the miracle of life overwhelmed me, and a palpable sense of spirituality enveloped us. Years ago I had become a cynic about religion. I had experienced so many different denominations. Each had come to feel like a way for the members to excuse their failures and absolve themselves of responsibility. In Elyssa, I found myself aware of the existence of possibilities. *Maybe God is just around, perhaps in our hearts or our spirits. Maybe He exists in the bond I feel with this infant. Maybe He is the ground we walk on, the water we drink, the rain that creates the rainbow. Maybe He is in a smile and a tear. Maybe He is the relationship we have with others. Maybe.*

Elyssa also revived a suspicion in me that we live many lives. *Even as a child, there were moments when I sensed that some of us are old souls who have been connected with each other for a very long time. If we have had past lives, what a shame that we can't remember them—that we don't consciously learn from them.*

Elyssa remained quiet as I pondered these heavy thoughts. She seemed not oblivious, but rather unconcerned. Peaceful. She lay quietly in my arms, gathering strength for the challenges and joys of her first days.

About the time Elyssa was growing into a toddler and beginning to look like my earliest memories of my little sister, I got a call from Teresa. She spoke in her usual, matter-of-fact tone, "I have to tell you something. I have been sick and have a tumor."

Her words snatched my breath away. My baby sister, the master of understatement, was telling me that I could lose her.

Teresa's tumor had begun behind her left eye then gnawed its way into the bones on the left side of her skull. Extensive tests had been run, and a surgery date was set. Now it was time for the family to pull together to care for her. My shift began immediately following her operation.

On the flight east, memories of our lives and the closeness we had shared flooded my thoughts. Through my tears I wrote on a Delta Airline napkin:

Raw fear.
What will I do if I lose her?
My sister,
My friend,
My hero,
My support,
The little one in red pants,
And wooden shoes (on the wrong feet).
Straight thin hair,
The pretty one, tall and willowy,

Possessor of the beauty I wish for.
My equestrian partner, riding double,
Sharing, laughing, crying, living,
Always willing to play the bad guy,
If only she could play.
The one whose opinion is so powerful,
She kept me putting one foot in front of the other,
With a smile.
I believed her praise of me,
Her disappointment could burn deeper than any.
My little sister,
Beautiful, strong, and smart,
Rising triumphant from the ashes of our past.

Craving the opportunity to be near her, I tiptoed into Teresa's hospital room. I observed her for a moment before she became aware of my presence. Thick bandages covered her eye and encircled her head. When she turned toward me, she smiled and held out her hand. I grabbed hold. I couldn't let go. With that one gesture, everything that mattered erased everything that didn't. I had my baby sister back, and she had me.

A week later, in the surgeon's office, I held Teresa's hand again while the nurse prepared to remove the stitches. She peeled off the bandages, exposing an incision that traveled from ear to ear and looked like a strand of barbed wire attached to her partially shaved head. A separate line branched under her eye. I cried quietly as I watched Teresa grimace with the pull on each thread. Because her eye remained swollen shut, the doctors were unable to predict whether she would see out of it.

When we returned to Teresa's home, she slept. It was the sleep of total exhaustion, the chance for her physical healing to begin. It was also the moment that triggered emotional healing for me. When she awoke, we talked. I told Teresa about Elyssa, about why she seemed like a part of us, and how she loved the farm and the horses.

A year later, I had the honor of introducing Teresa, the treasure of my past, to Elyssa, the treasure of my future. Teresa knelt down to meet Elyssa at her level. They inspected each other carefully. The seriousness of their greeting confirmed my impression of the similarities between them—Elyssa was Teresa's childhood. They shared the same diminutive body, small features, wild hair, and intense countenance. Notably, Elyssa lacked red stretch pants, but Teresa's tenacity, confidence, and bullheadedness were sufficiently prepotent to resurface in a generation twice removed. Neither would quit when the going got tough.

Teresa once dedicated hours trying to save an Amish farmer's horse that was no longer able to stand. The animal had already experienced days of muscle spasms that were severe enough to prevent its eating or drinking. Within moments of examining the creature, Teresa confirmed that the horse was infected with tetanus. The farmer had delayed calling a vet for so long that the situation was hopeless. Still, Teresa used every possible medical intervention to revive the gelding. Exhausted, she finally admitted to herself that the horse would need to be euthanized and she informed the farmer. He refused because the drugs were too expensive—if death was inevitable, the horse would have to die on his own. Teresa insisted, but the farmer again refused the humane solution to the horse's suffering.

When veterinary argument proved fruitless, Teresa stood up, and rising taller than her height, put her hands on her hips to lecture at a higher level. "If you do not put this horse to sleep, you are not a Christian man. The Lord would never accept your allowing His creature to suffer."

Startled but humbled, the farmer relented. My sister knelt back down. Gently and reverently she injected the animal with its final peace.

When it came to farm matters, Elyssa's outlook was the same. She knew that she knew best. She could barely walk, not even two years old, when she determined that the time had come to master the pitchfork. For more than a half-hour, she fought with a tool that stood three times her height. She grasped the handle halfway up, pushed the tongs into a small clump of manure, leaned back and hefted, only to have the targeted horse apple drop off midway to the muck bucket. Time after time, she repeated this process but the lever arm of the fork was too long for her to control. Instinctively, my hand reached out to help. Although she could not talk, Elyssa's stare made it clear that this was her battle. I was to remain nearby for moral support.

Mercifully, halfway to the bucket became such a short distance that when the clump of manure again dropped off, it fell into the bucket. Elyssa turned and looked at me, I clapped with relief, and off she walked. It struck me that I was the one with the huge smile. It would take more than a well-placed horse apple to erase the determination that still burned in Elyssa's countenance.

It is unclear whether Elyssa loves farm work for its own sake or because of its association with the horses. No doubt, however, the love of horses runs in her blood. She has demanded to ride ever since she figured out how to express her desires.

We have a pre-ride routine of gearing Elyssa up with proper footwear and a protective helmet. The boots were a bonus from my daughter's trip to Australia. Apparently, Outback kids ride early in life because miniature riding boots are readily available there. Elyssa's helmet is not the official black velvet variety of the horse show ring, but rather her half-sister's cast-off, pink biking helmet, which drops so far over Elyssa's tiny head that she has to tilt the hat to one side so that at least one eye shows when she sits astride a horse. Originally, Elyssa was satisfied to pet and hug her mount, cluck to him until he walked a few steps, then hug him again as she ordered me, "Down."

Once she dropped into my arms, she opened and closed a fist and said, "Bye-bye" to her equine pal.

Now she rides in front of me and relishes the rhythm of all the horse's gaits. She is fully confident that the horse is responding to her own, barely audible, barely intelligible commands to walk, trot, and canter.

Each day that Elyssa spends at the farm, she raids my refrigerator for carrots and apples to take to the horses. She can carry a good dozen carrots as she makes the rounds of the farm, and this is quite a feat. Her arms just barely encircle her bundle, the carrot tips ride under her chin, and the leafy carrot tops brush her knees. Progress is slow but steady. She has to set her load down as she feeds each animal its treat. Her favorites get several carrots. When my time is short, I'm tempted to cut the ritual short, but Elyssa refuses. Every horse must have its carrot, be called by name, and told good-night. She's like the postman—neither rain nor sleet nor snow will keep her from her appointed rounds. And she knows the exact spot for delivering the treat to each of the sixteen horses on her delivery route.

One carrot at a time Elyssa is turning the farm into a "dwelling place of happy souls." Still, I worry about her. It is not so easy to grow up these days, even under the best of circumstances, and hers are far from the best.

It has become a harsh reality for me that both my son, and Elyssa's Mother are deeply involved in pain pill addiction, as well as other drug use, and that Elyssa is living in a situation I cannot make sense of and cannot fix. I am used to digging in and working hard to fix problems, I vow to work hard to keep this child protected and safe. It is hard for me to accept that my hands are tied.

There are times when I have wanted to run away with Elyssa, to somehow ensure her the happy-ever-after life about which I always dreamed.

What I will do though, is make sure I am around, make sure she knows I love her and that I will be there for her. No matter what.

To Elyssa

Ominous sadness engulfs me.
How can my hands be so tightly tied?
I am helpless to affect your life,
In the way I believe is needed.

If only I could rescue you,
I am torn as I watch from a distance,
The insignificance attached to your life,
You, who are more than precious.

Your value is as a pawn,
In the selfishness of those not ready to parent,
What will it take to release you,
Into the arms of a waiting life?

No Matter What

"No matter what" came rushing headlong into my reality. I could not deny that Elyssa was in the care of a serious addict and that reasoning with an addict was just not possible. She was not safe. Her mother's drug use continued unbridled and my son, her dad was in California. I was glad he was away as I was hopeful the separation from his drug addict friends would help him to overcome his own problems.

Elyssa's diet consisted mostly of chocolate milk (which was often spilled and soured on her clothes and bed), and Top Ramen. She was often dirty and unkempt. I picked her up and spent as much time as I could with her but eventually, her mother refused to allow me to see her unless I was willing to pay.

In our town, along one of the main streets downtown is an overhead billboard. The billboard beckons passing motorists and pedestrians with the sad face and imploring eyes of a young child. The 800 number invites anyone with knowledge of child abuse or neglect to call. "It's the law."

Well, I am here to tell you that they do not want you to call, and they certainly do not want you to keep calling. They do not welcome the interruption those calls and concerns bring to their set routine. Oh, they are very polite at first and thank you for being a concerned and caring citizen. They were not, however, prepared or grateful for the concern of this grandmother.

I vowed to do something every day to rescue my granddaughter. I kept that promise. It took a year. A year of phone calls to the police, to the strike force (a division of the police who deal with the drug scene). A year of having officers tell me there was nothing they could do and to back off because my story was just one of hundreds they deal with. A year of calls to find out where my granddaughter, her mother, and whatever current boyfriend were living. They moved from one location to another, avoiding rent payments, bill collectors, drug dealers the law, and me. Always the tales from landlords were dismal, stories of many men sleeping on the floor with my tiny granddaughter in a corner, stories of drugs overshadowing the love of a mother for her child.

I called my son and told him things were bad and he needed to come home and help fight for custody. We continued the daily calls, rejection, etc. Nothing seemed to be moving in the direction to bring Elyssa to safety so I called the family services division as I thought they might have more clout on Elyssa's behalf. I was wrong. It seems a drug-addicted, neglectful parent has many more rights than an innocent victim of drugs.

The family I worked for on the farm assisted me many times over to help in my efforts including the initial attempts to prosecute Elyssa's mother and remove Elyssa from her care. They were there for me to confide in and provided a safe haven for me as I struggled with my new reality, one I could not comprehend.

Our school police officer went to Elyssa's various known locations to search for any evidence that could aid us in our endeavor. My friend and riding student, also a police officer, was vigilant in his support of me and provided me with names and numbers of those on the force to call. I called and called again. All to no avail.

I finally bit the bullet of pride and asked my sister, Teresa and her husband for help. They did agree to help me though I was sure that what they really wanted to tell me was, "I told you so." But they cared for Elyssa and desperately wanted her to be safe. I was so grateful but, in the end, I paid a heavy personal price for that call for help.

I had been so proud of my son and his determination to help with this fight for his daughter's well-being. We worked together following through with attorney suggestions, writing reports and keeping a constant written log of events.

Drug addiction seems to be a thing that sneaks up on a person. Perhaps, that isn't how it is for the addict but for those who love addicts, it just seems to move slowly where at first you don't see it, then you hope it isn't true and then, you know it is and, before too long, my son was back into his addiction and the fight for Elyssa's safety belonged to myself and my sister who was 2500 miles away.

Finally, because of several calls both my sister and I made to the District Attorney here in Utah, Elyssa's hair was tested for exposure and she was removed. After just a small bit of red tape and a period of panic and angst, Elyssa came to live with me at the farm. Legally, all was very fragile and I was terrified of my son and his addiction as it could jeopardize what had come at such a cost.

My sister worried as well and didn't believe that I could protect Elyssa from the influences of her dad's addiction. She procured her own attorney and filed for custody. A litany of degrading and hurtful e-mails ensued from her husband, not only directly to me but also to my friends and family.

My complete sadness was unexplainable. I felt abandoned in a time when I needed my closest friend, my sister. Now on top of all my worries for my son and his child, I lost my sister. We didn't talk. At all. I mourned.

Seasons of Missing You

So much grief,
And seasons of missing you,
I ache for the loss of you every day.
The desire to set the world right again,
Is clouded by the fact that…,
I cannot dig deep enough,
Into the depths of my being,
To find the nobleness,
I imagined myself to possess,
And the ability to leave,
This righteous anger behind.
Even knowing better,
In this,
I do not know how,
To do or be better.
So though we may both arrive,
At the end of our days,
With this cancer between us,
I have and always will love you.

When the final court date arrived to grant custody, Teresa flew in and stayed at a hotel, arriving at the courthouse with her attorney in tow. Teresa was beautiful and impeccably dressed in a dark skirt, pastel blouse and light green scarf draped perfectly around and over her shoulders. Elyssa's maternal grandfather was there as well and had also expressed interest in gaining custody. I was granted custody.

Teresa's attorney asked that Teresa be allowed to spend time with Elyssa. We first went to McDonald's for lunch. Teresa then spent the afternoon with Elyssa at my home playing outside in the sand with scoops and trucks and plastic horses. Teresa then drove herself to the airport in her rented car. Tears made a trail down my cheeks as she made her way down my drive.

It is important for me to make it clear, just in case the writing of this creates the idea that it was simple to rescue this child—it was nothing of the sort. There were court dates, hearings, supervised visits that were not adhered to, tears, angst, you name it. I kept a log, I have proof. "They" do not want you to call.

Pieces of Peace

A strong hand to hold,
Elyssa's smile,
A friend's "How are you?"
"I love you." From my child.

A rainy day rainbow,
The beauty of Mother Earth.
My horses running to greet me,
Pieces of peace.

Not "Happily Ever After,"
But for a moment,
Peace.

I suppose, we all have fantasies. Besides dreaming of Prince Charming, I also fantasized about buying back Milky Way Farm, but no such place exists anymore except in my heart. I dream of having my own small farm with a small horse barn, but at this time, for now, the farm where I lived was Elyssa's Milky Way Farm—all my hard work was her delight. Everyone who came there knew her, all the horses knew her. Beyond the perimeter fence, there are creeks and marshes she can explore someday. All that I so loved seems to be in her grasp.

Soon after Elyssa came to live at the farm new pony also arrived. Crystal was a thirty-year-old Welsh pony, long ago bleached white with age. In horse terms, Crystal measures twelve hands. In human terms, she was very, very small, but in little-kid terms, the height of her swayed back created the perfect arch, a comfortably safe distance from Mother Earth.

Crystal had been good and kind to her original owner for more than a quarter of a century, but now that her teeth were gone, she could no longer chew meadow grass or hay. Crystal had been retired at the farm in order to give and receive tender loving care.

Elyssa seemed to understand this bargain implicitly. As she scooted under the fence into Crystal's pen, she greeted the pony tenderly, "It's all right, Crystal, it's just me, Elyssa."

Elyssa carried with her a plastic cooking spoon with which she stirred the pony's mash. Then she served dinner to Crystal, one spoonful at a time. In exchange, Crystal stood patiently for Elyssa's grooming rituals—never complaining when the tar-based hoof moisturizer splattered and stained her furry, white legs.

Crystal and Elyssa

Under the moon, a late-night ride,
Set to the sweet music of you.
Singing, "Twinkle, Twinkle, Little Star"
You and the pony rode in the dark.

I had one arm around you,
The other held the rope.
Crystal's feet were sure,
Her eyes wise from many such children's rides.

You rode round and round the farm,
Calling out the name of every horse as we passed,
"Hi, Tribute and Angel, I'm riding Crystal."
Trot, Crystal, trot slow—Elyssa doesn't want to fall.

My daughter, Anna is the typical Northeastern college girl. She pulls her hair back in a long braid and wears baggy shirts and sandals. In some ways, she reminds me of me, but there is something steadier, stronger, and more self-assured about her. Anna's quiet and steady presence brings companionship and joy to my routine.

Perhaps it is our young horses that benefit most from Anna. She helps me "start" them, not break them, but rather teach them how to accept a rider and allow the loss of their free will without rancor.

Our method is the slow method. It requires hours of ground-work and heaps of patience. In each session, we seek a few steps of progress and laugh together at the inevitable problems. Our equine babies come to accept correction without feeling unjustly punished. They sense the joy between us, the aura of goodwill. They respond with trust.

Together, in this manner, Anna and I started Tribute, our two-year-old orphan baby. After hours of walking beside him while I sat quietly on his back, Anna began moving farther away to wean him from her presence. But Tribute wanted the security, his eyes constantly sought Anna, his energy tilted in her direction. I would swear I could hear him sigh with relief when she returned to his side and stroke his muzzle.

Tribute is the offspring of Astrolabe's father and a mare I had previously raised. I had purchased his mother, a stately, grey thoroughbred, which we named, Dare to Deviate, when she was just a weanling. We had trained her then sold her as a four-year-old eventing prospect. A couple of years later Deviate developed melanomas—a form of cancer that plagues grey horses. Her tumors metastasized much faster and grew far larger than usual. When unsightly lumps on her neck and face ended her show career, her owners offered to give her back to me rather than destroy her. Our veterinarian agreed that it would be possible to breed her in order to extend her useful life.

Deviate experienced an uneventful pregnancy. As she came to term, she didn't seem particularly large, but I could see the baby kicking and wasn't concerned because she was a maiden mare.

By the time the foal was due, Anna had been home for a couple of weeks of her summer vacation. She and I took turns getting up every two hours to check the mare. On Anna's watch in the pre-dawn hours, labor began. Anna woke me, and we ran to the barn together.

The foal's presentation appeared normal, front feet first. But as the baby's head came through the birth canal, we saw the first sign of a problem. Its head was misshapen, like it had been unnaturally compressed and then swelled so that its forehead protruded unnaturally. The mare's labor bogged down, and I called the vet. Anna and I worked along with Deviate. We wrapped towels around the baby's slippery, wet front legs so that we could maintain a grip as we pulled downward toward the mare's hocks.

Progress required more than our combined strength. We timed our efforts with Deviate's contractions until her contributions ceased. Then we redoubled our efforts to compensate for the mare's exhaustion. My daughter, normally quiet under stressful circumstances, stopped periodically and looked directly at me. Either to comfort me or herself, she repeatedly assured, "Everything's going to be okay."

I knew it was not okay. There was too much blood. When the colt finally delivered, he was too small. The placenta was complete but malformed, too thin to have provided appropriate nutrition.

Anna sat by Deviate's head and hand-fed her bits of hay or handfuls of water. In an attempt to cool her, Anna stroked the mare's neck with damp rags to wipe off the endless sweat. For the most part, Deviate responded quietly. Then her baby would whinny and set her off and Deviate would struggle to get up. Our hearts would break as her legs trembled and buckled, unable to support her weight. She crashed against the stall walls then fell back with a thud. We did our best to titrate her suffering with pain medication.

Deviate called to her baby who was desperate for her attention. He would scramble to his feet and careen around her. His tiny muzzle constantly sought her, touching her leg, her neck, her head. But no amount of maternal instinct was going to save her or even allow her son the first all-important drink of colostrum that would provide him the antibodies to survive all the diseases to which his mother had developed immunities. As the hours passed, the baby grew more and more frantic for food. He licked the stall walls and sucked our fingers. We did our best to milk the mare during her quiet moments. We filled a rubber glove and emptied the milk into his mouth.

Hours later, we accepted the inevitable. I emptied the bottle of painkiller into a syringe and injected it. Deviate rested her head in the straw and died.

I suppose it was fortunate that the baby so desperately needed help. I cradled him in my arms while Anna headed to a neighbor's farm to procure a milk goat. But getting the milk from the goat's udder into the foal's mouth proved a daunting task. The goat cooperated far better than the baby. When he flatly refused the standard livestock bottle, we resorted to a child's bottle. The foal would have nothing to do with the new, flat-topped, natural nipple designed to prevent later orthodontic problems. He finally accepted an old-fashioned nipple, in fact, he insisted on it.

Within hours of accepting the first bottle, he followed us everywhere. Still unsure that the earth would remain beneath him, he shuffled along on his spindly legs, nickering for milk. Every two hours, round the clock, we fed him.

The next night, a friend located a nurse mare for us. Exhausted, Anna and I agreed that it was the best news we had ever heard. Betty arrived at the farm with another orphan already at her side. Gently and with angelic patience, she demonstrated that she was willing to adopt a second foal.

We named our colt Daring Tribute in honor of his mother. When Tribute met Betty, he wasted no time in discarding the baby bottle for a real mother's nipple. But in those first critical hours of his life, Tribute had imprinted on Anna and me and would forever seek our company and find comfort in our presence.

Tribute remained the spoiled sweetheart of the farm throughout that spring and summer. Tribute galloped to meet everyone who came to his pen and followed them around, both relishing and demanding attention. He loved to have me sit with my legs under his head as he slept. I savored those moments as well, stroking his head and neck while his eyelids fluttered open and closed.

In our front pasture Astrolabe's full sister, Astrolabe's Angel, lives with Tribute. Angel is a two-year-old now. She is as classically beautiful as she is gentle. I have seen cars slow down as they drove by her pasture so the driver could get a better look at her.

I have just started riding Angel, and true to her nature, she has been a delight. Each step of her training has been textbook perfect. With the introduction of each new step, she has accepted and complied with a trust of me that is inspiring.

Angel

Little baby sister,
Into the world in the cold.
I pulled you out and dried you with wool,
Your curly, baby, equine coat.

Not a speck of white,
A peaceful girl.
Hard to come here to take brother's place,
Tough to make your way.

Your peaceful ways—always good,
A touch of mischief too.

Quiet and beautiful girl,
You eased into my heart,
Created your own bit of space.

You just let love happen,
Knowing that it would.
Little angel baby,
I love you.

As I ride my two young horses and spend time with the newest addition, Wings for Astrolabe, I am filled with a sense of pride and gratitude. These marvelous animals give me a true sense of peace in a world that often doesn't feel peaceful at all. I recently swelled with pride as I rode Tribute. He trotted, cantered, and jumped small jumps in a balanced and confident manner. I thought to myself, *You did all this yourself.* My next thoughts were more grounded:

I Trained Him Myself

I held you as you took your first breath,
And dried your newborn wetness,
As you lay on the golden straw.
Now you carry me with strength and grace,
—Obedient and strong.

I think as I swell with pride,
I raised and trained you myself.
My second thought—No,
I cannot take all the credit.

A host of others came before—a package deal
Equine teachers: Flicka, Dusty, Banjo
Books read and reread,
Instructors and teachers, too many to name.

What I have is an appreciation of the present that honors my past, honors the fact that experience has made me strong enough to deal with the future without a guarantee that all will be well. This inner strength has allowed me to let go of the dream of happily-ever-after in leu of the reality that happiness is a fleeting thing. At the same time, I realize that happiness would lose its value if it endured forever.

The fantasies are gone; or rather they are incorporated into the texture of my life along with the realities—my real world and the tool that I have with which to mold that world—me, me and the ripples I send out into the ocean of life.

There Is No Universe Big Enough to Hold This Loss

I watched an episode of M*A*S*H once where an injured young soldier's blood work caused solemn looks and uncustomary silence between BJ and Hawkeye. No jokes, no sarcasm, no smile. Hawkeye told BJ the only thing they could do for the kid was to patch him up and send him home to die. The boy had leukemia. In the '50s there was no treatment, no cure.

In May, 2007, my brother called and asked if I was where I could sit down. Fear shot through me-starting in my gut and bursting outward. Something was very wrong.

Teresa had leukemia. My only frame of reference was that episode of M*A*S*H. The world should have stopped. Mine did. My world stood still. There was nothing that was upright and there was not enough room in the universe to hold my sense of terror and sadness.

My Baby Sister Has Leukemia

The news declares a wreck on I-15,
A three-alarm fire and an impending storm,
An Amber Alert shows a missing child,
And my baby sister has leukemia.

My daughter wants help with training a horse,
My granddaughter needs a bedtime story,
And hugs and kisses and tucked into bed,
And my baby sister has leukemia.

There are bills to pay and chores to do,
I move as fast as I can but still can't keep up,
So many hats I must wear to make life work,
And my baby sister has leukemia.

So…the pace of life screeches to a halt,
Soon, however, heartbreak fuels action,
I lay myself down for a bone tissue test,
And my baby sister has leukemia.

Once I recovered from the initial shock, I spoke to Teresa and vowed to do whatever was needed or wanted for her to be okay, and to get through this. We are strong, we come from a strong family-yes, and stubborn too. In the long night that followed, I realized some things. I became very present to the fact that contained within in the initial silence, the pregnant pauses and the brief words between us, was the fact that the pain and hurt of our disagreements had fallen away. They were as nothing. They no longer mattered. I loved my sister far more than the hurt of her good intentions had caused me. These words reflect some of my ponderings:

Bygones

How does one let bygones be bygones?
How is it possible to let go of personal hurt and pride,
And put behind them the pain of personal hurt?
How does one release how important they think they are?

I don't see this as such an issue,
With casual friendships or superficial acquaintances,
But when love has bound the spirits of the two,
As in friendship, family or lovers, the connections and pain run deeper.

But… I think, perhaps, that,
Truly the very love that made the emotional pain so deep,
Is the same love that gives one the ability to just let go,
Leaving all the personal baggage behind…

To love, just love, letting bygones truly become bygones.

My vocabulary soon included words like; neutropenic, neutrophils, LMS, chemo, pic-line, transfusion, bone marrow, platelets, red and white blood counts, etc. Teresa and I spoke almost daily. Our love and her fight for life superseded any need to discuss the past. On the days she was too ill, I left messages. And I ached; for both of us.

Elyssa, such a bright and happy being, rose to the occasion as children do, and drew pictures for her great aunt and spoke of her getting better. I sent Teresa a pair of lucky underpants. Elyssa sent her a "lucky" rock. Elyssa was sure the rock would bring healing as it still had her love on it. Teresa was sure too.

Most Important Letter

Hand in hand we walk,
A newly addressed, crayon-adorned envelope,
Clutched in her tiny five-year-old hand.
To the post office, we go, the most important letter to mail.

Over an hour she has spent,
Coloring, spelling, cutting, and pasting.
Her positive nature and innocence,
Are incorporated and shine through each piece of work.

"Aunt Teresa is getting better,"
'Cause I send her stories, pictures, and letters, and games.
And, I even sent a special rock,
Purple, her favorite color.

She's Holding My Hand

Just days after receiving her lucky rock,
She returned home from her hospital room.
After fifty-three days to hell and back,
With her arm 'round the strength of her husband,
She slowly walked from one stall to the next.
She cooed softly and spoke to the gentle mares,
Stroking each velvet muzzle, scratching an ear,
So grateful to touch again,
The precious pieces of her life.

Hearing that she was home, her grandniece cheered,
"I knew it," She shouted, "My lucky rock worked!"
"I knew it would, 'cause when I first sent it,
My love was still on it,
And it went into her and made her get well.
So now, she told me, when she holds her rock,
She feels that she and I,
Are holding each other's hands."

A passive participant in this tale,
I am moved by the innocence,

And the healing power,
Of the pure love and faith of a child.

After months of treatments which included transfusions, and chemo, Teresa had a severe reaction to the blood in a transfusion. We almost lost her. My bags were packed and a plane ticket was purchased. Ready to go, I received a phone call. Teresa was out of the woods. The best news was, however, that she was also in remission and could soon go home. At Teresa's request, I postponed my trip so that I could come later in the spring when Elyssa and I were done with school and our family would be getting together for my brother's daughter's wedding.

A shadow of her former self and leaning on our brother, Teresa slowly walked from stall to stall with a, "Hi there," and a pat on the nose for each of her beloved horses. Our brother lived fairly close to Teresa, closer, at least than my 2500 miles or our older sister's 3000. It was so hard to not be by her side but such a comfort to know that he was there and to have him send updates.

He was with Teresa in her hospital room many nights and most weekends while he continued in his studies to become an attorney. Our brother is a hero. I am including here his e-mail communications to friends and family:

7/06/07
Good morning everyone!

This week Teresa had a bit of a breakthrough and some good bone marrow news!
First, the second round of chemo did its job. It totally wiped out her bone marrow…it sounds bad…but it is what needed to happen. It did such a thorough job that a couple of bugs came along and set her back a bit. She has pneumonia and a GI bug, both of which are under treatment. It was a rough week but the news about the bone marrow came on the same day that she began feeling markedly better! After about six days in bed, she began to get up and start her walking again… (It sounds like I am talking about my 90-year-old grandmother… But this is my little sister! An active vibrant equine vegetarian, I mean vegranarian, well, anyway, she is a horse doctor.) She made two rounds around the department (17 is one mile), the next day, she doubled that, and on the 4th Beth-Anne, Matthew and I took her outside for the first time in over a week. It was glorious for her to see the trees, the flowers, and the critters all going about their tasks. One of her favorite trees on our walk is a magnificent southern magnolia. The blossoms are so beautiful and fragrant and it was just what the doctor ordered. I wheeled her up to the path that we normally walk on and she walked one whole round on my arm… Beth-Anne and Matthew brought up the rear with the wheelchair…it was quite a sight. We said hi to the squirrels, the turtles, the ducks, the little dove, and sparrows…and then, it started to rain on us! We were in no hurry to get back as a summer rain can be good for the soul.

Daily, she is up and down. She still has a recurring fever and until that subsides she will remain in the hospital. As soon as she can get that licked she will be able to go home.

Again, I thank you all for your support, love, and prayers.

Ted
8/20/07

Just a quick note to everyone that Teresa got great news last week (many of you may already know) but she is in full remission. I am not sure what the next steps are, but I believe she will go back in for more chemo next month. More later… Wow! Thank you all so very much for your cards, concerns, thoughts, and prayers!

Ted
3/17/08
Good morning everyone,

Spring is in the air and we have so much to be thankful for (sounds like Thanksgiving), but especially the fact that Teresa is finished with Chemo, her bloodwork looks great, they checked her bone marrow and she is in remission!

The next step(s)…after Easter, they will harvest some bone marrow and freeze it just in case they ever need to do a bone marrow transplant sometime in the future…(Hmmm how does that work? Do they put it in a ziplock bag and have you take it home with you?—probably not.) I knew that you would all want to know the great news. It has been a long haul with lots of challenges and I can tell you that your thoughts and prayers helped to carry her to this point.
Thank you, from the bottom of my heart.

Ted

And then after passing through the "Valley of The Shadow," my sister came through. In remission now she could return home. I canceled a flight I had booked earlier, on her request and planned a later visit with Elyssa in the summer when we would all, as a family be together at my niece's wedding.

What a visit it was! Elyssa and I enjoyed the farm and Teresa's horses, we picked wild berries, played games, and went to see the Statue of Liberty. Teresa tired easily but loved life and living I reveled in being with Teresa and in seeing her joy in spending time with this child she so loved.

The wedding and being with family was glorious. We were all there, all four of us siblings, our half-brother, mom, and dad. Both of them!

My sister glowed with the happiness and beauty of it all. It was an event without equal. As A bystander I was acutely aware of the relationships and interworking of all these people that I so loved: My brother and his beautiful daughter as he clasped a simple necklace around her neck, his ex-wife and how I loved her and valued her friendship, my dad, the family patriarch as he used a cane to walk down the aisle alone, Elyssa sitting with Teresa wanting cake but behaving through the ceremony in spite of it and Teresa and I sitting side-by-side going through Kleenex blubbering away as the bride and groom washed one another's feet in a gesture of humility and took their vows. It was a perfect day, and then…we had cake.

Healing Tears

Such deep pain from so many years,
Ran in the tracks of our tears as they flowed,
Down from brimming eyes and over our cheeks,
And into the crumpled and shredded pieces of Kleenex
In my and my sister's palms.

And so much garbage fell away,
In the falling tears of so many,
As my father, the patriarch of our family,
Walked down the aisle of the church alone,
To the seats reserved for the grandparents.

He was frail and leaning heavily on his cane,
He sat in a pew all alone, In front of my mother.
But from his being shone so much pride,
In who we all had become,
And that all of us were together here,
In one place, at the very same time.

And tears of joy replaced those of pain,
As my brother walked with his child on his arm,
Angry words were forgotten, divorces and battles irrelevant,
As the service declared the purest of love,
Love more binding than any past ire,
That of God for his children and them for one another.

Back home, life settled into a busy routine of summer which included irrigating the pastures, gardening, caring for and riding the horses and then in the fall back to school for Elyssa (she was tested and would now be in the Accelerated Learning Academy). She was doing so well. I was relieved and proud. For me, it was back to teaching school and teaching lots of riding lessons.

Anna was now home from university. She was not enjoying the amount of work the farm entailed and voiced her opinion one day to the farrier who did all the horses' shoes at the farm. Unbeknownst to me, he shared this information with the folks who owned the farm and they took it that I didn't want to be there. I was given three months to move.

I was paralyzed. I just sat. What was happening to me was unbelievable. These were people I cared about and I thought they cared about me. I thought we were friends. I thought it was mutual. Silly me. I had nowhere to go and no means with which to get there. I could see no possibilities through my depression.

So for the first week, I dragged myself out of bed, did the farm chores, then dragged myself through the school day, and back home again for evening chores. I felt like I had been rung through a ringer and finally squeezed out the other side only to get wrapped around again and again.

But I had a child to raise, my daughter depending on me and a small herd of horses to care for. School was soon out for summer and Anna had been looking at places on various websites. I mustered up some courage, swallowed some pride and got in touch with my mom about the situation.

My mother really came through for me and on the very last day before the deadline, we moved onto a sweet little farm sixty-five miles away. This farm had been built in the early nineteen hundreds. The barn was a big old dairy barn and the house a quaint little Victorian. Elyssa was so excited and rode her bike around checking out the sheep next door, the tree swing and the outbuildings in the property. The horses all had room and pasture. My mother owned it, for now.

I purchased a sledgehammer, a saw, a good hammer and lots of nails. I spent hours breaking the concrete which had formed the stanchions for the cattle. We offered the steel pipes to anyone who would remove it and had junk hauled away. I built six stalls for the horses. They were beautiful! I also revisited my posthole digging expertise and put up new and safer horse fences as the previous fences were barbed wire that was probably close to 80 years old. The following summer, Mom and her husband came up and helped put in a riding arena and re-wire the barn. I had helped them find a couple of good and safe riding horses here for them to take back home.

After making payments on my home for three years, I re-financed and it became mine. It is home.

Elyssa and I returned to school in the fall. I now had over an hour each way to drive. After finding the best potty stops, they were a time to talk, listen to music, call Teresa, play games and giggle.

Leukemia also returned with the fall:

11/22/2008
Good afternoon all:
Today begins the next chapter in Teresa's fight with Leukemia. She is slated for a bone marrow transplant next Friday. So here is what will happen between now and then.
Today and tomorrow she will receive extremely potent doses of chemotherapy. That will be followed by three days of full-body radiation. The goal here is to absolutely wipe out as much of her own marrow (blood-producing tissue) as possible.

On Wednesday, a complete stranger will voluntarily go under anesthesia and have bone marrow extracted from multiple places on his body. The marrow will be prepped and flown to Philadelphia where it will be prepared for transplantation into Teresa. Now, this is amazing but Teresa will receive the transplant in the same way that she received a blood transfusion, intravenously! At that point, the new cells will find their place in Teresa's bones and start to do their thing. Teresa will receive anti-rejection, in addition to a myriad of other medications. For a period of several weeks, she will basically be living in a bubble (not literally) and will be completely exhausted. So much so that a trip to the bathroom will be exhausting. She will stay in the hospital for 4-5 weeks as she recovers. When she is healthy enough will then go home and have to live in an ultra-clean environment for a period of time until her body recovers.
Teresa is strong and determined. So is this leukemia. Her spirits are lifted by the love of her friends and the unbelievable selfless gift of a total stranger in another country.
I thought everyone would want to know and as always we are grateful for everyone's thoughts and prayers.
It is here that I want to pay homage to my brother and his endless hours spent loving and being by Teresa's side as well as dealing with the mixed emotions of the family.

Our Brother

A cool afternoon after a long-awaited night of rain,
Upon my sweet filly Angel, I rode along the path,
My spirit felt refreshed and thoughts flowed in and out,
As I trotted along, I received a call.
My dear brother on the line, going through so much,
Keeping the faith and lately, keeping peace,
With what you now bear, such a gentle and true soul,
You honor my love for our sister.

For the thousands of miles between us,
Which separate me from her,
You are the one who does what I long to,
Sitting by her side and holding her hand.

You've not any expectations,
A comfort and peacekeeper I know you are,
Thanks to you, from the bottom of my heart,
Our dear brother, so gentle and true.

A miracle occurred which seemed to coincide with Teresa's illness and my desire to be with her. Elyssa's mother successfully (after two and a half years in various treatment facilities and a halfway house) earned temporary custody of Elyssa. I am here to tell you, that was difficult at best. I was prepared to raise Elyssa as my own. Elyssa, however, was desperate for her mother.

Elyssa spent more and more time with her mom while I continued to transport her to school, have her for most weekends and help with homework at her mom's each day after school. Elyssa was a happy daughter and I was able to gradually shift roles to being grandma.

I began being able to plan to be away from home and with my sister as she continued her stays and treatments in the hospital. I wanted nothing more than to be with her though I was torn with all I had going on at home. The daily phone calls just weren't enough for all she was enduring.

On top of all else, my beloved sons were continuing down the road of drug addiction and both ended up in jail. "Too much", you say.

"You have no idea."

There were many times that I was with Teresa in the hospital back in Pennsylvania when I would receive a collect call from one or the other of my boys. I did not want to share any of this with Teresa. I didn't want to add any more burden or worry to her-she was already worried about her nephews so I would step out. I wanted desperately to have someone to talk to but was terrified at them knowing my shame. I wrote letters to judges, put hard-earned money in their accounts and attempted to get through it.

Teresa's treatments were brutal. First was the radiation, full-body, to completely destroy her own bone marrow. Teresa was terrified and so alone during these treatments. No one could be there and with her medical education, she was all too aware of the powerful damage that was possible to the rest of her body that would accompany the destruction of the cells that seemed determined to kill her.

The radiation was followed by the bone-marrow transplant, then the endless waiting to see if her body would respond positively or reject the transplant. While we waited for a miracle, there were transfusions of blood, of platelets, antibiotics for infections, medications for nausea, and constant fear of infections to be dealt with.

None of this comes close to the sadness, fear, and despair she, as well as all who loved her experience. On the other side of the coin, none of this comes close to the amazing displays of the best of humanity displayed by Teresa and by so many of the staff at the "Rhoads" wing of the University of Pennsylvania Hospital. Many of the nurses took special care to accommodate my sister's needs as well as the needs of those of us civilians who spent many hours, including nights, at their facility with their patients. I think we all knew the combination to the linen closet and were known by our first names by most.

In one such event, a hospital housekeeper who was particularly cheerful had a birthday coming up. Teresa caught wind of this and had her husband pick up a cake for her. This wonderful woman who wore decorated and colorful socks just to cheer the patients, cried-right there-tears running down her face. She said she had never had a birthday cake, imagine that!

After what seemed like far too many days, Teresa's counts began to rise. The transplant was indeed successful and so began Teresa's long road to recovery. Teresa had a small but lovely new apartment above her state-of-the-art horse barn. It was newly built and could be completely cut off from everything. With the medical staff's approval, Teresa was allowed to live there as her 300-year-old farmhouse was not sterile enough. She was so medically fragile that it was scary. At Christmas, she went home. That had been her goal. Her husband put a beautiful blue spruce outside the apartment window and decorated it with lights. It was a beautiful and tender gesture of love.

On the last day of January, 2009, Teresa called me. She said she had bad news and I feared the worst. She quickly said, "It's not me, I am fine. It's dad. He passed away last night in his sleep."

Dad had been incredibly important as Teresa fought for her life. She was far too vulnerable and weak to travel. She felt that perhaps it was a sign that Dad knew she would be okay and that he could go. We would take her with us in our hearts to our father's funeral.

So I traveled to Colorado where my father's wife, my half-brother, oldest sister and my brother and his children met with a couple hundred others to share memories and pay tribute to the man who raised me. I was proud to be his daughter. I was proud of the man my father was. I was proud of the relationship we had. I felt the loss deeply.

Later that year, in August, all of us siblings traveled east that August. We drove to our childhood home in Vermont to spread some of dad's ashes at the base of an ancient maple tree. I am sure we had tapped that tree for sap for many springs. Sure enough, there under the lowest branches was a rusty old sap bucket.

In A Childhood She Doesn't Remember

She took his ashes in her hand,
Made a fist and upon kissing it, said,
"Bye, Dad, I love you."
She then slowly relaxed her hand,
Letting him sift gently through her fingers.

So he is there 'neath the great old maple,
Where he himself had once gathered sap,
O'er many a spring in the days of his youth,
In childhood, she doesn't remember.

We then drove to Connecticut and had a small ceremony in his home town in Connecticut where Teresa was presented with a flag and the rest of his ashes were buried beside his mother.

Back at Teresa's farm, under the cover of a massive tent, as the fireflies dotted the grass and the horses grazed in the warm August dusk, live music bounced off the trees, sunflower centerpieces adorned the tables and incredible food was offered and we danced. Teresa danced. Her doctors and nurses were there and her family. Her best friend was there with her brand new baby daughter who was named after Teresa. She wore a beautiful ensemble with the skirt pinned up to accommodate the weight she had shed but she glowed and she danced. We all danced, and laughed and cried with relief at Teresa's life. It was glorious-a perfect day.

I went home wrapped in the glow of that evening. I returned to a new year of teaching school. Teresa returned to caring for her horses and planning for the new foals who would be arriving the following spring.

My daughter continually looks on-line for horses who need rescuing. In October she came across an incredibly well-bred Thoroughbred mare. Teresa was impressed and felt that the mare would be a great asset to her herd of brood-mares. She, in turn, had a mare that had not raced well and was difficult as a brood-mare. I figured I could re-train her for eventing. We decided to trade. Anna and I would drive the new horseback to Pennsylvania at Thanksgiving when I had a short break from school. Teresa would then travel back with us and the beautiful mare she was giving to us.

This trip was beyond amazing. Teresa was coming to MY home. We had so much fun on that drive. We marveled at the beauty of our country and we laughed so hard sometimes we had tears running down our cheeks.

We pulled into my little farm in the early afternoon. The weather which had been cold enough to freeze water in our absence was now beautiful and warm enough for just sweats. We settled the mare into her new home and with the sun shining down on us, my sister and I rode together again. We rode. It was a miracle. A miracle that I had kept in front of me for almost three years was unfolding in front of me. I wanted to turn cartwheels, jump up and down, scream, cry. We rode. Together.

And Me

Three days we journeyed mile after mile,
Across this county we so love,
Laughing, joking, playing twenty questions,
She, taking in the sights and beauty of each region,
Then awed at the beauty of the rugged west,
And me.

The sun shone down on this November day,
On she, my sister who had traveled,
Both a journey through hell fighting leukemia,
And now, in winning that war,

Has come to see my life,
And me.

We rode together this November day,
As adults, not as children as in days gone by.
She who a year ago had less,
Than a twenty per-cent chance,
Of living to see this day,
And me.

For the past year, I have looked to this day,
Three hundred and sixty-five days,
Every day thinking, saying, knowing,
That she could not leave me here,
'Cause we would surely ride together again,
She, my baby sister,
And me.

Her recovery had ups and downs, tears and laughter. Teresa had the awe-inspiring ability to see human miracles and needs all around her in spite of what she was dealing with. She often called to tell me of people in her life who moved and inspired her. One was a woman she met while at the hospital for treatment. They shared their lives as they received their respective doses of blood and chemo. In between little naps, they also managed to complete a crossword puzzle together. The woman had been a pediatrician who did a lot of work for underprivileged children overseas as well as here in the US. Teresa also shared stories of a pair of sisters who were working for her at the farm who were adding such joy to her life as they learned from her, the master horse-woman and equine veterinarian. She was happy to be contributing to others.

When Teresa got to the point where she was holding her own but just not thriving, the decision was made to remove her spleen. Following that surgery, her recovery took a huge forward thrust. She resumed her joy in the horses and her life. Every moment was a precious gift. She delivered the new foals in the spring, prepped the yearlings for sales and monitored the two and three-year-olds at the track. The mares were sent off and bred for the next year. Life was moving along. Sweet, blessed, comfortable life.

May, 2010. Leukemia's ugly self rises again. My hysterical sister is on the line and I, in immediate emotional shutdown knew it was bad, very bad news. We talked until she had calmed. I was terrified, she wanted to sell everything and give up. I told her it was important to keep life in front of her, to keep planning for the horses and her business. I felt she needed things to look forward to, a future to live for.

Then as we spoke, I got on the internet and found some treatments that were being done for others who shared similar circumstances. She calmed and began to talk of upcoming events that she was looking forward to including a James Taylor concert (she invited me) and the sale, in New York of one of her yearlings. Sure, it was bad but there were still some viable options. She was young and strong and, and she was my sister. And I needed her.

Teresa immediately began another litany of treatments to prepare her body for a second infusion of the donor bone marrow. In between, she attended the concert (I didn't go) with our brother, nephew, and best friend and prepared to go to New York. Two weeks later, I had the privilege to accompany Teresa on that trip to Saratoga New York where a prize racehorse of hers was being sold. Until we arrived at this pristine upstate town, I had not realized how very important this event was to her. She was there to sell her horse, yes, but more than that, she was there so that she could show the upper crust of the thoroughbred racing world that she had "made it." That this girl who at eighteen left college to work with the horses by day sleeping in a loft at night; this girl who lived off crackers and ketchup given to her to a local café; this girl had made it, she was here with thoroughbred racing's royalty and a horse bred well enough to be accepted into this prestigious sale. Teresa showed me who people were that she had learned so much from. We watched as Bobby Flay purchased a filly for over two-hundred thousand. We met Bob Baffert, a top trainer and Calvin Borel, one of our top jockeys. But, best of all, we had an exclusive meeting with Rachel Alexandra who outran the colts and was voted Horse of the Year in 2009.

She was feverish and scared the morning after the sale. I drove her straight to the hospital from New York. Two weeks later, she left us. My brother, her best friend, her husband and I were there. James Taylor's "Close your Eyes" played softly on her friend's phone and she slipped away in the early morning light.

I lay on a couch as we waited for them to take her body away. With my eyes closed lying there, I suddenly was aware of blue and white lights circling beside me. I clearly heard her say, "I'm not thirsty anymore."

I touched her hand as she was lifted from her home and then helped carry her body as she was laid to rest back home the next day in a steady summer rain, in the very courtyard where her wedding had taken place.

To Touch A Spirit Muzzle

I am haunted by the unknown,
The death that has no answers,
And as I finally find sleep,
All I feel is deep, soul-deep anger.

But then I see you in the pre-dawn,
In that place between asleep and awake,
I am not dreaming but dreamy,
But aware and know it is you.

You stand, your spirit self,
In the midst of swirling white and blue light,
Soft but blinding, bright all the same.
Your essence permeates the moment.

You in the midst of spirit horses,
I saw those who had gone before,
They reaching toward you,
You, palm forward to touch a spirit muzzle.

The Grace of Forgiveness

Through everything, it had been easy to hold on to the resentment I held and fostered toward my mother. This bitterness continued to be fueled by my sister's illness and my mother's lack of compassion, nurturing, and love as well as her continued selfishness surrounding Teresa's battle for life. I am not sure that these are the right words and some of the words and emotions might be used in order to fuel my own sense of self-righteousness and self-importance in caring for Teresa, but that is how I felt.

When Teresa passed there was incredible tension as Teresa's husband strove to protect her memory from the woman he saw to have hurt her so deeply in her life. He was bent on punishing my mom. On the other side of the coin, Mom was desperate for something, anything from the rest of us to explain Teresa's husband's behavior at the burial service. There was no easy way to tell her without digging up the past and its accompanying pain. I for one was flabbergasted that she didn't know. In my memory, we had had these discussions many times over.

Finally, after the burial service, Mom, being resigned to her own misery and to not getting the satisfaction she so longed for, retired to the guest bedroom in my brother's home where she was staying. Emotions were high but I went into the room, shut the door and sat with Mom. I told her that I never wanted to dig through the past involving Bunny again. I also told her that I wanted to thank her for Teresa's life and that I knew she had not wanted to keep the pregnancy. She looked up then with tear swollen eyes, "I didn't know anyone knew about that."

"I know, Mom," I said, "I just wanted you to know how grateful I am that I had Teresa in my life, thank you." At that moment, with my mother's swollen eyes looking at me and an ocean of loss in my heart, I felt truly grateful for my mother. I was grateful for her sacrifice in choosing to bring Teresa into the world in spite of herself and the entrapment she had felt in her world.

She is my mother, she gave me life. I am grateful. With that gratitude came openness to forgiveness and newfound grace toward my mother. It didn't condone the past but it also didn't carry any meaning with it about me, it didn't mean I wasn't good enough and it didn't mean I wasn't loved. My mother did indeed love me, and she did, indeed love my brother and sisters.

In time, and with the incredible experience gained from Landmark Education, I have also realized that I had hung on to all the meaning I had attached for myself around my mother, Bunny, my past, leaving the horse farm, etc., truly believing that I was flawed, lacking and never good enough. I had used it, to some extent, to serve my own purpose. I was dragging all those past meanings into a future and living out those meanings in my present and even into my future. What a silly waste of time, and at such a personal cost.

The Last of Bunny

After using *The Secret's* philosophies to get through the years of my sister's illness and passing, I was still left lacking the power to live the life I wanted for myself. I felt I could not do this, that I was not enough for this loss. Following Teresa's passing, I spent the first year posting quotes, encouraging donations and sharing information on the site supporting the foundation established by her husband. *The Rhoads Six Foundation* was established to grant veterinary scholarships in Teresa's name. The idea was to establish the fund with enough that the scholarships would be awarded long after we were no longer around. It was good to be involved in something to remember my sister but it did not provide the peace I longed for.

By the second year, I was just plain depressed. I missed her so completely in every aspect of living. I just went through each day often wallowing in the grief I felt. My long drives to and from work were the worst.

In desperation, I contacted an online psychic who communicated some beautiful things to me from Teresa. I then went to see a local psychic/medium. This session truly brought me comfort and much-needed peace. I knew that the sadness and sense of loss would be with me. I welcomed it as a token of my love for her.

In the meantime, my brother had been encouraging me to take a course that he declared had changed his life. I finally agreed and truly, Landmark Education has the ability to transform people's lives. This education transformed my life and the lives of my family. One of the distinctions of the education is to clean up and complete one's past.

In order to further clean up my past and make way for new possibilities, I found her. I found Bunny.

She no longer went by the name, "Bunny" so my quest to find her was a bit difficult but I did find her. When the first contact number was disconnected, I almost gave up emitting a sigh of relief.

"Well, I made the effort," I said to myself giving myself credit for what I had not accomplished. I was off the hook. I busied myself with cleaning the kitchen, and then the barn. I mowed the yard. I had no peace. I knew by my angst that I wasn't done.

Back in front of the computer, I searched a bit further, found another contact and dialed. I reached her on the first ring.

"This is Barbara."

"Bunny?"

"This is Barbara."

"Is this the Barbara who used to go by, Bunny?"

I felt weak and my hands were suddenly cold. I sat down.

"Yes."

"This is Karen."

"Karen?"

"Yes, I just called to ask your forgiveness as I have spent many years blaming you for my failures and for not living up to my potential."

The ensuing silence was deafening, to say the least. I got up and started wandering through the house.

"Well, I need to ask your forgiveness as well. I wasn't a very nice person back then."

From there we exchanged a bit of small talk including the passing of Teresa. And, I was done, forever. I would no longer be dragging my "abused child" past around with me. I was free.

Epilogue

There's a tiny speck in the world,
That tiny speck is me.
One in seven-billion,
Taking up my bit of space.

One ant on the world's anthill,
I'll make it matter to take up this space.
I will do more than just exist,
More than just consume and waste.

My little corner of the anthill,
Will be left better,
Simply because I was here.

I am stronger now, but there are times when the remembering hurts and new situations cause the scars to twinge. So much of my life, I longed for someone to hold on to; someone to help keep me from drowning. Instead, as another person seemed to offer me an anchor—just as I reached to grip their hand, I felt let go of. It seemed to me that they turned away. I came to feel that rather than holding on to one another in order to add strength to life's journey, people tended to become more like driftwood bumping and bruising each other, then slowly drifting apart. Some make it to shore, others just float on the tide.

How fragile we are in the midst of how strong we believe we have become. Even as we acknowledge the gifts we have received from our past, it takes only one small thing to open the gates that allows past insecurities to flood back into our lives.

It is my father who showed me how to see the rainbow in the rainstorm. Because of him, I stop to see the beauty hiding in ordinary moments, and remember to look for what is in the world to be amazed by.

It was my mother who spun the thread of love for horses and an intensity about life that was strong enough to span four generations—from her to her daughter, from me to my daughter, through my son to my granddaughter. The love of horses, the riding and the rhythm the touch and the smell, the beauty, and the divine became the constant. The pendulum of life swung for each of us in different directions, but it always came to rest in the presence of our horses.

So too with our approach to life. The intensity, determination, and the drive to excel permeate us all. It is for me to not only honor the intensity Mom passed on to me, but teach my children and grandchildren to channel this legacy in a way that will create a positive impact on life.

My siblings have chosen to become educated, productive members of society. We all suffered bumps in the road, and our successes were probably delayed by our tumultuous past.

Linda earned a Master's degree and has been a teacher for twenty years. Ted was a computer network engineer and radiologic technologist, managing radiology centers for a major university hospital. He has now earned a law degree and helps victims of religious abuse. He has recently moved and teaches at a radiology school in California. Teresa was an equine veterinarian and raised Thoroughbred racehorses.

To paraphrase the words of Maya Angelou, "We did what we knew until we knew better, then we did better."

I have saved some of the "stuff" which has formed the reality of my life. A vial of dirt from my Vermont home and a blanket Bunny bought me. The color-coded *Bible* sits on my bookshelf, though I never open it. In a shoebox in the closet, I keep the letters written to me by Phillip's father. On a shelf in my bedroom, I have a replica of an Astrolabe. Letters to the babies, I will never hold, lie near a charm given to me by a now-dead lover. I've kept locks of my babies' hair, both human and equine and a lock of Teresa's hair tucked into an antique cross. A large box holds treasures from each of my children. I keep these odds and ends from my life to remind me of where I have been and to keep me grounded to now. They are items I can put my fingers on and hold—things to touch, to hold in my hand, objects to show, stories to tell.

What We Keep

Things; tangible, solid, touchable,
Bits and pieces to hold on to,
Objects to remind us,
From where we have come.

Places, people, experiences,
All that shapes who we are,
And guides what we will become.

For me it is locks of baby hair;
My three cherubs now grown,
Dirt. Home. The place from where I came,
The ground that holds me steady,
Anchoring me when I feel lost.

Stones of love and of places I love,
A letter addressed to a never-born child,
A belief, a song, an impossible love,
Tokens are all I have.

I now deal with the harsher realities of life with less anger and bitterness. Now I accept that those are part of being human and living life. Now I am quick to take action when those realities appear. At times, I am sad, but being bitter only ate away at my own spirit. The handhold I have on the cliff of life feels a bit less precarious. I am not ready to relax and let go yet; even though I now believe I would land on my feet.

Other more important dreams will arise in front of me and I now know how to make life happen instead of letting life happen to me. I don't try; I work hard and persevere.

I conduct my life with dignity. I want the ripples I create to make a difference. My life's dreams have been amended a number of times. Instead of becoming a veterinarian, healing horses' bodies, I pick them up from killer pens and have a part in healing their spirits. I will not be an Olympic equestrian, but

I am an effective horsewoman.

As a teacher, I tell my students, "All you have to do in life is live and die. Everything in between is up for grabs, determined by your own uniqueness and the choices that you make. Anyone can eat, breathe, procreate, make waste and take up space in the world. Do more with the time you have than just take up space. Make it matter that you are here."

One of the most inspiring passages, I know, comes from *The Little Prince* by Antoine Saint-Exupery. The passage drives home the message of connection and responsibility. It is a story of how important we are to one another, a story about the importance of taking the risk to love, and once we take that risk, being responsible for ourselves as well as those we have taken that risk for.

The Little Prince asks a fox to play with him.

"I can't play with you." The fox said, "I'm not tamed."

The little prince doesn't understand and repeatedly asks what he means by "tamed."

Finally, the fox answers, "It is something that's been too often neglected. It means to establish ties." The fox continued to explain, "For me, you are nothing more than a little boy just like a hundred thousand other little boys. I have no need of you. And you have no need of me. For you, I am only a fox like a hundred thousand other foxes. But if you tame me, we will need each other. You'll be unique in the world to me and I will be unique to you." The fox continued, "My life is monotonous, but if you tame me, my life will be filled with sunshine. I'll know the sound of your footsteps that will be different from all the rest. Other footsteps send me back underground. Yours will call me out of my burrow like music." And then, "you see the wheat fields over there? I don't eat bread. For me, wheat is of no use whatever. Wheatfields say nothing to me, which is sad. But you have hair the color of gold, so it will be wonderful once you've tamed me! The wheat which is golden will remind me of you. And I will love the sound of the wind in the wheat. Please tame me."

So the Little Prince tames the fox and when it was time for the

Little prince to leave the fox said, "I shall weep."

It's your own fault, I never wanted to do you any harm but you insisted that I tame you.

"Yes, of course."

"But you are going to weep!"

"Yes, of course."

"Then you get nothing out of it?"

"I get something, because of the color of the wheat."

And, for me, some of his most powerful words are written as the fox tells The Little Prince, "You are responsible forever for what you have tamed."

If I help a child to make important life choices, if I retrain a throw-away horse, if I raise children who in turn also make their lives better—then, I have affected lives forever.

So, I have told you my story, and I am eternally indebted and grateful to those who have shared their stories with me. I thank my friends and family, as well as those who have written the books, composed and played the music, and woven the poetry that has inspired me along the way. So many connections are made in a lifetime, those connections, both positive and negative, get us to the places we are and aid us in who we choose to become.